Insect Ecology

AUSTRALIAN ECOLOGY SERIES

General Editor: Harold Heatwole

Other titles in series

Reptile Ecology: Harold Heatwole

( )

Insect Ecology

( )

E.G. Matthews

**University of
Queensland Press**

Printed and bound by Dai Nippon Printing Co. (HK) Ltd.,
Hong Kong

Distributed in the United Kingdom, Europe, the Middle
East, Africa, and the Caribbean by Prentice-Hall Inter-
national, International Book Distributors Ltd., 66
Wood Lane End, Hemel Hempstead, Herts, England

National Library of Australia
Cataloguing-in-publication-data

Matthews, E. G.
    Insect ecology.

1 (Australian ecology series).
    Index.
    Bibliography.
    ISBN 0 7022 1250 4.
    ISBN 0 7022 1251 2 Paperback.

    1. Insects — Australian — Ecology. I. Title.
    (Series).

595.7050994

Contents

List of Illustrations

Black and White

Colour (following page **160**)

Preface

Ecology is the science involved with the interactions of organisms and their physical and biotic environments. This field has always been a source of fascination to professional biologists, naturalists and conservationists. In recent years, as human population has progressively increased, environmental problems have also become of vital interest and importance to the public as well. It has now become imperative that ecological principles, and the ecology of specific regions be understood by a wide variety of people. The present series was designed to aid in filling this need.

It is felt that these volumes will serve as a source of information for those university students, teachers and the interested public who require a basic factual knowledge for broadening their understanding of ecology, or those conservationists, agriculturalists, foresters, wild life officers, politicians, engineers, etc., who may need to apply ecological principles in solving environmental problems. In addition, these books are expected to be a valuable reference work and source of stimulation for professional ecologists, botanists and zoologists. The writing is at a level that will neither encumber the layman with unnecessary jargon (although he may need to consult reference works and dictionaries in order to understand some of the terminology) nor be too elementary to be of interest to the professional ecologist.

The study of ecology can be approached on various levels. For example, one can emphasize the biotic community and analyze the kinds and numbers of organisms living together in a particular habitat, the way they are organized in space and time and the interactions they have with each other. This type of ecology is known as synecology.

Another way of studying ecology is to use Systems Analysis. In this method, the biotic community and the physical environment which together make up what is known as an ecosystem, are looked upon as a functioning unit. In this approach the main emphasis is on the cycling of energy, minerals, or organic materials within the ecosystem and the factors influencing these processes rather than specifically upon the organisms themselves. Often mathematical or theoretical models are constructed and tested.

Both of the above approaches are synthetic and take an overview of entire communities or systems and do not emphasize individual species. By contrast the following two approaches are concerned mainly with individual species, or at most groups of only a few species.

The population approach is concerned with (1) fluctuation in abundance and distribution of individuals of a given species in an area, (2) the contributing phenomena such as birth rates, death rates, immigration, emigration, longevity and survival, and (3) the influence of the physical environment and of other species on these characteristics. Of major interest are mechanisms regulating population density and factors influencing population stability.

The final approach is one primarily concerned with the effect of the environment on the individuals of a species, e.g. how they are affected by temperature, moisture, light or other environmental factors. This approach is known variously as Autecology, Environmental Physiology or Physiological Ecology. The keynote is adaptation to specific environments.

In looking at *Ecology in Australia* in the volumes of this series, all of the above approaches will be employed. Certain topics like Ecology of Grasslands, Ecology of Forests and Woodlands, or Ecology of Deserts lend themselves to a community approach; grasslands, forests, and deserts *are* types of communities and if studied as an entity must be approached on the community or ecosystem level. On the other hand, where specific taxa such as reptiles, birds, or mammals are treated the population and/or autecological approach is used. Which one is emphasized varies from group to group, depending on the information available.

The volume on insects combines the synecological and autecological approaches with emphasis on the former. The major biotic communities in Australia are examined in terms of (1) the role insects play in their functioning and (2) their effect upon insect adaptation and evolution.

Some new interpretations of previous concepts have arisen from the writing of that volume and appear for the first time in it. It is hoped these will stimulate discussion about, and investigation into, the ecology of this important group of organisms.

In each book in this series, regardless of the emphasis, the available information on a particular field is critically reviewed and summarized in order that the reader might be brought abreast of current knowledge and developments. Recent trends are indicated and the way for future development prepared by emphasizing conspicuous gaps in knowledge and pointing out what appear to be fruitful avenues for research.

Harold Heatwole
Armidale, N.S.W.
February 1974

Introduction

Ecology is a diverse science which permits a variety of approaches. My approach to the subject of this book has been to focus on the diversity of insects — not to list or describe this diversity, but to look for general principles and common patterns which underlie the varied roles insects play in different ecosystems. In doing this I have chosen to place emphasis on the ways insects utilize available energy, on how natural selection forces the adoption of certain adaptive strategies, and on how insects interact and coevolve with other organisms with which they are associated.

This approach is intended to complement the other existing books on the ecology of Australian insects, which have adopted the population and autecological approaches.

On reading a descriptive account of what an insect does, I am constantly nagged by the question: why? Why does an insect behave the way it does? Why does it have certain structures and colours? In my opinion, the answers to these questions are to be sought in the context of the ecosystem — the forces, both biotic and physical, which operate on the individual in its community environment. It is in an attempt to formulate more precise questions (and a few tentative answers) that this book has been written.

Theodosius Dobzhansky (1966 and other papers) has drawn attention to the two contrasting philosophies biologists follow, often subconsciously, in attempting to answer "why?": reductionism and compositionism (or holism). The reductionist tends to explain natural phenomena, including evolution and species distributions, in terms of organismal traits and molecular events such as mutations, chromosomal changes, biochemical and physiological properties, and morphology. The element of chance plays an important part in the reductionist's explanations. The compositionist (naturalist, or Darwinian), on the other hand, believes that all of the above phenomena are regulated in turn by natural selection. His explanations will always be in terms of natural selection, and he will assume that there always is an explanation in these terms, even if it is not immediately obvious. The events and structures which preoccupy the reductionist will be considered by the compositionist to be mechanisms on which, or through which, natural selection exerts its influence and it is the selective influences, not so much the mechanisms, which interest him in his constant search for answers to the question "why?". He will not be satisfied merely with descriptions of events or structures and will not accept the possibility that there could be no reason (in terms of selection) for any phenomenon.

Reductionism in the form of non-evolutionary and descriptive "explanations" is the major obstacle to our understanding of ecological principles (Janzen 1973a). At the same time, too vigorous an effort to escape reductionism may lead us to succumb to the opposite fallacy, which is teleology or determinism. The latter philosophy assumes that the course of natural events is somehow goal-oriented. In this book I have tried to steer a middle course between the Scylla of reductionism and the Charybdis of teleology.

Throughout this book I will be looking for common patterns and for unifying concepts in terms of adaptive values. I am not attempting to assemble all current knowledge of Australian insect ecology, and particular facts may be omitted if they are redundant in illustrating a principle. On the other hand, work done outside Australia may be included to help explain concepts. In general, recent summaries or reviews are cited, but not always the articles on which they are based. Consequently, the present book is not a complete coverage of the literature but an introduction to it.

Insect control (by man) and economic and medical

entomology are not directly treated, although many data from the literature in these fields are included. I have also found it necessary to omit the subjects of parasites of vertebrates and of inquilines in the nests of ants and termites as being too specialized. These types of associations are examples of animal-to-animal coevolution, the general principles of which are discussed using examples from the interactions with insectivorous vertebrates and with parasitoids. The subject of coevolution with plants is given a prominence which reflects its overwhelming importance in the life of insects.

The willing cooperation of all Australian biologists approached in the course of preparing this book has been most gratifying. Most of these are mentioned by name in the text as providing personal communications, but I am also indebted particularly to the following individuals for offering extensive help and in some cases unpublished manuscripts: Dr. E. B. Britton (Division of Entomology, CSIRO), Dr. S. W. Cowling (Division of Land Use Research, CSIRO), Dr. P. J. M. Greenslade (Division of Soils, CSIRO), Mr. G. F. Gross (South Australian Museum), Dr. K. H. L. Key (Division of Entomology, CSIRO), Dr. K. E. Lee (Division of Soils, CSIRO), Mrs. J. Lowry (University of New South Wales), Mr. G. B. Monteith (University of Queensland), Dr. R. A. Perry (Division of Land Use Research, CSIRO), Dr. J. J. H. Szent-Ivany (South Australian Museum), Dr. D. F. Waterhouse (Division of Entomology, CSIRO).

E. G. Matthews
Adelaide
June 1975

CHAPTER 1
Some General Principles

Before proceeding with a survey of patterns of adaptation of insects to specific ecosystems, it would be desirable to review some general principles. I shall concentrate in this chapter on the general ways insects play the ecological game of survival in a heterogeneous and dynamic environment, on prey-predator and plant-herbivore interactions, and on speciation as an adaptive strategy.

1.1 THE GAME OF LIFE

It is convenient to view species as players in a game and some of the concepts of Games Theory have found their way into ecological writing. This should be seen as a way of organizing thoughts about how animals and plants adapt to their environments — as a sort of analytical tool to help reconstruct, in the imagination, a model which is a simplified representation of what exists in reality. On the other hand, the proponents of the games analogy insist that it is not an analogy at all, but a precise description of what actually happens in evolution, providing the rules are carefully defined.

It should be emphasized at the outset that every move is opportunistic, in no way goal-oriented, and governed by a combination of natural selection and chance, with only the former providing direction. The payoff of the existential game can be a quantity of energy, but the real "aim" of the players (species) is not to maximize their energy winnings, but to maximize the duration of their part in the game. The only way to leave the game is to become extinct. One way for the player to survive in the short run is to increase his fortune (population size), but in the long run his duration of play depends only on his ability to minimize his stakes — the proportion of his energy supply committed to each play (an event or perturbation). This minimization of commitments is achieved through an overlapping sequence of responses to the event. Each response in the sequence entails increasing stakes, and the higher-stake responses continue in operation only to the extent that lower-stake responses have failed to counter (or take advantage of) the influence of the event. The lowest-stake response is a behavioral one at the individual level, whilst the highest-stake one cosists of permanent genetic changes at the species level. If the low-stake, short-duration response is adequate, the remaining responses do not run their full course (see Slobodkin and Rapoport, 1974). I will be pointing out later (section 1.6) that insects have recourse to the genetic responses much more frequently than most vertebrates, but nevertheless this strategy has paid off with some very long periods of continuous play. This phenomenon requires some further explanation in terms of the games analogy.

I will also be using the concept of r and K selection (MacArthur and Wilson 1967; King and Anderson 1971; Pianka 1972) as a common thread running through the book. Here again, this provides only a unifying framework on which to hang facts and ideas, and whilst I believe the concept has validity, it is by no means necessary to formulate questions and answers in its terms, and the reader should feel free to re-state the same facts and ideas on some other basis if he so wishes.

R selection is said to predominate during colonizing episodes which arise after some environmental change has altered or destroyed the former habitat, and favours a high population growth rate (r is the symbol used to represent a population's unrestrained rate of natural increase), whilst K selection predominates during periods of prolonged stability and favours a more efficient utilization of resources (K represents the carrying capacity of the environment).

Whereas the ultimate strategy adopted by the players is always the same (that of staying in the game), the successful tactics for pursuing it are different under the two types of selection, as we shall see presently. I shall follow the usual terminology and refer to "r and K strategists" rather than "tacticians".

1.2 TWO KINDS OF STRATEGISTS

A species, when first moving into a suitable environment which contains an abundance of food, is subjected to "r selection", which can simply be defined as a situation of high food density and low population density. Such a situation may occur when there are changes in weather or other physical factors, when a species has managed to reach an environment previously inaccessible, or sometimes through human activity, such as the planting of a food crop. R selection will favour species with a rapid intrinsic rate of natural increase (r), since the most successful species in an r environment will be the one most quickly able to build up its numbers to exploit favourable conditions. Initially there are no constraints on this build-up as the influence of competitors and predators will not yet be felt, and little energy need be invested in individual defence. There is no advantage in food specialization.

As the species subjected to r selection builds up its numbers, and competitors and predators also build up theirs, the environment becomes crowded, the carrying capacity (K) is approached, and the conditions of r selection no longer prevail. As individual resources become scarcer, it is no longer so important to multiply rapidly. In fact, it may benefit the species to keep its numbers down so the fitness of existing individuals can be maintained. It is now more important to compete successfully with other species, to avoid predators, perhaps to defend territories, to expend more energy on individual and progeny defence, and to spend more time on courtship (the latter is a device to ensure conspecific matings — necessary when there are closely-related species about). It becomes mutually advantageous to co-operate with other species (form symbioses) and to specialize in one kind of food (to minimize wasteful conflict and maximize efficiency).

In short, *r* selection typically favours fecundity, mobility, and polyphagy. *K* selection favours intrinsic population density control, lack of mobility (for reasons which will be explained later), food specialization, individual defence, competitive ability, and symbiosis.

A few species can adjust to both *r* and *K* selection, notably flour beetles (*Tribolium* spp.) which adopt some *K* strategies, such as population density control (see below), when their environment becomes crowded. The granary or flour bin is rather a special situation, however, and most species which succeed under *r* selection are not able to compete with other species under *K* selection, and they tend to emigrate. *R* strategists, as such species are called, are thus particularly good at moving, or getting moved about — not only to retreat when their environment gets crowded, but also to be on hand when new, favourable situations arise. In order to succeed as an *r* strategist, a species must exist in an area subject to frequent and unpredictable changes (for example, the temperate zone, arid areas, or the culture steppe). However, a few *r* strategists can survive in even the most stable general environment if they are adapted to those aspects of that environment which do change unpredictably. For instance, if we take one of the most stable known environments, the tropical rain forest, there is still change there in the form of tree fall, animal deaths, landslides, and the falling of fruits and objects acting as small water containers (to select but a few *r* situations). Some of the terms long used in the literature to describe *r* strategists are: fugitive, tramp, weedy, colonizing, opportunistic, mobile, or vagile species.

In general, the relative influence of *r* or *K* selective forces depends on the degree of stability of the environment. Stability does not necessarily mean a lack of fluctuation. Temperate climates are unstable not so much because of seasonal changes, but because given seasons can differ unpredictably from year to year.

Stable environments will contain a high proportion of K strategists. However, for the largest number of such species to occur it is also necessary for the conditions of stability or predictability to have been in continuous existence for a long time. K strategists are adapted to one particular environment (including the complex of species with which they are associated) and have usually been evolved *in situ*. Their evolution is the culmination of a long process of interaction with a particular set of factors. Even an apparently unstable environment can produce its quota of K strategists if its fluctuations have been within circumscribed limits long enough — for instance, the Australian arid zone.

Greenslade (1972) has introduced the concept of "beyond-K" selection. This type of selection operates in environments which may have something in common with r environments in that they are dominated by harsh physical limiting factors. However, unlike r environments, these factors are highly stable and predictable. Their stability permits species to become closely adapted to them, whilst their severity has the effect of keeping out most competitors. Furthermore, the specialized adaptations required to meet this severity, once evolved, enable beyond-K strategists to out-compete most potential invaders. If a given beyond-K environment has persisted long enough unchanged, it can contain some extraordinarily ancient relict species. The sorts of environments which are beyond K are mountain streams, high mountain tops, the marine littoral and intertidal zones, and caves (Chapter 5). The more severe and ancient deserts are probably also included, as are the arctic and antarctic zones.

Thus r, K, and beyond-K environments select for different adaptive strategies and, in general, species are able to adapt to only one such set of selective forces, although some special, small habitats may contain the same species throughout their succession. Also, species occurring at an intermediate stage in the process of ecosystem maturation may show both types of adaptation in combination.

The two main types of selection, then, can be thought

of as extremes of a continuous spectrum of change which can be related in part to ecological succession, maturation of communities through evolution, and a transition from variable to equable climates or other physical conditions.

The study of a species of *Drosophila* by Birch *et al.* (1963) is pertinent in this regard. They compared the value of r (the intrinsic rate of natural increase) of five different populations along a geographic transect running from New Britain to Sydney, finding that r increases steadily from north to south (although the Sydney value was a little lower than that of Brisbane). They interpreted the result in terms of the relative fitness of the different populations, but this is not a valid interpretation. Fitness can only be compared between individuals in the same environment, and not between populations in different environments. Undoubtedly, all the populations of this fly are equally well adapted. What the study does show is that adaptation to more temperate areas may require a higher capacity for increase, to cope (one presumes) with the vicissitudes of temperate climates.

Under the conditions of K selection a number of theoretical alternatives are open to species to adjust their numbers. If they are r strategists they will usually emigrate. If they are flexible r-K strategists they will adopt self-regulatory measures dependent upon population density. The best-studied examples of the latter are the flour beetles *Tribolium confusum* and *T. castaneum* (the former a little more r-adapted than the latter) (King and Dawson 1972). These beetles have a surprising array of intrinsic density-regulating mechanisms, including egg and pupal cannibalism by larvae and adults, reduced fecundity and fertility in aged populations, and the secretion of an inhibitory quinone gas in crowded situations. Cannibalism is prevalent among insects and is not only a regulatory mechanism but also improves the fitness of surviving individuals (Mertz and Robertson 1970). It may be an important factor in keeping the number of emerging adults relatively constant in a given food volume in spite of an excess of eggs laid in it, and has been observed even in phytophagous insects such as some butterfly larvae (Common and Waterhouse 1972), the codling moth (Clark *et al.* 1967), and chrysomelid beetles (Eickwort 1973). For the general subject of population self-regulation see Brereton (1962), Monro (1967), Wynne Edwards (1970), May (1972). As for full K strategists, they will have low fecundity in the first place (coupled with a high individual survival rate), having invested energy toward more efficient resource utilization (examples are the morabine grasshoppers, section 2.3.3, thynnid wasps, section 3.4.2, and others). These species do not have the flexibility of r or r-K strategists and should the conditions of K selection no longer prevail, they will usually leave the game (become extinct).

The biosphere as a whole will have many more K (localized) than r (widespread) species, and within a given taxonomic group there will tend to be more K than r species (section 1.6). Where the group as a whole has entered the beyond-K adaptive zone, this proportion will be even higher but the total number of species in it will drop precipitously (Greenslade 1972). Such groups are represented today by relatively few relict species. In Australia, the order Plecoptera, the family Peloridiidae (Homoptera), and the genus *Tettigarcta* (Homoptera) would be three of many examples of the latter, all more or less restricted to montane formations. Evans (1959) lists others, many of them under the heading of southern relics with aquatic larvae. The frequent emphasis on the aquatic nature of relict insects misses the main point, which is that certain sorts of aquatic environments are beyond-K (Chapter 5) and that it is this aspect of such environments, not their aquatic nature, that permits the survival of relics.

1.3 THE EFFECTS OF PREDATION

In the following two sections I shall be concerned with the interactions between insects and other organisms, and the evolutionary influence that these interactions have had on insects. The present section deals with the effects of predators and parasitoids, and the next one (1.4) with the influence of plants.

The most important predators on insects in general are, first of all, vertebrates — particularly birds, but also amphibians, lizards, small mammals, and fresh-water fish. To the extent that most of these predators rely largely on vision to catch their prey, their evolutionary influence on the external aspect of insects has been most profound.

Parasitoids, which are also insects, are probably second in importance. A parasitoid differs from a predator in that it spends its entire feeding life in just one host, and from a parasite in that it always kills the host eventually. In addition, it shows certain other characteristics, such as reduced multiple infections and reduced mixed-species infections, which have been enumerated by Kuris (1974).

Finally, invertebrate predators, particularly spiders, and parasites (nematodes and other vermiform groups, protozoans, bacteria, and viruses) are important in all environments. A parasite usually causes multiple infection of its host and usually does not kill it, whilst a predator kills many prey individuals in its lifetime.

The effects of predation are felt at three levels by prey species: (1) at the population density level in contemporary time, (2) at the species level in evolutionary time, and (3) at the community level, through increased community diversity and stability. These effects will be discussed in turn, but following the investigations of Pimentel (1968) it is no longer possible sharply to separate contemporary and evolutionary time in discussions of population density regulation.

1.3.1 STABILIZATION OF PREY POPULATIONS

Pimental (1968), drawing on observations of field natural history and experimental evidence, pointed out that relative stability and low densities are both the norm in natural populations. Wildly fluctuating "plagues" are usually the result of interference by man producing temporary situations which favour a certain species, but the very abundance of that species exerts powerful selection pressures on its food organism which, within only a few generations, will result in the evolution of increased resistance or other defences in the latter. This in turn reduces the population levels of the predator or herbivore (which is itself evolving counter-measures) and in a relatively short time this "genetic feed-back" will produce a fairly stable situation. This stabilization occurs in evolutionary time, but it is to be recalled that this can be quite brief in organisms with short-lived generations.

In section 1.4.1, 4.6.2 and elsewhere I have suggested that the defences of plants may be as important a factor in controlling herbivore populations as it is in influencing their evolution, if only because overcoming these defences draws investment from the herbivore's limited energy budget away from other requirements of survival and reproduction. It is interesting to note that even until very recently (Wilson 1968), discussions of the control of insect abundance in natural and artificial ecosystems omit any reference even to the possibility that plants are anything but "food", able to influence herbivore population levels only through their rela-tive supply or abundance. The recent awareness of what is undoubtedly the most important mechanism of population control in natural communities (coevolution by genetic feed-back) arose only when evolutionary principles were applied to ecological practise and theory (Pimentel 1968).

Even within the context of contemporary time (that is, without any genetic changes taking place), there are stabili-zing factors at work in predator-prey relationships. These take the form of frequency-dependent predation pressure (Murdoch 1969; Hassell and May 1973; Readshaw 1973). The basis of the frequency dependence varies according to the type of predator. In the case of insect parasitoids and predators, it is largely the result of matching prey abundance by a corresponding increase in predator density through population build-up. In the case of vertebrate predators, par-ticularly birds, as well as some invertebrates, the tendency of many of these to feed selectively on the most abundant of several alternate prey items, through the formation of search images or some equivalent behavioural mechanism, concen-trates predation pressure in direct proportion to the prey's frequency of availability. While there is some doubt about the validity of the search-image and avoidance-image concepts as originally formulated by Clarke (1962), the evidence for the existence of some similar mechanism, at least in vertebrates, is convincing (Ayala and Campbell 1974). Because of their greater search range, birds are also able to congregate at sites of local prey abundance (Readshaw 1973).

Some theoretical models which do not reveal any stabilizing effect in the predator-prey relationship have failed to allow for this non-random or aggregative behaviour in the predator's response to unequal prey distribution (Hassell and May 1973). Also, it is necessary in constructing a realistic model to include all three levels of ecological interaction (plant-herbivore-carnivore) instead of just two of them (May 1973).

If the tendencies in both contemporary and evolutionary time are toward the stabilization of populations at relatively low levels, why then do we get plagues? We can understand the general factors which bring about irruptions if we remember that, as a rule, organisms are kept in check by the defences of their food species, the effects of their competitors, and predation, all acting in combination. Sudden increases in numbers may therefore occur in two different sorts of situations: (1) in the exceptional cases where these are not in fact the normal constraints on population build-up, but where the weather usually exerts control, as in very unstable climates (section 2.3.2), and (2) where unusual circumstances (usually human interference) remove at least two of these constraints simultaneously. For instance, in forests where defoliating insects may become abundant (sections 4.3.3, 4.3.4), these insects must on the one hand benefit from stresses suffered by the food plants which draw energy away from the plant's defences, while on the other hand the insects must also be capable of practising either absolute or (more usually) selective predator satiation (this depending only partly on predator abundance). That is, they must be able to remove predator pressure at high densities through having exceeded their predators' ingesting capacity or toxicity tolerance limits (section 1.3.2). Since it appears that a break-

down in the plants' defences is the more usual triggering
stimulus for plagues in forest biomes, we must conclude that
it is in general a more important controlling factor for
herbivorous insects than predation.

1.3.2 PREY-PREDATOR COMMUNICATION
The continuous pressure of predators selects for the evolution
of various defensive mechanisms in the prey species, and as
mentioned above, those which curtail predator population
increase can evolve very quickly. In the present section we
will be concerned mostly with long-term evolutionary effects
on insect prey species, particularly with regard to communication between them and their vertebrate predators – a
communication on which many insects depend for survival.

The most effective defence for any prey individual is to
escape detection altogether, but where predation is by visual
animals, this is only possible if the prey inhabits sheltered or
subterranean habitats, or (if exposed) remains more or less
immobile in the daytime. In the latter case, it will evolve a
camouflage, or procryptic pattern and shape. Even so, many
insects with such procryptic patterns will also display signal
colours or emit sounds when they are exposed to inevitable
detection (for instance, many grasshoppers in flight,
phasmids and mantids under attack, and various beetles
when disturbed). These are signals to predators which come
into play when procrypsis is temporarily ineffective. Procrypsis may also be temporarily abandoned as a defensive tactic
when population density becomes high. This is because the
area-restricted searching behaviour of predators enables them
to perceive normally-overlooked items when these are concentrated, once they have found the first one (Tinbergen,
Impekoven, and Franck 1967; Readshaw 1973).

Insects which must necessarily be active in the daytime,
such as most pollinators and other diurnal foragers, will display signal colours permanently on the surfaces exposed
during flight or walking. If it is possible for these colours to
be masked when the insect is at rest, they usually will be (as
in many butterflies). The signal colours do not increase the

conspicuousness of the insect when in use (this will be high anyway because of movement), but they are presumably of some disadvantage when it is at rest. Nevertheless, the conflict in selection pressures has almost invariably been resolved in favour of signal colours in those diurnal insects which have only one surface which they can expose (beetles, for instance). Some beetles have solved this dilemma by being able to achieve both a procryptic and a signalling effect with the same surface. They achieve this by using diffraction gratings, which appear dark in the shade but return flashes of colour in the sun (Hinton 1973).

The near-universal coincidence of signal colours and sounds with situations which invite inevitable perception by predators demonstrates beyond any doubt that such signals have a defensive function in themselves. They are by no means restricted to very toxic or otherwise strongly defended insects and their significance must therefore be sought quite apart from the "warning" function conventionally attributed to them.

Whilst controversy continues to surround this subject, there can be little doubt that the principal pressure selecting for the evolution of signal colours and sounds in animals necessarily exposed to predation is the type of frequency-dependent selection known as apostasy, or apostatic selection (Clarke 1962; Ayala and Campbell 1974; Otte 1974). The effectiveness of this defence results from the predators' reliance on a search-image for prey selection. A search-image is formed by a predator as a result of a number of favourable experiences with prey items conforming to that image. The predator will subsequently attack without hesitation all such prey items as long as they continue to be available at frequencies sufficient to maintain the image. It will also sample items not conforming to it, but these are approached with sufficient caution and hesitation to increase their chances of escape. At least some birds are known to evince a hesitation or even fear of novel items (Coppinger 1970). The function of most insect signals, therefore, is simply that of being sufficiently different from other such signals for the sender to appear novel, and thus avoid being the subject of a search-image.

Conversely, sampled prey which are found by experience to be unpleasant to a predator will induce the formation of an avoidance-image. Any prey individual conforming to that image will subsequently not be attacked by an experienced predator for a length of time which varies according to its hunger state, its species, and the unpleasantness of the experience. The more distinctive the colour pattern of an unpleasant prey item, the more easily it will be remembered as such by a visual predator. This can be demonstrated experimentally. The "unpleasantness" of a prey item, which leads to avoidance-image formation, can be unpalatability as a result of a toxin, or it can be a mechanical weapon or simply an effective escape mechanism (Gibson 1974 and references therein).

Generalized predators, that is, those feeding on a large variety of prey species, must necessarily form search and avoidance images, or adopt some equivalent mechanism, in order to "classify" their potential prey into three categories: rewarding, unrewarding, and unknown. Their subsequent attitude to members of these three categories will differ significantly, the first being attacked without hesitation, the second being avoided, and the third being attacked cautiously. The function of the classification mechanism is to enable predators to exploit highly varied food efficiently, and in order to be effective it must be flexible and responsive to changes in relative prey density.

Most vertebrate insectivores are generalized to the extent that within their search range or stratum they will pursue, with greater or lesser enthusiasm, all available insects except those they have learned to be unrewarding. Specialization among such insectivores generally takes the form of restriction to particular sectors or strata of the habitat or particular hunting techniques (for instance, foliage gleaning at a certain height, picking over leaf litter, or pursuit in flight).

Insects respond to the selection pressure of generalized visual predators and their frequency-dependent classification

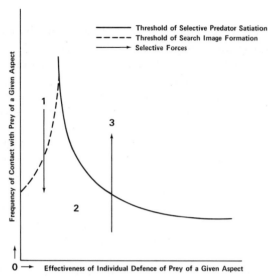

Figure 1 The hypothetical classification system used by a generalized predator which feeds on highly diverse prey, such as insects, and which relies for prey selection on its ability to associate relative reward rate (palatability and catchability) with the aspect of prey items. The three categories in the classification (numbered) are (1) known to be rewarding, applied only to items of a given aspect which have a high contact frequency and low individual defence; (2) unfamiliar or unremembered items, those which have a contact frequency which is too low, when combined with their individual reward or punishment rate, to be specifically remembered as being rewarding or unrewarding; and (3) known to be unrewarding, applied to items which combine frequency and punishment dose sufficiently to be remembered as such. Items in category (1) are unhesitatingly attacked, those in (2) are attacked with caution, and those in (3) avoided.

As a result of selection by vertebrate visual predators, insects necessarily exposed to such predation react in evolutionary time by using signals to modify the aspect of genetic units (species and morphs) so as to place themselves as often as possible in categories (2) and (3), depending on a combination of their abundance and individual defence capabilities. For relatively poorly defended species, selection favours a reduction of frequency of a given aspect through divergence in appearance between species and morphs (left arrow). For relatively well defended species selection favours an increase of frequency of a given aspect through convergence of appearance between similarly-shaped species (mimicry) (right arrow).

Insects will thus convey either distinctiveness or similarity by using the "language" of their predators, which consists either of primary colour patterns or sounds. This is why, as an example, all diurnal insects necessarily and repeatedly exposed to predation (butterflies, for instance) are always colourful (from Matthews, 1976).

systems by evolving signals which are distinctive for each morph, species, or mimicry complex, as the case may be. Any two prey individuals which share the same aspect will be in the same class, as far as the predator is concerned. In the case of an abundant palatable species of which search-images are easily formed, there will be an advantage for some individuals to appear different from the rest and thus be classified as "unknown" rather than "rewarding". They will have a greater chance of escaping. Where two or more palatable species are involved, if they share the same aspect they will be treated as one abundant species which will quickly be classed as rewarding. Any one of them which becomes distinct from the others will probably remain "unknown" and benefit thereby.

Therefore, evolution and maintenance of aspect diversity, whether within or between species, will reduce the chances of search-image formation by reducing the frequency of contact associated with any one particular aspect. This message of distinctiveness is conveyed to the predator in the latter's own language, which in the case of vertebrate visual predators tends to be primary colours.

In discussing species-specific "startle" displays in mantids, Key (1974a) points out that such a display "can succeed [in startling] only if one form of it is relatively rare". This is of course another way of stating what has been said above. Startle displays, such as those seen in many orthopteroid insects, serve to induce hesitation in a predator only so long as they are unfamiliar. This will lead to selection for a different display in each species, exactly as in butterflies and other day-flying insects. Since escaping detection through procrypsis is always the most effective defence if feasible, the relatively palatable orthopteroids will usually resort to displays only as a second line of defence.

It is important to understand that the partial protection afforded by a predator's hesitation and caution in the face of the unknown and unfamiliar, is in itself a strong defence. It need not be backed up by weapons or toxins (although these may be effective as a third line of defence, in some cases). In the context of any particular natural community, the true back-up defence is provided by the very toxic species of the community, whose existence is what leads the predators to rely on their classification system in the first place. This is the real ecological importance of the strongly defended prey species, such as the danaine butterflies, which indirectly extend a degree of protection to all other butterflies in the community (providing the latter are not common enough to induce search-image formation). Because their presence extends at least a small measure of protection to rare species, the strongly toxic insects have a diversifying influence analogous to that of dominant predators (section 1.3.3).

Prey species which are actually unpalatable or otherwise have active defences against a predator, will benefit by sharing the same signals, since this will augment the number of unpleasant contacts associated with any particular signal and speed up the process of avoidance-image formation. Nevertheless, a complex of mimetic species sharing one aspect will benefit as a whole from appearing clearly different from other, less well-defended species. The signals involved are therefore serving the same purpose as before — to convey distinctiveness.

It was mentioned above that procrypsis is not an effective defence when the insect increases in density beyond a certain point. The first step in the breakdown of this defence occurs when the predators' area-restricted searching behaviour comes into play, and this takes place before the insect consumes its vegetation cover or has to expose itself through movement. When the latter two events occur, procrypsis becomes totally ineffective and is abandoned as a defence in favour of signal colours. This phenomenon represents a defence strategy switch which is not common among insects as it requires the combination of great density fluctuations with relatively feeble individual defence. Most defoliating insects that regularly reach high densities are well enough protected not to need to resort to procrypsis at low densities (see section 4.3.4), or it may be that they have simply not evolved the density-dependent colour changes seen in certain other insects. Among the latter are well-known African

Fig. 2

Figures 2−5 Density-dependent predator satiation. (2) Diurnal aggregation of larvae of the sawfly *Perga affinis* Kirby about to begin migration to another tree after defoliating their present host, a *Eucalyptus blakelyi* Maiden near Canberra. Insects can only take this sort of advantage of a plant's lowered defences due to unusual stresses, if at the same time they are able to practise predator satiation. Sufficient mobility to transfer to new host plants is usually necessary as well. [Photo John Greene, courtesy Division of Entomology, CSIRO] (3) Larvae of a chrysomelid beetle, *Paropsis* sp., on *Eucalyptus*. As in the previous case, predator satiation is achieved through the multiplication of individual defence capabilities by aggregation. [Photo John Greene, courtesy Division of Entomology, CSIRO] (4) Close-up of *Paropsis atomaria* Olliff on *Eucalyptus blakeleyi* Maiden. One individual is everting the caudal defensive glands which discharge a substance containing cyanide. [Photo John Greene, courtesy Division of Entomology, CSIRO] (5) Migrating hoppers (nymphs) of the plague locust, *Chortoicetes terminifera* (Walker). Because of relatively feeble individual defences, predator satiation is achievable by these grasshoppers only at very high population densities during the migratory phase. At lower densities there is a defence-strategy switch to procrypsis, with corresponding colour changes. [Photo B. Lewis, courtesy Division of Entomology, CSIRO]

Fig. 3

Fig. 4

Fig. 5

locust species and some Australian phasmids (Key 1957) (Figs 13 and 14) and some lepidopterous larvae (Common and Waterhouse 1972). Readshaw (1965) noted that the phasmids when at high densities, appear to escape predation by birds, their usual enemies. This would either be as a result of absolute predator satiation, as Readshaw believed, or as a result of selective predator satiation, whereby the birds have ceased feeding altogether on the phasmids and have turned to other food. It is only if these insects can induce selective predator satiation (that is to say, avoidance-image formation) that there would be any function for their conspicuous coloration at high densities. Most probably, this satiation would not be brought about by a greater individual distaste-fulness at high densities, but by a cumulative toxic effect produced by a summation of many individual small doses of toxicity, this effect only being achievable when the insect is abundant.

Not all insect colours are the result of selection by verte-brate predators, although nearly all the visible ones are (visible, that is, to vertebrates). In some insects, the surfaces bear a superimposed ultraviolet pattern which is used by the insects themselves for intraspecific (sexual) communication. Many butterflies and some cetoniine scarabs are known to use UV patterns, which like all courtship signals are species-specific (Ghiradella et al. 1972; Scott 1973; Hinton 1973). This permits the same surfaces to send signals along different channels to quite different receivers.

The emphasis until now has been on visual signalling because we, as visual animals using semaphores and flags our-selves, can most readily understand this medium of communi-cation. However, everything said so far probably applies also to sonic and olfactory communication with predators, including selection for divergence and convergence of signals depending on the circumstances. Chemical signals are a little different from the others in that they combine a signalling with an active defence (repugnatorial) function in one message. They often constitute an arthropod's main defence (for a survey, see Eisner 1970). One specific case that may be mentioned here provides an example of seasonal variation in the concentration of a defensive substance, probably in response to the relative intensity of predation pressure at different seasons. In an Australian ant of the genus *Dolichoderus,* the concentration of the terpenoid dolichodial varies from a maximum of 31 per cent of body weight in spring to a minimum of 11 per cent in winter (Cavill and Hinterberger 1960).

Both chemical and sonic signals are more frequently used for intraspecific communication in insects than are visual ones. Sonic signals in the Orthoptera, in particular, are produced by males and serve to space out the individuals, prevent ipsi-sexual courtship, and attract females of the same species. All three of these functions require that the signals be species-specific, and we have seen that this is also a requisite for most predator-selected signals. It follows that the nocturnal sounds of insects may have a defensive function as well, replacing the silent semaphoring of the diurnal species. Here again, conspicuousness is inevitable because of the need to signal for intraspecific purposes, hence a signal component directed at predators would not increase the chances of detection.

The stridulating noises of many beetles, which come into play when the insect has been disturbed, are believed to have a defensive function (Lane and Rothschild, 1965; Eisner *et al.* 1974). They are particularly prevalent in cerambycids, tenebrionids, and scarabs and are probably signals aimed at predators which rely on sound for recognizing their prey (small mammals, perhaps?).

The most interesting and well-studied cases of prey-predator sonic communication involve certain moths which send signals to bats. Arctiid, ctenuchid, and noctuid moths have tympanal organs, and some sphingids have modified labial palpi, which detect the echolocating signals of bats. Most Arctiidae and Ctenuchidae, which are probably unpalatable, also have tymbal organs which then return a sound with both a sonic and ultrasonic component. Noctuidae use in-flight contact of the wing apices for this purpose. Bats in

Figure 6 Supernormality in mimicry by an undescribed paraoxy-piline mantid from Arnhem Land. The female (figured here) runs rapidly with ants of the genus *Rhytidoponera* in the latter's foraging trails, imitating their movements, and is in appearance a close but supernormal mimic of the ant. That is to say, the mantid exaggerates the characteristics of the ants by being larger and highlighting the reflected sheen from the ants' body surfaces through the use of more distinct white markings. Visual predators having learned to avoid the ant will probably react with even greater aversion to the mantid's supernormal sign stimuli. [Photo Division of Entomology, CSIRO]

flight veer away from an insect when they hear these sounds (Dunning and Roeder 1965), and crawling bats will back away from a moth when the latter "clicks" (Dunning 1967). Most of these moths also produce defensive odours which by themselves deter crawling bats, but when both prey and predator are in flight it is unlikely that chemical defence alone could be effective in avoiding damaging contact. The moths also display signal colours, at least on the underwings, and thus possess three different communication channels able to send messages receivable by all possible types of predators under different circumstances.

It is interesting to note that mimicry also occurs in the olfactory and acoustic communication media, as expected (e.g., Lane and Rothschild 1965). Groups of unrelated animals and even plants may combine to produce the same (or same-tasting) substance to simplify the lesson to be learnt by the (presumably omnivorous) predator. Thus, some Lepidoptera, coccinellid beetles, braconid wasps, and nettles may all produce the same odour (Rothschild 1960). Likewise, analysis of sounds produced by moths shows some evidence of mimicry in one component: pulse repetition rate. As long as this is much higher than that used by the bats' own echolocating signals, it elicits an avoidance response in bats hearing it (Dunning 1967). It follows that palatable species could imitate these high pulse repetition rates and thereby gain some protection in flight as does one relatively palatable arctiid tested by Dunning. However, as I have previously explained, we need not expect that palatable species sending such signals are necessarily mimics.

A type of mimicry known as aggressive mimicry, where a predator sends false signals to a prey individual in order to lure or lull the latter, has been shown to occur in lampyrid beetles ("fireflies"), where the females of some species specialize in preying on the males of other species by luring them with imitated mating flashes (Lloyd 1965: Nelson et al. 1975). Remarkable Australian examples of such "femmes fatales" are provided by the web-less argiopid spiders of the genera *Celaena* and *Dicrostichus* which lure male noctuid

moths to their death (McKeown, 1963). A curious case
of possible aggressive acoustical mimicry of an insect
by a vertebrate involves the Cicada Bird, *Edoliisoma
tenuirostre*, which has a call very similar to that of a cicada.
While this Australian bird will feed on a number of insects, it
will subsist almost entirely on cicadas at certain times
(Chaffer 1930).

1.3.3 THE DOMINANT PREDATOR EFFECT

The existence of aggressive predators may have a diversifying effect on ecosystems, particularly those which are
already complex. This dominant predator phenomenon
was first noted in a marine community and has subsequently
been recognized in other communities. Two simple examples
are presented here, one acting at the second-order consumer
level and one at the first-order.

Among the ants of the Flinders Ranges, South Australia,
it was noted by Greenslade (1973) that in the immediate
vicinity of nests of the dominant diurnal predator, *Iridomyrmex purpureus,* certain other ants — small, specialized,
uncommon, or nocturnal — were more abundant than they
were away from the *Iridomyrmex* nests. In places where the
latter were absent, the other ants mentioned appeared to be
susceptible to predation or interference by a third group of
"subdominant" ants. In other words, the dominant predator
reacts with and drives away the subdominant ones, thus permitting the group of small and specialized ants, with which it
does not react, to survive in its vicinity. There are far more
species in this latter group than among the subdominants;
hence diversity of the whole ant fauna of the community is
increased by the presence of *I. purpureus.*

In plant communities where a dominant plant species
normally suppresses the activities of other species, the introduction of a specialist herbivore on this dominant plant
increases the diversity of other plants by reducing the influence of the dominant. This occurred when a chrysomelid
beetle was introduced to attack the weed *Hypericum perfora-
tum* (St John's Wort) in England (Harper 1969). Some chry-

somelids specializing on this weed have also been introduced into Australia (Wilson 1960). To understand the correlation with the ant situation above, it is necessary to think of the chrysomelid as equivalent to the dominant predator, the *Hypericum* as a subdominant, and the other weeds as the third group (not interacting with the beetle).

The diversifying effect of dominant species, whose influence may ramify throughout a community in numerous and often unsuspected ways (not seen until careful observations are made), is one that must be taken into account in any analyses of community structure and in formulating conservation policies. One of the first tasks should be to identify the "keystone" species whose diversifying and stabilizing influence is out of all proportion to the amount of energy that they actually process. These keystone species, of which several probably exist in each complex community, are likely to be predators but could be herbivores and, as we have just seen (p. 16), they could even be strongly toxic prey species.

1.4 THE PLANT–INSECT INTERFACE

1.4.1 INSECTS AS HERBIVORES

Ehrlich and Raven (1964) called attention to the profoundly important process of coevolution between insects and plants, with numerous examples from the butterflies. They described this process as a step-wise reciprocal selective response whereby, as the first step, a plant subjected to herbivore attack adopts defences which are effective against the herbivore. These defences tend to be chemical, although they can also be mechanical (e.g., pubescence-forming trichomes). A large variety of substances is available to plants for chemical defence (see Whittaker 1970). When confronted with this defence, herbivores must either narrow their food spectrum to undefended plants, or evolve chemical counter-measures to eat the defended ones (which then become undefended to them). In either case, a narrowing of the food spectrum takes place – specialization occurs. Those species evolving chemical counter-measures embark on a course of ever-increasing specialization as the food plant evolves more efficient defences. The ultimate step in this process is to have a herbivore restricted to one species of plant, as in some birdwing butterflies (*Ornithoptera*) (Straatman 1962). There are many examples among insects of restriction to a few related host plants (or unrelated ones relying on the same defensive substances, see section 3.5). The narrowness of food plant choice among Australian butterflies may be gauged by perusing the food-plant list in Common and Waterhouse (1972). Among grasshoppers, the pergomorphids display some notable examples of food specialization. For instance, species of *Monistria* and related genera are usually restricted to a few strongly-defended host plants, and themselves use chemical defences, while in Arnhem Land *Petasida ephippigera* appears to be restricted to the very few species of *Pityrodia* (Dicrastylidinaceae) — only recently discovered and highly localized — and one species of *Dampiera* (Goodeniaceae) (Calaby and Key 1973).

If the plant's chemical defences can be circumvented experimentally (for instance, by altering the insects' chemoreceptors), it can occasionally be shown that the plant tissues are not themselves toxic to an insect which normally does not eat them (J. J. H. Szent-Ivany, personal communication; Common and Waterhouse, 1972), but it should be understood that there is no way that food-plant specialization can evolve except by selection against individual genotypes that make the wrong choice of oviposition sites, and this has to be initially through differential larval mortality or reduced adult fitness. A result of this selection is to favour adults which use either the toxic compounds themselves or some other factor completely correlated with them to avoid unsuitable plants. It is possible that the insect's reliance on a correlated factor may enable the plant on rare occasions to dispense with the toxic principle, or it may be simply that an insect has not yet responded to the recent entry of a new suitable food plant in its habitat.

The theoretical reasons why some insects persist with a

monophagic strategy in spite of the fact that they are capable of feeding on other plants have been suggested by Levins and MacArthur (1969). Monophagy is a rewarding strategy as long as the probability of failure to find the normal host plant in the time available is low, and the proportion of suitable to unsuitable alternate plants is also low. Substantial changes in either one or both of these factors are required to bring about a switch in strategy.

In any case, monophagy and oligophagy are mediated by the insects' reliance on chemical stimuli to recognize host plants for oviposition and feeding, and by the plants' reliance on a chemical communication system which informs the insect of their specific identity without the latter's necessarily having to chew into the tissues.

Some insects can deal with strong toxins through detoxification. For instance, an arctiid moth can detoxify the highly poisonous substance cycasin, elaborated by cycads (Dethier 1970) (see also section 4.3.6) and the bird-wing swallowtails, Troidini, can detoxify aristolochic acid and feed on *Aristolochia* exclusively (von Euw *et al.* 1968).

Insects specialized to feed on toxic plants can sometimes use the plant's toxin for their own defence; for instance, the Zygaenidae (Lepidoptera) can use hydrocyanic acid from food plants (as well as manufacturing their own) (Jones *et al.* 1962), and the wanderer butterfly, *Danaus plexippus,* uses digitalis-like cardiac glycosides extracted from Asclepiadaceae (Reichstein, von Euw, and Rothschild 1968).

Particularly interesting are cases where two different plant substances from different plant species are used by the same insect for two different purposes. This is seen in the danaine butterflies and the arctiid moths again, where cardenolides from Asclepiadaceae are used by both sexes for defence, and pyrrolizidine alkaloids derived from Boraginaceae and some other plant families are used by male butterflies, at least, as female flight-arrestants and aphrodisiacs (Rothschild, von Euw, and Reichstein 1973; Edgar, Culvenor, and Pliske 1974). That the substances come from two different host plants is most curious, and Edgar and co-

workers postulate that an ancestral species of the lepidopterans in question must have fed on plants containing both
substances. They suggest that the subsequent evolution of the
plants into two groups, each containing only one of the substances, was a form of defence against these specialized
herbivores.

Sometimes closely-related species may feed on food
plants which are quite different both taxonomically and
chemically, such as the two Australian species of salt-and-
pepper moths, *Utetheisa lotrix* and *U. pulchelloides,* which
feed on various Leguminoseae and Boraginaceae respectively
(J. J. H. Szent-Ivany, personal communication), whilst in
other cases different races of the same species may feed on
different (but chemically similar) host plants (section 3.5).

Seed eaters may be confronted with special chemical
defences in the seed coat or pod, or in the embryo proper. In
tropical forests, most seed eaters become specialists as a result
(sections 4.3.6 and 4.6.2). Among substances found in certain
legume seeds in Central America is a free amino acid known
as L-dopa, used in the treatment of Parkinson's disease, and
highly toxic to insects (Rehr, Janzen, and Feeny 1973). Other
substances in seeds are mentioned by Janzen (1973b). The
most intimate plant-insect relationship is that which involves
gall-making insects. Here the communication is again chemical
and may include the use of nucleic acids (section 4.3.1).
Examples of true mutualism between plants and insects are
the plant-pollinator relationships (section 1.4.3), the fig-
agaonid relationship (section 4.3.1), some insect-fungus
associations (sections 4.3.1 and 4.3.7), those between ants
and some acacias, and between ants and some Rubiaceae.

1.4.2 PLANTS AS INSECTIVORES

An unusual facet of the plant-insect interface is the one where
the tables are turned, so to speak. Four families of higher
plants in Australia include predators on insects: the pitcher
plants (Nepenthaceae, Cephalotaceae), sundews (Droseraceae),
and bladderworts (Lentibulariaceae) (section 4.4.4), whilst at
least one fungus group (*Cordyceps*) kills subterranean insects

(section 2.4.2). Other plants trap and kill insects apparently as a consequence of adaptation for seed dispersal by birds, and possibly also as a means of defence against seed eaters. Such is the "insect-catching grass" (*Cenchrus australis*) described by Lea (1915), and the trees *Pisonia brunoniana* and *P. grandis* which trap insects and sometimes even birds with a very sticky seed-coat. *Lomatatia* (Proteaceae), a bird-pollinated plant, has cyanogenic flowers said to kill insects (Cribb 1969).

Some insects have become specialized to feed on the trapped prey of pitcher plants and sundews (section 4.4.4).

Although not predators, some flowers trap their pollinators, temporarily or permanently, to make sure that the latter will well and truly perform their function of picking up pollen or depositing it, as the case may be. Cribb (*op. cit.*) and Jones (1970) mention orchids of the genera *Pterostylis, Caleana,* and *Corybas* which trap small Diptera temporarily or permanently, and Common and Waterhouse (1972) cite a case of an introduced asclepiad (*Araujia* sp.) trapping *Pieris rapae,* sometimes killing it. Of course, the efficiency of the trapping mechanism must be adjusted to the strength of the principal pollinator so as not to kill it the first time.

1.4.3 INSECTS AS POLLINATORS

This facet of the plant-insect interface is mutualistic and it is advantageous to the plant that the pollinator become, at least temporarily, a specialist since a pollinator visiting only one or a few species of plant at a time ensures successful cross-pollination.

Plants will therefore tend to evolve flowers which are distinct from the flowers of other species, as this facilitates the evolution of flower constancy, or oligolecty, in the pollinators. The pollinator itself benefits from constancy to one flower species at a time, as it then needs to be programmed for only one set of stimuli, thus reducing its search time and energy expenditure (Levin and Anderson 1970). For this reason, at any one time flexible pollinators tend to become constant on the most abundant flower species — the apostatic effect again, known in this case as the "dominating flower phenomenon" — and thus favour that species to the detriment of minority species (exerting a diversity-reducing effect opposite to that of apostatic predators, and favouring flower mimicry in some situations). If conditions do not permit the evolution of species-specific pollination, different plants can share the same pollinators by arranging to deposit pollinia on different parts of the same bee, as in some *Asclepias* (Macior 1971) and *Stylidium* (Carlquist, 1969), or they can use a "lock-and-key" mechanism between the pollinium and the receptive part of the strobilus, as some orchids do. They can also stagger their flowering times, as occurs in some alpine zones.

The arid tropics produce the opposite effect, with a large number of pollinating species competing for flowers which tend to bloom simultaneously in response to moisture. In this case, the level of oligolecty (restriction of number of flower species visited) is undoubtedly greatly increased (section 2.4.3), and in Northern Australia some bees have adopted the unusual tactic of flying at night (T. F. Houston, personal communication).

One way of bringing about pollinator constancy is to use insects or other animals which do not normally pollinate at all, and which are therefore not being used by other plants. Such tactics are employed by the Australian orchids — *Cryptostylis, Prasophyllum, Calochilus,* and *Caladenia* spp. which induce (by chemical means) male ichneumon wasps of certain species to "copulate" with them (Erickson 1951; Cribb 1969; Jones 1972). One species of *Diuris* orchids similarly attracts a male bee (Erickson, citing Edith Coleman) and one *Spiculea* attracts a male thynnid (Rotherham 1968). The orchids *Pterostylis* attract and temporarily trap small nematocerous Diptera, *Prasophyllum* spp. may attract staphylinids and chrysomelids, a *Microtis* attracts a weevil (E.C. Zimmerman, personal communication, based on material collected by D. Jones of Victoria) and one *Diuris* attracts a *Liparetrus* (Scarabaedae) (Erickson 1951 *op. cit.*). An arum lily, *Typhonium* sp. of Queensland, smells of fresh faeces and attracts dung beetles and flies (G. B. Monteith, personal communication), whilst other Araceae may attract snails for pollination (Cribb 1969). Some of the advanced gasteromycete fungi are well known as attractors of blowflies and dung-beetles which then disperse their spores. Ant-pollinated flowers are known elsewhere in the world and probably occur in Australia as well.

At least in the cases studied overseas, the attraction of most orchids for insects is highly species-specific and in some cases also male-specific; this specificity is often vital in maintaining reproductive isolation among sympatric orchid species. Visual aspects of the flower, sometimes including prey-mimicry, play an important part, but the specificity is also reinforced chemically (Dodson *et al.* 1969).

The many species of the Australian genus *Stylidium* (Stylidiaceae) appear to specialize in bombyliid flies and perhaps other Diptera, although a few species attract a variety of insects. These plants have a pressure-sensitive column in the flower bearing a brush-like stigma which is sprung against the abdomen of the fly, picking up any attached pollen grains, while anthers simultaneously bend inward to deposit more pollen. Self-pollination is avoided by a fifteen-minute delay in re-sensitizing the triggering mechanism, reducing the chances that the same insect will still be around to pollinate the same flower. These remarkable plants are surveyed by Erickson (1958) and Carlquist (1969), who observed several instances of species-specificity in pollination. They would provide excellent subjects for a detailed study of plant-insect co-evolution. In most cases the insect pollinators are unknown or have not been accurately identified.

It is quite clear from evidence assembled by Baker and Hurd (1968) and others, that the earliest "flowering" plants (both angiosperms and gymnosperms such as Bennettitales) were pollinated by beetles, as are primitive groups today (the arum lilies and orchids are probably secondarily beetle attractors). The earliest flowers attracted beetles by pollen alone. Later beetle-pollinated flowers offered a better "caloric reward" in the form of nutritive tissue to be chewed. Nectar (and bees) came much later. A prime example of a primitive magnolia-like group still pollinated by beetles in Australia is the genus *Eupomatia* (containing two species, sole living representatives of the Eupomatiaceae). These are pollinated by species of the weevil genus *Elleschodes* (Hotchkiss 1958).

The caloric reward offered by a plant will be the minimum necessary to achieve the desired amount of cross pollination, but plants which produce synchronized flowers at intervals, and which therefore must rely on generalized pollinators, need to produce a generous reward to attract a large number of insects, only a small proportion of which will have previously visited a conspecific plant. On the other hand, flowers morphologically modified as a result of coevolution to be available to only a few specialized pollinators, need produce only a small daily reward (extended over a whole season). Such specialist-pollinated plants can exist at very low densities and be relatively inconspicuous (native orchids, for instance), since their pollinators will seek them out, sometimes over great distances (section 4.6.2).

Highly evolved and bilaterally symmetrical bee-pollinated flowers often rely on ultraviolet colours to attract their pollinators. Some have UV nectar guides which change in intensity according to the flower's state of nectar depletion. Many bee-attracting flowers which appear yellow to us are really yellow+UV (bee's violet) (Macior 1971). In contrast bees cannot see red. Red flowers are believed to be specialized for pollination by birds, but this colour is also visible to some butterflies.

Since flowers have been evolved strictly for attracting pollinators (but see Hinton 1973), the great majority of them insects, the question arises as to why flowers should also provide man's own standards of beauty in colour, form, and fragrance. Similarly, the patterns and colours of day-flying insects considered beautiful by man, have been evolved in response to selection pressure by birds and other visual predators (section 1.3.2). Could insects, birds, and man share the same standards of what is visually attention-catching, and therefore attractive? This seems probable, and the existence of a "pan-aesthetic sense" among all higher animals has been suggested by Leppik (1972). What this simply means is that beauty often may be largely equivalent to communication — that which is visually and olfactorily aesthetic is that which conveys a message — and the most informative combinations of patterns, colours, and odours are those which are most removed from randomness or entropy. This provides a universal standard.

1.4.4 INSECTS AS SEED DISPERSERS

The great importance of seed dispersal by ants in certain xeric habitats in Australia has been pointed out by Berg (1975). Some 1500 Australian species of plants in 87 genera and 24 families have evolved special ant-attracting structures (elaiosomes) on their seeds or fruits. This compares with only about 300 known species of ant-dispersed (myrmecochorous) plants in the rest of the world, making Australia the "world centre" for this kind of plant. Unlike those known elsewhere, the Australian myrmecochorous species are nearly all woody shrubs growing in dry sclerophyll forest or dry shrubland, and at present we do not know for certain what the factors are which selected for the independent autochthonous evolution of ant dispersal in so many different plants.

Some 30 species of ants belonging to nine genera are adapted to collect elaiosome-bearing seeds in the very limited areas studied by Berg, showing that this is an exceedingly important facet of the plant-insect interface in Australia.

1.5 WHY ARE THERE SO MANY INSECTS?

The subject of species diversity in natural communities has received much attention in recent years (following the lead of G. E. Hutchinson's classic paper of 1959) but there is still considerable disagreement concerning its usefulness as a concept and whether it can be accurately measured. The most widely-used index was formulated for quite a different purpose by a communications engineer, C. E. Shannon. It takes into account the number of species present in an area (species richness or abundance) and how individuals are distributed among those species (species evenness or equitability). The reader interested in researching this topic in more depth would perhaps do best to start with the critique of Hurlbert (1971).

Quite apart from the problem of devising a biologically meaningful index, there are the difficulties involved in obtaining samples which accurately reflect the situation in the field. Normal sampling procedures in insects are strongly biased (e.g., Greenslade 1964; Roff 1973), and even if this is taken into account, there is the problem of deciding when to cut off the sampling at a point which approximates an estimate of the asymptote of the species/area curve. This point will differ in different habitats.

Nevertheless, numerous papers dealing with species diversity continue to appear in the ecological literature, and it is evident that in spite of criticisms and caveats, many ecologists continue to find the concept and its application useful.

Aside from ecological diversity, there is the question of taxonomic diversity, usually concerned with the distribution of species among the genera of a given higher taxon. As in the case of ecological indices, there are some common patterns in taxonomic diversity which require explanation (Anderson 1974). Both ecological and taxonomic diversity patterns reflect the fact that there are a great many more rare species than common ones (section 1.6).

In this section I will be concerned mostly with the broad question of the number of species of insects in the entire biosphere, the factors which appear to bring about diversity in insects, and the distribution of insect species according to trophic level.

To begin with, it should be pointed out that no realistic estimate of the total number of insect species is available. The number of formally described species is somewhat less than a million at the time of writing, but this is a grotesque underestimate of the true situation. This is not only because many areas of the world, and many taxonomic groups, remain unexplored or poorly known, but also because most insect species are not discoverable by standard, morphology-based taxonomic procedures. A recent estimate for Canada calculates the ratio of such "cryptic" species to morphological species at about 2·5:1. If we take into account the number of unnamed morphological species in the world (perhaps equal to those presently named), and if the above ratio is generally applicable, the result is a rough estimate of four to ten million biological species of insects in the world.

Of course, the interests of biological science are not served by any attempt to name and describe all those species. This activity should be restricted to occasions when it will further the solution of some biological problem.

However inaccurate may be our estimate of the number of insect species in the world, or in any part of it, it is quite clear that insects outnumber all other organisms put together. This brings us to the question at the heading of this section:— why are there so many insects?

In seeking an answer, we must temporarily set aside discussion of the factors which cause an increase in biotic diversity in general, very briefly summarized at the end of this section. The present question more precisely framed, is: why have insects responded to the forces which generate diversity by producing more species than other animals also subject to those same forces?

I believe that there is a variety of reasons acting in combination. These are: (1) the high level of organization of insect sensory and neuro-motor systems; (2) their minimal learning capacity and short generation time; (3) their small size; and (4) the nature of the coevolutionary interactions which involve insects.

The first reason is the basic one, and the only other group of animals which matches insects in organismal development is the Vertebrata. A high level of organization enhances the ability to perceive small environmental differences and react to them; it effectively maximizes the apparent (perceived) environmental heterogeneity. The problem is therefore reduced to a comparison between insects and vertebrates, and the other three reasons apply specifically to this comparison.

It is axiomatic that learning ability is most highly developed in vertebrates and that no invertebrate group as a whole matches most vertebrates in this respect. The reason for this has been pointed out by Slobodkin and Rapoport (1974) in their discussion of optimal strategies in evolution. Learning is a behavioural adaptation to cope with events which are irregular and unpredictable in occurrence, but which recur with sufficient frequency within the lifetime of a single individual to make it worthwhile to evolve the individual ability to adapt to them. Animals are unable to learn if each of the major perturbations in their environment during their lifetime are unique. The life spans of insects are simply too short to permit the evolution of learning ability beyond a rudimentary level.

When faced with a new situation, a learning animal may well find that the appropriate response is within its existing repertoire, whilst the non-learning animal may not be programmed to respond appropriately. If the new situation persists, the non-learning population will need to be "reprogrammed", that is to say, to undergo genetic changes. To adapt to local environmental perturbations, insects must evolve mechanisms which permit them to undergo rapid genetic changes. Genotypes so evolved must in turn be protected by barriers to gene flow against loss of adapted alleles to other environments where the same conditions do not occur, as well as against the influx of non-adapted alleles.

In other words, the development of semi-isolated and fully-isolated genetic units (races, semi-species, and species) is some animals' way of adapting to the environmental heterogeneity which in others is dealt with through individual non-genetic tactical adjustment (Slobodkin and Rapoport 1974). Speciation (or, more correctly, genetic heterogeneity) in insects is an adaptive strategy; more will be said about this in the next section.

The third reason mentioned above, small size, can partly account for the greater number of insect species (in comparison with vertebrates) since a greater number of niches per unit area of the earth's surface, can exist for small animals than for big ones. The environment for the former is more "coarse-grained". The rate of extinction should also be less for small animals, as a given amount of energy can support a larger population, enabling them to absorb environmental perturbations with a proportionately smaller commitment of resources.

The fourth reason involves coevolution, which in insects is primarily with plants. The nature of the plant-insect interface is governed by all the previous factors mentioned, particularly small size and highly developed sensory receptors. The two apposed surfaces of the interface are, on the one hand, the secondary plant substances, and on the other, the chemosensory receptors of insects. The extreme sophistication with which both groups have been able to elaborate and detect the chemical substances involved have enabled insects and higher plants to create a structural and molecular "fine texture" on the interface between them. The importance of this interaction was first stressed by Ehrlich and Raven (1964), who see plant-herbivore coevolution as the principal diversity generator in terrestrial environments. As a diversity generator its effect on vertebrates is limited because, in the first place, most vertebrate herbivores are large polyphagous animals which cannot be tied to a single host plant species, and which have to vary their diet in any case in order to be able to deal with the toxicity of individual plant species. In the second place, their behavioural and physiological flexibility enables them to by-pass or ignore many of the intricate chemical defences of plants. The most diverse terrestrial vertebrate groups are not herbivores but insectivores, probably because coevolution occurs between insects and their vertebrate predators (section 1.3.2) to a greater extent than between plants and their vertebrate herbivores. Evidently, insects are more of a "match" for vertebrates in this regard than are plants.

Independent confirmation of Ehrlich's and Raven's thesis can be obtained by correlating insect species numbers with major trophic levels. One can go through the lists of families and numbers of included species in *The Insects of Australia* and find that the herbivorous groups contain far more species than all the others put together. According to my rough estimate, about 32,000 of Australia's 54,000 described insects (as of 1968) are herbivorous or fungivorous. In fact the disproportion is probably greater, since many species in the most species-rich groups are undescribed. For instance, there are about 10,000 Australian weevil species (a herbivorous group), less than half of which are described (E. C. Zimmerman, personal communication). Furthermore, as Pimental (1968) pointed out, many supposedly saprophagous species are really feeding on microorganisms and fungi.

The proportion of herbivorous to non-herbivorous species will not hold for any particular insect group, as some groups are simply not adapted for herbivory. It is the total number of insect species that must be considered, and classed according to trophic adaptation and not taxonomy.

When this process is continued for the remaining 40 per cent of insect species, the result is also illuminating. No less than a further 12 per cent are parasitoids (Kuris 1974), and an undetermined but probably disproportionate further percentage are parasites and inquilines in the nests of social insects, leaving a surprisingly small number of predators and decomposers. Insect herbivores, parasitoids, parasites, and inquilines all have one characteristic in common: a high degree of host specificity as a result of coevolution between eater and eaten. It is this interaction — coevolution — which generates the diversity, not the plant food as such. The greater influence of the plant-insect interface is simply due to the greater quantity of energy that passes through it in comparison with the other interactions which involve coevolution.

The detritus food chains have relatively little diversifying influence, in spite of the fact that much more than half of all energy flows through them. This is simply because dead organic matter does not defend itself, and no coevolution can occur except among the consumer species themselves through competition, and between the consumers and microorganisms.

With regard to predator-prey relationships, there is some degree of specificity in insects which is behaviourally mediated as a rule. Certain types of prey, such as spiders and ants, require a high degree of specialization in their predators. One extreme example of prey specificity is seen in the sphecid wasp *Sericophorus viridis,* which was observed near Canberra by Matthews and Evans (1970) to feed exclusively on the males of the blowfly *Calliphora tibialis* (itself a specialist predator on earthworms).

In short, the reason why there are so many insects is that their advanced organization, combined with small size and reliance on molecular-based interactions with food organisms, permits them to exploit a great array of minor variations in ecological opportunities, at the same time that their minimal learning capacity and short generation time dictate that their exploitation of these variations be at the genetic rather than the individual behavioural or physiological level.

The opinion expressed here that coevolution is the fundamental basis for organic diversity is not shared to the same extent by other observers. Current concepts on diversity, very briefly summarized, explain the rate of build-up of a fauna in a given area as being first of all governed by the rates of immigration and extinction of species, which are in turn dependent on the size and heterogeneity of the area in question and its accessibility to other areas (MacArthur and Wilson 1967). Under given conditions, the number of resident species reaches an equilibrium which is at first independent of any interactions between species (a non-interactive equilibrium) but which soon becomes an interactive one, permitting a greater number of species to coexist (Simberloff 1969). The slow process of organic diversification which begins once the initial interactive equilibrium has been reached is seen as being influenced by a number of factors, of which interactions (coevolution) are only one. The others are time, stochastic (chance) factors, energy flow, and the physical environment (MacArthur 1968). Except to the extent that time is necessary for coevolution to take place, I have suggested above that these other factors are secondary. Among the interactions themselves, competitive displacement and symbioses are seen to be on a par with predation, whereas I believe (as argued above) that the latter, if understood to mean eater-eaten relationships between living organisms, is overwhelmingly more important than the others.

The theory of island biogeography of MacArthur and Wilson (1967) has been applied with some success to continental biocoenoses where immigration and extinction rates are disproportionately important, as in caves and mountain tops (Chapter 5), and there is growing evidence of its applicability to insects on host plants, the latter being essentially biotic islands.

1.6 TACTICS IN THE STRATEGY OF SPECIATION

I have suggested that speciation may itself be adaptive in organisms which routinely adjust to different environments at the genetic level. This idea is contrary to current concepts of speciation, which is believed by most biologists to occur only as a result of the formation of extrinsic barriers to gene flow between the potential sibling species, either as a result of climatic events which break up a previously continuous range into fragmented refuges (Brereton et al. 1969) or as a result of the "founder event" (Carson 1970; see also Mayr 1965). The latter takes place as one or a few stray individuals become transported to an isolated habitat or island and their progeny then undergo genetic changes departing from a base which contains only a fraction of the parental population's original gene pool. A strong element of chance enters into both these mechanisms, in which natural selection has no control over whether speciation will occur in the first place, but only acts ex post facto after physical isolation has been imposed by an external event. There can be little doubt that these allopatric mechanisms are important in consolidating genetic differences between populations, but it appears likely that in insects the environment, at a much earlier stage, will select for a "propensity" to speciate, by whatever means, by selecting against individual vagility. This would have the effect of enhancing the efficacy of any barrier involved. By the same token, the rate of speciation can be greatly retarded by selecting for individual vagility.

A parallel controversy concerns the nature of the primary barriers to gene flow which are needed to bring about partial or complete reproductive isolation. It has been generally believed that these barriers must be geographic or micro-geographic, that is, they must bring about a spatial isolation of the two potential species, which must therefore be allopatric. Recently, Australian entomologists in particular have proposed that an additional speciation mechanism may operate, termed stasipatric or parapatric (White *et al.* 1967; White 1970), and there has been a revival of the old theory that speciation may occur sympatrically (Bush 1974). However, even in these mechanisms, as they are currently explained, natural selection is seen as playing only a minor role, or none at all, in the earliest stages of speciation, which are believed to be initiated by spontaneous genetic or chromosomal events. I believe this to be highly unlikely, and that the particular genetic mechanisms involved are themselves selected precisely because they do lead to speciation (or, more correctly, to a segregation of adaptive gene frequencies).

There is universal agreement that speciation is impossible without an interruption of gene flow between the incipient species. If natural selection is to control the rate of speciation, it can only do so by controlling the rate of gene flow between the populations involved. Genes are, of course, carried in individuals, and reduction of gene flow between populations simply means selection against the genotypes of individuals which move out of the zones to which they are adapted. This will occur with maximum intensity where populations need to become very closely adapted to local conditions, which are *ipso facto* unique. The more closely they become adapted to their own environment, the less successful they will be in the environment of other populations, and the stronger will be the selection against mobile genotypes. Given stability, this process is self-accelerating and will lead to ever-decreasing vagility. This will in turn lead to a fragmenting of populations along cleavage planes which correspond to relatively unfavourable environmental features. To the observer coming along at this stage, it will seem as if these cleavage planes, or barriers, have themselves caused the fragmentation to occur. In fact all they have done is to facilitate a process of genetic segregation which is taking place anyway. (Since this was written, a paper by McDonald and Ayala (1974) has been published demonstrating experimentally that environmental heterogeneity is matched by genetic heterogeneity through natural selection in a species of *Drosophila*, and a paper by Ehrlich and Raven (1969), previously overlooked, was found to contain much the same ideas as those expressed here.).

Whereas speciation is often thought to occur most rapidly where environmental, particularly climatic, conditions are most unstable, the present interpretation arrives at just the opposite conclusion and predicts that speciation will be most rapid in stable environments (those under K selection).

It cannot be concluded from this that the rate of evolution will be faster among K strategists than among r strategists, since speciation and evolution are not at all equivalent. Speciation can occur with minimal genetic changes, whilst extensive genetic change may occur without speciation. The conditions which give rise to evolutionary novelties are still not understood.

The adaptive function of barriers, then, is to help reduce gene flow between conspecific populations inhabiting areas on either side of the barrier which are sufficiently different, as far as that species' adaptations are concerned, to require that the populations evolve correspondingly different adaptive gene combinations. Normally, a barrier is allowed to be only partial. This permits a certain amount of genetic interchange which may be beneficial in renewing the heterogeneity of the gene pool.

Over a wide latitudinal range, or along an altitudinal transect, it is the usual case for related insect species to replace one another, apparently in response to temperature and humidity gradients. All taxonomists are familiar with this phenomenon. This is undoubtedly because the lack of behavioural flexibility in insects, previously stressed, is matched by a lack of physiological flexibility, which requires that different (rather narrow) ranges in physical factors be matched by somewhat different genotypes.

When a phytophagous or parasitic species has the opportunity to adapt to a variety of hosts, the individuals feeding on the different hosts may differ genetically. This has been shown to occur in fruit flies (Tephritidae) (Bush 1974) and in mosquitoes (White 1974), at least. In the former case, the genetic differences between host races are minimal and affect only those key loci involved in host selection. The integrity of the host race is maintained through non-random mating occurring on the host itself. In this case, the barriers to gene flow are behavioural rather than geographic, and since the loci involved in host selection are few, it is theoretically possible for this process of genetic segregation through non-random mating to culminate in full speciation rather rapidly, should this be of selective advantage.

It has been shown in a few rare cases, involving mostly Hawaiian *Drosophila*, that speciation has occurred without any apparent change in the chromosomes. This and the minimal changes seen in closely-related species of tephritid fruit flies indicate that speciation can occur without the fundamental restructuring of the genome which has traditionally been thought to be a necessary accompaniment. It would be entirely incorrect to conclude thereby that the discredited theory of the "hopeful monster" (saltation) had been vindicated. The minimal allele differences that characterize tephritid semi-species involve precisely those loci that help maintain the host race barriers, and this has not been brought about by accident but as a result of a long-term genetic structuring which serves to facilitate host race formation as an adaptive strategy.

So far we have been considering cases where the physical or biotic environment is sufficiently heterogeneous to provide discontinuities which can act as partial barriers to gene flow. But what if there are no sharp boundaries which can be used as markers for such gene filters, and yet the environmental differences along the gradient are too great for a uniform genetic combination to be adaptive over the whole range? It seems that the first stage in the adaptation to this situation is selection for an absolute minimum of vagility. This would have the effect of making a barrier of anything that could possibly serve this purpose. But if vagility has been reduced to the minimum compatible with survival, and this is still not sufficient to preserve locally adapted genotypes, then one more mechanism is available. It involves the establishment of partial genetic barriers where no environmental markers exist, through evolution of a chromosomal mechanism that serves this function.

Some of the morabine grasshoppers and some phasmids provide examples of this strategic extreme. In the former, at least, vagility has already been reduced to what would appear to be an absurd minimum. In one species, movement by individuals over more than 3 m in their lifetime is unusual (White 1957), although movements of up to 11 m have been recorded since (Blackith and Blackith 1969). An upper limit of about 300 m is possible (Key 1974b).

Correlated with this minimal vagility is a tendency for the chromosomes to be unstable and fragment, forming re-arrangements. The species of morabine in question, *Moraba viatica,* has races characterized by different chromosomal arrangements separated by relatively sharp boundaries, only a few hundred metres wide, which run across apparently homogeneous areas and do not coincide with any environmental features. These barriers are maintained by a slight reduction in the viability of hybrids between the adjacent chromosomal races. White *et al.* (1967) postulate that hundreds of thousands of rearrangements have arisen in the history of this species, but that the only ones selected for are the few which are unusually favourable in the areas in which they arise. In spite of reduced hybrid viability, these new rearrangements become fixed in a local population, perhaps during a contraction phase when a peripheral population is small enough for some random fixation to occur (Key 1968) or through the effect of meiotic drive (White 1970).

In any case, such adaptive chromosomal arrangements spread from their points of origin to a line where they impinge on others spreading in the opposite direction. Depending on which arrangement is most adaptive in the zone of contact, the front between them will shift one way or the other until an adaptive equilibrium is reached, that is, until the selective forces do not favour one arrangement over the other. There the front will temporarily become stationary, maintained by reduced hybrid viability. There is every indication that a phasmid species of the genus *Didymuria,* with at least ten chromosomal races, exhibits exactly the same phenomenon (Craddock 1974).

The reduced hybrid viability is not sufficient, however, to prevent all genetic exchange across the boundary. The contact zones between chromosomally different populations have been called "tension zones" by Key (1968), who likens them to semipermeable membranes in that they allow some genes through in either direction, but not those involved in the rearranged chromosomes. Since the genetic adaptation to local conditions is embodied in the rearranged chromosome (otherwise it would not have been selected for), then the tension zone has the effect of preserving precisely those genotypic features which need protecting, whilst allowing through those genetic characteristics which are generally useful to the species as a whole.

White *et al.* (1967) interpret the chromosomal phenomena just outlined as a process of incipient speciation, termed "stasipatric", but it is unlikely that the genetic events observed in *M. viatica* necessarily or inevitably lead to speciation. Rather, they represent a genetic strategy to preserve local genetic identity, evolved in some species under strong *K* selection in a distribution range which displays no environmental discontinuities at the same time that it is sufficiently heterogeneous to require local genetic adjustments. Under these circumstances, a species must create its own genetic discontinuities between units of coadapted gene combinations. At the stage observed in *M. viatica*, the subsequent course of events could go either toward the maintenance of chromosomal races for an indefinite period, or toward full speciation by a progressive pile-up of genetic differences on either side of the tension zones, as suggested by Key (1968, 1974b).

If partial barriers, of whatever type, are converted to full barriers to gene flow, it will be because this is of selective advantage, either because of a polarization of the environmental differences which selected for the genetic divergence in the first place, or because the group can adapt more efficiently to the existing environmental heterogeneity by breaking up into independent genetic units. The suggestion made earlier that the process of genetic fragmentation is self-accelerating under stable conditions indicates that it will automatically culminate in full speciation unless conditions change. This is a question that requires further attention, but at present we will assume that this is not always the case and that allopatric, parapatric (stasipatric), and sympatric mechanisms of genetic segregation through non-random mating do not necessarily lead to speciation, so that the term itself is misleading and deterministic, since it implies a goal. Strictly speaking, it should not be used except in retrospect, but no other convenient, generally understood term is available.

Speciation, then, may be seen as the culmination of a long process governed by natural selection which is initially manifested as a reduction in gene flow between units of a population which must diverge genetically in order to adapt efficiently to environmental heterogeneity. In most cases this reduction in gene flow is brought about by selection against mobile individuals, and this will result in geographic barriers not previously recognizable as such. This is the allopatric mechanism. In the case of host race formation, however, the same segregation effect is produced by non-random mating on the host, and the genetic control of host selection is concentrated in only a few loci whose mutations are allowed to be expressed phenotypically by a relaxation of normal mechanisms of genetic homeostasis vis-a-vis these particular loci. This is brought about by selection and bestows on the species an exceptional flexibility in adapting to host heterogeneity. This is the sympatric mechanism. Finally, if the allopatric mechanism is insufficient to produce the necessary genetic heterogeneity (even after vagility has been reduced to a minimum), because of the absence of suitable environmental discontinuities, the species must create its own genetic discontinuities through the medium of exceptionally unstable chromosomes. This is the parapatric mechanism.

If the speciation processes are seen thus, many of the known facts, such as the coincidence of frequent chromosomal rearrangements and minimal vagility, and the simple genetic control of host race formation, fall into place as parts of processes governed from their inception by natural selection. Chance, external events of a catastrophic nature, and topography play minimal roles in speciation except on islands. A traditional preoccupation with insular speciation events has led to widespread misconceptions.

Once speciation has occurred, the newly-formed (sibling) species can freely and extensively overlap each other's ranges. This bestows on each genotype a greater advantage than when it was represented only by a race, and permits efficient sympatric exploitation of environmental heterogeneity. Any lingering tendency toward interspecific interactions is quickly selected against as a result of gamete wastage or hybrid inviability, and intrinsic pre-mating barriers are erected (generally as ritualistic courtship). This process has long been well understood. The sibling species will be ecologically different even before overlap, because this is what led to their speciation in the first place, but as in the case of reproductive interactions, remaining competitive interactions involving key components of the niche may be selected against as being wasteful, and ecological differences between the species may be reinforced. This process is known as habitat divergence or competitive displacement (MacArthur and Levins 1964). An example of this process in two sibling species of the grasshopper genus *Psednura* has been described by Key and Balderson (1972). The two species occupy different habitats when sympatric, but they are found in the same sorts of habitats when allopatric.

However, competitive displacement need not necessarily occur, since the process of genetic feedback (section 1.3.1) can permit two competing species to coexist, perhaps indefinitely (Pimentel 1968; Ayala, 1971). This is because as one species becomes dominant, its members will be competing with themselves increasingly, while the other species will be competing mostly with the dominant one. The "underdog" species will thus be constantly improving its competitive ability while the dominant one is undergoing self-destructive intra-species competition. This will eventually reverse the relative positions of the two species and likewise reverse the process. The extent to which this phenomenon is prevalent in natural ecosystems remains to be determined, however. In theory, the eventual avoidance of all interspecific competition, as a result of competitive displacement, would seem to be the least wasteful solution for both species.

This chapter has briefly reviewed some of the basic principles of evolutionary biology which I believe must be grasped if we are to understand what is going on, and what has gone on in the past, in natural ecosystems. The frontiers of knowledge are still moving very rapidly forward, and concepts which were considered axiomatic even a few years ago have had to be modified or questioned. The biggest advances recently have been made in our understanding of plant-herbivore and predator-prey interactions and coevolution, and of the adaptive role of speciation. We see that natural selection plays an even greater part than was thought previously, and descriptive studies in ecology (as in biology as a whole) are becoming increasingly redundant if not placed in the perspective of evolutionary time.

CHAPTER 2
Arid Australia

2.1 GENERAL CHARACTERISTICS OF THE BIOME

According to the generally accepted definition of arid lands approximately three quarters of the land area of Australia is arid (Slatyer and Perry 1969). Aridity is defined in terms of the effectiveness of the rainfall, not its absolute quantity, but in general the limits of the arid zone coincide with the 750 mm annual isohyet in the north, the 500 mm one in the east, and the 250 mm one in the south. The existence of well-defined dry seasons (winter in the north, summer in the south) produces seasonal arid conditions (with evaporation exceeding precipitation) for insects inhabiting exposed habitats outside the arid zone proper. Such insects may have extra-ordinarily wide distribution ranges.

On the other hand, even in areas which receive very little rainfall, there can be localities which collect a disproportionate amount of water ("run-on areas") because of the terrain. In the arid zone, such areas are frequently occupied by groves of mulga (*Acacia aneura*). Unlike larger animals, insects can exploit the smallest of these relatively favourable habitats.

Most of the rain that does fall is insufficient to directly affect plant growth. For instance, in the Broken Hill area, 70 per cent of the rainfall is in this category. However, such rains are sufficient to cause decomposition of litter and the release of labile (unabsorbed) nutrients into the soil. These nutrients thus accumulate until the next heavy rain, and absorption of the nutrients by plants at that time produces vigorous growth. Because nutrients are thus quickly used up, a second period of heavy rain closely following the first has a minimal effect (Charley and Cowling 1968). Productivity and nutrient cycling in arid lands is therefore intermittent and occurs in surges controlled by rainfall.

Aside from the paucity of rain, there is another characteristic of arid-zone precipitation that is of vital significance to the biota — its unreliability (variability). For a given area, this factor is measured as the average percentage deviation from the annual mean for each year over a given period. Only the southern coasts of Australia and the far northern coast have a variability of less than 20 per cent (Leeper 1970). Most of the arid zone has over 30 per cent variability and the North West District of Western Australia has over 40 per cent. In view of the overriding importance of rainfall as a limiting factor in the arid zone, this variability adds greatly to the instability of the environment, and has important consequences for insect ecology.

Storage of water in arid lands occurs primarily in creek beds below the ground surface and in the surrounding soil (section 2.4.7), not in the vegetation. As has been seen, nutrients tend to be stored in labile form in the soil as well. Arid formations are thus the most physically-dominated of all the ecosystems treated in this book except for some of the beyond-K environments discussed in Chapter 5.

The natural vegetation of Arid Australia (as this zone is called by Slatyer and Perry 1969) consists of various woodland formations, mostly tropical (12.4 per cent of Australia's land area), shrublands (32.5 per cent including 24.3 per cent mallee), and grasslands (29.1 per cent, including 22.6 per cent spinifex), altogether covering 74 per cent of the continent. The entomofauna of these formations is discussed in section 2.4.

2.2 COMMUNITY STRUCTURE AND ENERGETICS OF ARID BIOMES

Studies of arid-zone productivity in Australia are very recent and only incomplete results have been published so far, mostly in scattered reports of symposia and conferences. It has therefore been impossible to obtain a general summary of the subject.

It does appear that soils, particularly in the spinifex areas, are exceptionally infertile (Ross 1969) and one could expect very low general productivity in this formation.

Present knowledge of the productivity of mulga formations has been reviewed in a series of articles in *Tropical Grasslands,* Volume 7 (1973). Production of forbs and grasses important to grazing animals is inversely proportional to shrub (*Acacia aneura*) density (Beale 1973). Response of plant growth to adequate rain depends considerably on the location of the plants, increase in biomass following rain being very much greater, proportionately, in unfavourable areas where biomass is initially lowest (Ross and Lendon 1973). In the most favourable area (run-on groves supporting high vegetation biomass continuously) production increase following rain is minimal.

Rodin and Basilevich (1966), in a world survey, stress the disproportionate amount of biomass occurring below ground in desert communities in the form of root tissue, and this is partially borne out in Australia by Charley and Cowling's (1968) estimates of biomass in a saltbush community. The above-ground/below-ground fraction of organic matter is only about 6 per cent, although much of the latter consists of organic matter in the soil rather than roots alone.

Secondary productivity also depends on a complex of variables, including the species of herbivores present, their productive efficiency, and the proportion of plant growth available to them. In African savannah, where numerous species of mammalian herbivores select different food species and vary their selection at different times of year according to protein content, production of these animals can be very high (Lee 1975), and may possibly serve to raise the proportion of primary productivity consumed by herbivores from the usual maximum of 10 per cent to that of 45 per cent suggested as a maximum by MacFadyen (1964).

The proportion of primary productivity going to insect grazers in arid lands has not been estimated, but circumstantial evidence indicates this to be as high as, or higher than that going to vertebrate herbivores, even when large ungulates are present. Blocker (1975) estimates that a density of 6 to 7 grass-hoppers per square yard (0.84 m^2) over a 10-acre (4.05 ha) area is equivalent in herbage consumption to one cow; grass-hopper densities can reach 30 to 60/0.84 m^2 under some conditions in the United States. Under arid conditions there, three grasshoppers per 0.84 m^2 can consume 50 per cent of available herbage. In some Australian grasslands, Lee and Wood (1971) conclude that termites alone exceed native mammalian herbivores in biomass per unit area by 30 to 230 times, whilst Watson et al (1973) estimate that in a mulga-grass area near Alice Springs, termite biomass is comparable to that of cattle (1.0 to 1.5 g/m^2) and greatly exceeds that of kangaroos (0 to .15 g/m^2). They stress that the mammals choose green feed, if available, and that there is little inter-ference between them and termites except during droughts.

Although termites and grasshoppers are the principal arid-land herbivorous insects, there are many others as well. Blocker (1975) mentions particularly hemipterans, harvester ants, scarab larvae, chloropid flies, and thrips as groups which may occasionally reach plague proportions in rangelands in the United States. He stresses that the effect on primary production by these insects can exceed the damage directly caused through ingestion. For instance, grasshoppers often do not eat all the grass that they cut down, and sucking insects, because of their selective feeding on key nutrients in the sap, can decrease potential photosynthetic fixation by plants by a quantity much greater than that of the energy that they actually remove.

The fate of energy ingested by herbivores depends on a further set of variables. In general, poikilothermic herbivores have a low assimilation efficiency (a range of 27 to 50 per cent is given for insects by Menhinick 1967). A notable exception is shown by termites which, because of their symbiotic micro-organisms, can raise food utilization to more than 90 per cent (Lee 1975). On the other hand, productive efficiency of poikilotherms (that is, the assimilated energy that goes into tissue production) is much higher than in homoiotherms, where much of the assimilated energy goes into respiration. To compensate for this, homoiotherms are supposed to have a more efficient digestion ($\pm$ 70 per cent of assimilation, according to Engelmann 1966).

Studies on bioenergetics seldom go above the herbivore level, since man, as an omnivore, is primarily interested in the first two trophic levels. However, van Hook (1971) considered spiders in a grassland ecosystem, and it is interesting to note that spiders have a digestive efficiency of up to 99 per cent (Moulder and Reichle 1972), suggesting that carnivores in general may be much more efficient in their utilization of food, thereby compensating for the greatly reduced amount of energy available to them.

Energy ingested but not assimilated is returned to the system as faeces (egestion). The proportion egested per caloric intake should be higher in poikilotherms than in homoiotherms (see above). However, since the former are nearly all small animals their faeces tend to go directly to micro-organisms, without the involvement of large decomposers. This is also largely true of bird droppings. In the case of mammals, however, faeces are often concentrated in deposits of sufficient size to reward exploitation by large decomposers, primarily insects (section 2.3.6). As far as coprophagous (faeces feeding) insects are concerned, the important factor is not the total production of faeces in the ecosystem, but that proportion of production originating with medium-sized and large mammals. Introducing large mammals into areas not containing insects adapted to handling their faeces produces a bottleneck in the recycling of faecal material, as micro-organisms alone cannot efficiently decompose large dung pads.

Finally, energy not consumed by members of higher trophic levels passes directly to the medium and large decomposers (birds, insects, millipedes, isopods, and earthworms) and to the small ones (fungi and bacteria). A generally accepted average estimate of the proportion of production thus going to decomposers in most ecosystems is 90 per cent (MacFadyen 1964; Odum 1969). It hardly needs to be said as a consequence, that in any ecosystem the decomposers are very much more important than the grazers with regard to the quantity of energy processed. The decomposer industry also increases the efficiency of the system, as it returns materials to the producers. Grazers, on the other hand, are very much more important in determining community structure and in governing the direction of evolutionary forces (Chapter 1).

Litter decomposers in Australian arid communities may be more efficient than previously supposed, if the estimates for saltbush by Charley and Cowling (1968) are typical. These authors note that litter breakdown, which occurs mostly after rains, is surprisingly rapid. In this type of formation litter decomposition is attributable mostly to micro-organisms and micro-arthropods. However, it is probable that over the greater part of Arid Australia, particularly in the mulga and spinifex formations, termites are even more important as litter feeders as they can be active between rains.

2.2.1 THE ROLE OF TERMITES IN THE ENERGETICS OF THE ARID ZONE

It has already been mentioned that in Australian grasslands termites may greatly exceed native mammalian herbivores in biomass. It is not known whether they are responsible for a greater consumption of living plant tissue, although in specific formations such as spinifex even this appears likely. All termites utilize cellulose as their source of energy, but whether the cellulose is obtained from living or dead plant tissue depends on the termite species, on the relative supply of each source available, and on the geographical area. Individual species, whilst often showing preferences for one type of food, nevertheless frequently display flexibility in this regard (Watson *et al.* 1973).

Termites show several unusual features which set them apart from other decomposers. Foremost among these is their digestive efficiency, which may reach 90 per cent and which can be attributed to the fact that they combine two "links" in decomposer food chains — the large and the small decomposers — into a single unit. Their contained symbiotic microorganisms break down ingested food to the extent that the faeces contain only a small proportion of lignin and other polyphenols. Ingested lignin is largely digested by an as yet unknown process (K. E. Lee, personal communication).

Also unusual is the tendency of termites to form "closed systems" in which nutrients are locked for a considerable period of time. This is because the faeces are incorporated into the mound and not passed to the rest of the environment except by weathering, which can take 50 years or more. Watson (1972) records a mound of *Nasutitermes triodiae* which is known to have been in existence for about 100 years. The result of this "hoarding" is that at any given moment a significant proportion of the organic matter, plant nutrients, and exchangeable cations (3 to 22 per cent, depending on the substance) contained in the combined A_1-horizon mound layer is stored in the mounds (Lee 1975).

The rapid and nearly complete decomposition of structural polysaccharides by termites eliminates a potential recycling "bottleneck" which normally operates to stabilize ecosystems, since these polysaccharides are usually decomposed very slowly by free micro-organisms (Lee and Wood 1971). On the other hand, the storage and slow release of materials resulting from polysaccharide decomposition by termites must have a considerable homeostatic influence on the ecosystems where these insects are abundant, and thus compensate for the reduction in the usual stabilizing mechanism. At the same time, it should be recalled that termite mounds release periodic (and predictable) surges of energy in the form of millions of alates (winged individuals), practically all of which die in a short time. Thus the mediation of termites transforms much of the irregular and unpredictable, rainfall-controlled surges of productivity in arid zones into slow, steady release and predictable bursts. Instability is thus converted to stability, adding yet another vitally important influence of these insects in arid areas.

Even during periods between swarms, there is a significant contribution by termites to arid-zone food webs, in which the principal predators are probably ants (Greenslade 1970) and vertebrates. The significance of termites as a reliable long-term source of food is demonstrated by the existence of some highly-evolved and apparently ancient vertebrates, such as the numbat and *Myobatrachus* (a frog), which are specialized to feed almost exclusively on them.

More direct evidence of the importance of termites as food for vertebrates in arid areas comes from a study of the food habits and other niche components carried out by Pianka (1969) on Australian lizards of the genus *Ctenotus,* many of which are closely associated with spinifex communities. Of fourteen species of lizards studied (with as many as seven being sympatric in some places), nine depend largely on termites for food. Pianka itemized the stomach contents into twenty-six categories, of which the single category of termites made up 80 to 95 per cent of the numbers, and 53 to 82 per cent of the volume of food items ingested by these nine species. In three of the remaining species termites averaged about 10 per cent of the food, whilst two species did not eat them at all. Although it is unwarranted to extrapolate unduly from Pianka's study, his data do suggest that termites provide the staple food for the majority of non-flying arid-zone insectivores, and that the special hunting techniques required, lead to a high level of specialization on the part of termite predators.

2.2.2 PHYSICAL EFFECTS OF TERMITES IN ARID ECOSYSTEMS

In Australian arid areas it is the burrowing activity of arthropods which has the greatest effect on soil turnover. Earthworms, so important in more humid climates, have no significant influence. The most conspicuous burrowing arthropods are termites, ants, spiders, scorpions, crickets, beetles, bees, sand wasps, and root-feeding moth larvae. All of these except termites tend to confine their activities to the A horizon, although honey ants, geotrupine beetles, and hepialid moths, in particular, are known to dig to considerable depths (2 to 3 m or more). Denudation of the surface also frequently follows from ant activity. However, it is termites which have the most consistent influence both through denudation and through bringing up materials from deep horizons (Lee and Wood 1971). The latter activity leads to a slow but continuous physical overturning of the soil.

Soil particles incorporated into mounds or caps by termites are tightly packed and cemented by excreta, forming a surface extremely resistant to weathering and unavailable for seed germination. Watson and Gay (1970) and Watson *et al* (1973) describe how these properties of *Drepanotermes* mounds and other factors have had a severe "degradation" effect in one semi-arid mulga association in southwest Queensland. The process was begun by man's pastoral management, which caused a reduction in the number of mulga shrubs. This resulted in proliferation of grass, particularly after rains, with a consequent increase of harvesting termites that placed a hard cap of compacted earth over their nests. During dry spells the termites were forced to continue feeding on grass tussocks, whereas normally they would have switched to mulga debris. The resulting exhaustion of food reduces termite populations considerably, but the old mound caps persist (for about 70 years) and impede the regrowth of grass or other vegetation in the area which they cover. During the next wet spell new termite colonies are founded in clear spaces. As this process continues more and more land becomes covered with old termite mounds and the carrying capacity of the whole system becomes correspondingly reduced. Clearly, human interference removed the principal stabilizing factor in this system, i.e., the mulga shrubs which serve as alternate food for termites during droughts.

It can be concluded that termites have a greater influence than any other single group of animals on the production, flow, and storage of energy, and on the physical transformation of the soil, in Arid Australia. Their sociality enables them to operate continuously and thus have a much more profound influence than that of the more spectacular, but intermittent, outbreaks of plague locusts.

2.3 GENERAL ADAPTATIONS OF INSECTS TO ARID CONDITIONS

Bodenheimer (1954), Pradhan (1957), Cloudsley-Thompson (1964), Bourlière and Hadley (1970), and Edney (1974) have discussed in general terms the adaptations shown by adult insects in arid environments. Such accounts tend to focus on adult morphology, physiology, and habits. Here I pay more attention to the insects' life cycles, foraging tactics, developmental stages, behaviour, social organization (if any), and population dynamics.

All accounts of desert insects agree that digging ability is an important adaptation, at least in part of the insect's life cycle. It would be difficult to find any species which does not spend at least one stage in the soil. The significance of the soil as a refuge is traditionally explained in terms of shelter from heat and dryness. This is of course true, but in any biome all organisms must find shelter at times, at least from predators. The reason that the soil is disproportionately important in arid regions is that it is often the only available shelter, since the above-ground portion of the vegetation is relatively sparse. Also most organic matter, and hence food, in deserts occurs below ground (section 2.2).

The significance of excavation as an arid-zone adaptation bestows exceptional importance on the soil type as a determinant of distribution limits. In particular, sandy areas, which provide abundant subterranean shelter opportunities, appear to be far richer in their general insect fauna than rocky or stony areas such as desert mountain ranges.

Vertebrate burrows are important in providing shelter and food for insects in arid areas. I have trapped the coprophagous tenebrionids *Brises* spp. (present also in caves) and various Aphodiinae in burrows of rabbits and hairy-nosed wombats in the Nullarbor Plain. Richards (1971) also reports *Endacusta* sp. (a phalangopsid cricket), *Trox amictus* (Scarabaeidae), and the cockroach *Paratemnopteryx rufa* from burrows in the same area. Many mosquitoes use rabbit burrows as daytime shelters (Marks 1972).

Some of the more specific adaptations of insects to arid conditions are discussed in the following sections.

2.3.1 DEVELOPMENT GEARED TO RAINFALL

Although it is adaptive for arid-zone insects to time their development so that their feeding stages coincide with growth flushes, there is no simple way in which this can be achieved by using moisture as a triggering stimulus. This is because light rains that fall in deserts are usually insufficient to induce plant growth, and any premature hatching under these conditions would be abortive. Diapause, in particular, is seldom if ever induced or broken by moisture factors alone (Cloudsley-Thompson 1964).

The non-diapause eggs of the plague locust, *Chortoicetes terminifera,* can be induced to hatch by humidity and there are safeguards to minimize the dangers of premature hatching (Wardhaugh 1972). In the summer, egg pods are laid deeper in the soil, so that they will not be reached by the moisture resulting from light rains. This also protects them from excessive heat near the surface. With the onset of winter, egg pods are laid more shallowly, but at that time light rains will be more effective because of lower evaporation rates. Even so, a portion of the eggs in these pods are in diapause and will not hatch until later. This type of "insurance" through only partial hatching has been noted in other arid-zone insects (Andrewartha and Birch 1954; Pradhan 1957). The environmental factors which are used as cues to determine the type of egg pod to be laid are temperature and photoperiod – not the absolute values of these parameters, but the direction in which they are changing (Wardhaugh 1972).

If the dormant stage is the pupa or adult, emergence is geared to the onset of soaking rains, as in the cicada wasp *Exeirus lateritius,* which may wait two to three years as a pupa if conditions are dry (Tillyard 1926), and the moth *Chlenias inkata,* recorded by Tindale (1961) as passing more than three years as a pupa in captivity. Desert-adapted Collembola revive very quickly after months of inactivity when the soil becomes wet (section 2.4.9). The synchronization of hepialid moth activity with rainfall is described in section 2.4.7.

When an insect is in diapause, its tissues are much more tolerant of desiccation and heat than when it is active (section 2.3.5).

In the plague locust, which has been more widely studied than other arid-zone insects, rainfall exerts its influence: (1) by inducing oocyte formation indirectly through green feed (Clark 1970); (2) by determining the number of generations per year (from one to four); and (3) by inducing outbreaks (Casimir 1962). Too much, or too continuous rainfall, on the other hand, has a detrimental effect by causing some drowning of eggs (Hogan 1965) and in producing so much vegetation that the amount of bare ground suitable for oviposition sites is reduced (Key 1945).

2.3.2. THE *r* STRATEGY IN DESERTS

Rainfall in Arid Australia is unreliable and consequently areas are continuously changing in an unpredictable manner. The instability inherent in this situation favours an *r* strategy (section 1.2), involving high mobility of propagules and populations and the capacity to build up population densities rapidly. This strategy increases the probability that favourable areas will be located and unfavourable ones abandoned, and that the former can be fully exploited in bursts of productivity.

The two principal tactics of the *r* strategy — nomadism and rapid population build-up — are best seen in plague locusts, which are associated with arid areas all over the world. Nine species of grasshoppers are listed by Key (1938) as occasionally reaching outbreak proportions in Australia. Beside *Chortoicetes terminifera* these are *Austroicetes cruciata, Gastrimargus musicus, Locusta migratoria, Austacris guttulosa, Phaulacridium vittatum, Oedalus australis, Brachyexarna lobipennis,* and *Praxibulus laminatus.* These grasshoppers sometimes have, in both adult and nymph ("hopper") stages, solitary and gregarious phases which differ behaviourally, physiologically, and morphologically. As previously discussed (section 1.3.2), when passing into the gregarious kentromorphic phase the populations may perform a "switch" in defence strategy from predator avoidance with cryptic coloration to predator satiation with signal colours.

In *Chortoicetes terminifera*, the plague locust, there are certain areas in the eastern part of the country termed "outbreak areas" (mapped by Key 1945, but supplemented and modified by more recent work) where conditions are particularly favourable for the locusts from year to year and where, once climatic conditions improve further, population build-up is most likely to take place. These favourable conditions are largely dependent on soil type; the locusts require a mozaic of relatively bare, compact soil for oviposition and a darker, poorly drained (self-mulching) soil supporting various grasses which provide food and shelter. Trees are detrimental to locusts (Clark 1950), and even continuous grass is unfavourable in that oviposition sites are lacking (Key 1945).

Locusts, even when in the solitary phase, are naturally nomadic and adults often travel long distances at night, particularly during atmospheric depressions. This mobility enables them to locate rainstorms, oviposit, and build up populations at the same time that the plants are growing in response to the rain. Outbreaks occur partly as a population build-up *in situ*, and partly as a result of large-scale immigration over long distances from the relatively permanent outbreak centres. Once an outbreak concentration has occurred, there is a mutual stimulation mediated by a pheromone, which results in the subsequent generation being of the gregarious phase. Even the hoppers are nomadic (Fig. 5). Such hopper bands are believed to survive better than an equivalent number of solitary nymphs as a result of increased foraging area and better protection from predators, who become selectively satiated toward the mass (section 1.3.2).

Population fluctuations of the locust by a factor of up to 2,000 may occur in the Channel Country of Queensland (Clark and Davies 1972). Even much smaller fluctuations would probably give sufficiently dense populations to bestow the benefit of predator satiation.

At least three species of wasps, including the egg parasite *Scelio fulgidus,* can parasitize swarms quite heavily (Clark 1970) and apparently follow them about (Hogan 1965). Birds also feed on the adults and nymphs (Andrewartha and Birch 1954), but there is no evidence that any of these predators exert any significant influence on the control of locust populations at high densities. Hogan (1965) found a median mortality from *Scelio fulgidus* of only 5 per cent, whilst average mortality from non-biotic causes was 39 per cent.

The bushfly, *Musca vetustissima,* provides another example of an arid-zone insect capable of extensive movement and density fluctuations. Although not itself a strong flier, at temperatures above 18° C it is almost constantly on the wing (particularly when protein supplies are inadequate) and is carried hundreds of kilometres a day by strong winds (providing these are warm), thus repopulating southern areas in which it was not able to survive the winter (Hughes 1970a; Greenham and Hughes 1971; Hughes and Nicholas 1974). Because prevailing winds are in the wrong direction, the bushfly is unable to invade Arnhem Land during the favourable winter period, and this area is usually free of it.

Once having invaded favourable areas, the fly can build up local populations rapidly by breeding in dung (section 2.3.6). In this species, large-scale population movements are a response to seasonal temperature fluctuations aided by winds, and not a specific response to rainfall. However, it can be expected that within its area of permanent breeding (roughly north of the twenty-ninth parallel and south of the fourteenth), the fly's mobility aids it in quickly locating areas of suitable moisture.

The bushfly can rapidly expand its populations when food is abundant, and is able to regulate its numbers quite precisely in relation to available food. When protein supplies are inadequate, there is much more flight activity, thus increasing the chances of emigration to other, more favourable areas. In dung pads of a given size, the number of emerging flies is surprisingly constant regardless of the number of eggs initially laid in them (Hughes and Walker 1970).

Other highly mobile insects in arid areas include some of

the dragonflies mentioned in section 5.1, and the water beetle *Eretes australis,* abundant in water holes and occasionally moving in mass flights (Hale 1928).

A relatively new tool available for the study of insect flight is the portable radar unit recently adopted for locust research. It has shown that, providing temperatures are favourable, there is a great deal of insect flight activity in horizontal layers at night, whereas in the daytime flying insects tend to converge in vertical columns up to 2 km high. At such heights, even mild winds can carry them 300 km in a day (Roffey 1972). The passage of a weather front is marked on the radar screen by a dense band of "blips" representing thousands of insects concentrating on the warm side of the front.

The air over a portion of South Australia was sampled (with the use of an aircraft) at 100 to 600 m altitudes by White (1970). He stressed the importance of daytime thermal currents in carrying insects up into the atmosphere. Taylor (1974) noted that migratory aphids use daytime atmospheric lift to break through the boundary layer (the level above which wind speed exceeds the insect's flight speed) to reach the necessary altitude for long-distance dispersal.

2.3.3 THE *K* STRATEGY IN DESERTS

We have seen in the previous section how some insects continually advance and retreat across a dynamic environmental mozaic. This is probably the most effective way to maintain a high average biomass in arid lands, but it is not the only way to survive. Other insects adopt the opposite strategy of remaining in place and closely adapting to a local set of circumstances.

The prevalence of flightlessness among desert insects has been stressed in the overseas literature, but quantitative supporting evidence is lacking. I believe rather that any mature community type will select for reduced mobility among *K* strategists (section 1.5 and 1.6), and that unneeded wings will atrophy in the interests of energy conservation. Permanently flightless insects may be found in all of

Australia's natural communities. If flightlessness is particularly prevalent in a desert, it is probably because that desert has been in continued existence for a long time, not merely because it is a desert.

There are indeed some spectacular wingless insects in Central Australia, including the flattened helaeine tenebrionid beetles (Fig. 9), spinose ground weevils, very large and colourful cockroaches (Fig. 10), some wingless genera of large gryllacridid "crickets", and several others. Detritivorous, herbivorous, and carnivorous diets are all represented in the above groups, the gryllacridids in particular being omnivorous (H. Mincham, personal communication) but probably playing a largely predatory role.

However, the only K strategists in arid and semi-arid regions of Australia which have been well studied are the morabine grasshoppers. They are so typically extreme-K in all their major attributes that a brief look at them here is instructive in gaining an understanding of this strategy. Their genetic adaptations have already been discussed (section 1.6).

The morabine grasshoppers (family Eumastacidae) are characterized first of all by an extraordinary lack of vagility (section 1.6). Although seldom strictly monophagous, the insects tend to restrict their diet to just a few plant species. There is one generation a year, with no diapause. Fecundity is very low in the species studied, the maximum recorded number of eggs per female being twenty-one (White 1957). A population may contain only a few dozen individuals.

The host plants of some species have been investigated by Blackith and Blackith (1966), who stress the importance of distinguishing between plants that serve as staple food and those which serve as shelter and emergency food during droughts. The latter, generally termed "indicator plants", serve for survival rather than growth, but are just as essential in the environment of the species as are the principal food plants. In general, it is the young shoots of plants that emerge after rains that are preferred as food for growth and maturation, particularly by winter-maturing species in the south. In the acridid *Phaulacridium vittatum*, it has also been found that only a fraction of the host plants can support growth and reproduction, the rest serving only for adult survival (Clark *et al.* 1967).

Two groups of grasshoppers, therefore — the acridid plague grasshoppers and the eumastacid morabines — provide us with examples of both extremes of arid-zone adaptation. The first are nomadic, greatly fluctuating in population densities, polyphagous, and represented by only a few species, whilst the second are sedentary, probably constantly at low population densities, oligophagous, and represented by a multiplicity of species (about 240 according to K. H. L. Key, personal communication).

2.3.4 SOCIALITY

Social organization in animals permits the effects of environmental fluctuations, both physical and biotic, to be buffered to a large extent. Physical fluctuations are damped by creating a controlled microclimate in the nest and by storing water. Biotic stability is enhanced by storing food. The maximum benefits of sociality would thus be expected to be felt in the most variable environments, and it is no accident that the most successful and influential organisms in desert habitats (termites and ants) are among the few insect groups with social organization.

Some grass- and litter-feeding termites store large quantities of material inside their nests (Fig. 7) that often temporarily serves as insulation as well as food (Lee and Wood 1971). Watson *et al.* (1973) estimate that an average nest of *Drepanotermes perniger* contains 200 to 500 g of stored dry grass when foraging ceases, and that this lasts through the winter. Metabolic water or water obtained from the water table and carried in the crop is stored in the clay and carton structure of the nest. Nest clay has a 25 to 32 per cent moisture content and the atmospheric relative humidity inside the nest is 95 per cent at all times (Lee and Wood 1971).

It is well known that certain ants of the genera *Melophorus, Camponotus,* and *Leptomyrmex* obtain honeydew

Figure 7   Food storage in a harvesting termite, *Drepanotermes rubriceps* (Froggatt) at Amburla Station, Northern Territory. The mound is broken open to reveal storage chambers containing fragments of the grasses *Eragrostis* and *Monochather* spp. [Photo J. A. L. Watson, courtesy Division of Entomology, CSIRO]

Figure 8   Larva and adults of a species of *Platydema* (Tenebrionidae) in the nest of a zebra finch. Every nest of this bird examined in northern South Australia contained these beetles, which are probably scavengers and are specialized to this habitat. [Photo the author]

from homopterans and nectar glands and store it inside some of the workers (repletes), whose abdomens become greatly distended and about the size of small grapes. The honeydew may be as important as a source of water as it is of food, and may last up to two years (Tindale 1966). Seeds are stored by harvester ants, which can exploit the herbaceous vegetation of deserts (honey ants are dependent on woody plants). Wheeler (1910) mentions three Australian ants as harvesters (*Pheidole longiceps, Meranoplus dimidiatus,* and *M. diversus*); Brown and Taylor (1970) also mention that some species of *Chelaner* are harvesters.

Temperature fluctuations inside the nests of termites are buffered by: (1) the insulating effect of the earth and carton walls; (2) the presence of air circulation passages in the walls; and (3) to a certain extent by other aspects of nest architecture. The most spectacular example of the last is shown by the "magnetic" termite of the Northern Territory (*Amitermes meridionalis*), whose tall mounds, elongated in a north-south axis, minimize heat gain during the hot part of the day and produce air circulation by the alternate heating of each side. It can be expected that temperature and humidity fluctuations are buffered in the underground nests of ants, as in any burrow, and desert ants may burrow deeper than their counterparts in moister and colder areas. Aborigines are reported to have to dig down to a depth of 2 m on occasion for the repletes of *Melophorus* (Bodenheimer 1951). The mound structure at the entrance of nests of *Iridomyrmex purpureus* absorbs the heat of the sun in the early morning, allowing the ants to begin foraging early (Greaves and Hughes 1974).

Greenslade (1970) suggests that a more dispersed nest may be an adaptation to cope with reduced food density in arid regions, as such a nest type occurs in the inland variety of the meat ant, *Iridomyrmex purpureus.* Meat ants are able to exploit new opportunities rapidly by transforming satellite colonies into independent ones through the expedient of accepting a new queen from the parent colony (Greaves and Hughes 1974).

There is a tendency for the nests of both ants and termites to be overdispersed in arid areas, that is, for the colonies to be more or less equidistant from one another, rather than randomly distributed or clumped (Brian 1965). This type of dispersion (seen only in some species) could only be brought about if there were an antagonistic inter-action between members of different colonies that increased in intensity in the vicinity of the home colony. Lee and Wood (1971) found such territorial behaviour in a number of Aus-tralian termites, but particularly in *Amitermes vitiosus* (Fig. 26). Interspecific overdispersion can also occur and be even more accentuated than it is intraspecifically.

The theoretical conditions for overdispersion in social insect colonies are: (1) that the structure of the environment be two-dimensional, that is, dominated by a single plane; (2) that this plane be relatively homogeneous; (3) that the food supply be relatively abundant (so that the establishment of very dispersed foraging territories is not necessary); and (4) that individual workers be small in relation to total nest biomass (so that the loss of a worker through territorial defence is a proportionately minor sacrifice) (Carroll and Janzen 1973).

2.3.5 PHYSIOLOGY AND MORPHOLOGY

The attributes of adult individuals are those which have tradi-tionally received most of the attention in earlier works on desert insects. However, it is unlikely that physiological and morphological adaptations to heat and desiccation are as significant as the behavioural ones previously discussed. Most insects are adapted to withstand dry conditions in the adult, at least, and other habitats such as stored products may offer more severe conditions in this regard than do deserts. Never-theless, a brief and probably incomplete list of heat and drought adaptations at the individual level follows. A thorough survey is presented by Edney (1974).

(1) Hydropyle cells in the cuticle of grasshopper eggs. These absorb water from the surrounding medium against an

osmotic gradient, and have been described in the eggs of *Austroicetes cruciata* by Andrewartha and Birch (1954).

(2) Greatly increased tolerance of tissues to desiccation during diapause, as in the weevil *Otiorrhynchus cribricollis* (Andrewartha and Birch op. cit.). A Nigerian chironomid can tolerate a 15 per cent moisture content for three years during diapause (Hinton 1953).

(3) The production of metabolic water, particularly as a by-product of cellulose digestion. This is well known in termites (Lee and Wood 1971).

(4) Reabsorption of water from faeces. Khare (1973) discusses a "hydro-filter" device known in several groups of beetles whereby water flows out of the faecal mass in the colon back into the Malphigian tubules whence it returns to the body cavity after extraction of the soluble toxins; the Malphigian tubules have become reassociated with the gut for this purpose. Water can be reabsorbed against the osmotic gradient in the rectal lumen of some desert locusts (Edney 1974).

(5) Impermeability of the cuticle. This is in fact a general characteristic of insect cuticle, but in some cases sealing sclerites slide over the permeable membranes when the insect contracts (Hinton 1953).

(6) Excess feeding to extract water from food. Buxton (1924) found that desert insects obtain water by feeding on dead plant matter which has absorbed water during the night, and Clark (1970) states that nymphs of plague locusts eat large quantities of dead feed thereby obtaining more water.

(7) Tolerance of high temperatures. Those insects adapted for walking on the ground during the day, such as some thysanurans, may be expected to be able to tolerate high body temperatures. The highest recorded lethal temperature for an active insect is 50 to 53°C for a Mediterranean tenebrionid (Cloudsley-Thompson 1964); the diapausing Nigerian chironomid mentioned above tolerates 103°C when dehydrated (Hinton 1953). In general, an upper temperature tolerance limit of 40 to 50°C (after 30 minutes exposure) is to be expected in non-diapausing eurythermic insects (Edney 1974).

(8) A subelytral cavity in beetles. Best developed in wingless species, a more or less sealed air cavity above the abdomen of desert beetles is believed to reduce transpiratory water loss, and also to act as a buffer zone to delay radiant heat transfer from the elytra and thus permit "short jaunts" across hot sands (Hadley 1970). Edney (1974) doubts whether the subelytral cavities function effectively in these ways.

Hinton (1961) has raised the interesting question of how insects (particularly their immobile stages such as eggs and pupae) living in dry environments, can avoid drowning when subjected to occasional, heavy rains. It would seem that adaptations to these two opposite eventualities are contradictory and pose a dilemma. The principal morphological solution to this dilemma is the plastron, which occurs more often in terrestrial insect eggs than in adults of aquatic insects (Hinton, op. cit.). The plastron combines a large diffusion interface in water with a small spiracular opening which minimizes water loss when conditions are dry. Under aquatic conditions a high oxygen tension in the water is required.

2.3.6 THE SPECIAL PROBLEMS OF ARID-ZONE COPROPHAGY AND NECROPHAGY

There is a sufficient number of native and domestic mammals and smaller vertebrates in the arid zone for their faeces and cadavers to be a significant source of energy. However, physical conditions create special obstacles to the utilization of this energy.

Leaving necrophagy aside for the moment, there are three general tactics adopted at the level of the large decomposer for tapping the faecal energy source in any environment: (1) using the original latent moisture of the faeces to breed with the maximum possible speed on the surface (flies); (2) burying the faeces to conserve the moisture content longer and to take advantage of soil moisture (dung beetles); and (3) eating the faeces in their dried state (termites and tenebrionids). Only tactics (1) and (3) seem to meet with any consistent success in arid areas. They are discussed in turn.

(1) Rapid breeding on the surface. To be successful, this tactic requires the insect firstly, to be on hand at the moment of defaecation, and secondly, to breed rapidly. The bushfly, *Musca vetustissima,* is a good example of an insect which has developed both gambits. It is constantly hovering about a potential producer of its food and can oviposit instantly when defaecation occurs. While I believe, with Hughes (1970b), that this is the principal reason for the fly's annoying habits, this behaviour provides an important additional benefit in enabling it to acquire protein food, necessary for ovarian maturation, from the mucus, blood, or pus of its host (Hughes *et al.* 1972); water is possibly obtained from sweat and urine. Protein-poor food reduces the number of eggs produced, but not their viability.

Having been able to take maximum advantage of the original moisture content of the faeces, the insect undergoes rapid development. Although normally requiring an average of 120 hours for development, too-rapid desiccation of the dung due to weather conditions, overcrowding, or disturbance by competitors such as dung beetles results in the dung being abandoned prematurely (after only 70 hours) by 30 per cent of the flies. The emergent flies are dwarfs, but still able to survive and reproduce (Hughes *et al.* op. cit.). Aside from size reduction, the flies are able to make other developmental compensations for reduced energy intake.

(2) Burial of faeces. This strategy is adopted by beetles with a longer developmental period than that of flies. They compete successfully with the latter if the dung can be buried before the maggots have consumed it. However, because of the longer development time, the present tactic depends on a reliable external source of moisture in the soil. Consequently, the great variability of rainfall in Arid Australia virtually eliminates dung beetles from consideration in the zone covered by this chapter except in specialized habitats such as irrigated pastures. It is interesting to note, however, that on the fringes of the arid zone in Northern Australia some dung beetles have adopted the bushfly's tactic of being on hand at the moment of defaecation, not by hovering about their

hosts, but by clinging to the fur about the anal region. Six species of the genus *Onthophagus* and at least five species of macropods are involved in this association; the beetles have evolved this behaviour several times independently (Matthews 1972).

Also, on the western fringe of the zone, between the Murchison River and the North West Cape, endemic dung beetles have been able to survive for reasons which are not entirely clear. Here I found several different genera adopting the same general feeding-burrow architecture. It is probably the standard "arid-zone design" for dung beetle burrows. Basically, it consists of a shallow chamber or (as described also for an eastern species by Bornemissza 1971b) a shallow depression, into which faecal pellets are quickly brought from the surface to preserve their moisture while a vertical shaft is sunk from this chamber. This type of double burrow was first described for a Central Asian dung beetle by a Russian investigator in 1913 and correctly interpreted by him as an adaptation to arid conditions. In Western Australia I was also able to note that very old, entirely desiccated faecal pellets could be used by dung beetles if the soil was thoroughly moist. Once buried, microbial activity (and hence the food value) of the pellets is restored by the moisture. This tactic is, of course, limited to times of rainfall and cannot be relied upon to sustain dung beetle populations in most parts of Arid Australia.

(3) Feeding on dried faeces. As mentioned above some dung beetles can utilize desiccated faecal pellets by burying them in damp soil, thereby restoring their moisture. However, neither dung beetles nor flies can feed on excrement which remains dry. In the case of herbivore dung, this is left to termites to consume, and the surprising extent of this consumption has been documented by Ferrar and Watson (1970). No less than 48 species of termites have been recorded in dung in Australia, most of them members of the genus *Amitermes*. Dung-feeding termites are omnivores, not harvesters or specialized wood-eaters. The areas involved are mostly Northern and Central Australia, and wet dung may sometimes

be attacked as well as dry. The process of dry-dung consumption is slow, as it takes about three months to destroy average dung pads from cattle.

Ferrar and Watson (*op. cit.*) point out that coprophagy in termites is underestimated, since most collectors do not think of looking in dung pads for them. I suspect that in most of Arid Australia during periods when conditions are too dry, even for bushflies, termites are the most important coprophages, at least as far as cattle dung is concerned. Their importance with regard to marsupial pellets has not been investigated yet.

I have frequently seen tenebrionid beetles of the genus *Helaeus* feeding on dried human faeces in desert areas at night, and believe that the coprophagous role of tenebrionids has been underestimated.

(4) Cadavers in arid areas. The problems previously discussed in connection with the exploitation of faeces apply also to vertebrate cadavers, but to a lesser extent, since the original moisture content of these cadavers is of course much longer-lasting because of their skin cover, and larger mass. This permits definite successional stages in decay to become clearly evident, with a somewhat different insect fauna at each stage (Fuller 1934; Bornemissza 1957). The earliest successional stages ("putrefaction" and "black putrefaction") are inhabited predominantly by blowfly (calliphorid) larvae together with their predators such as the metallic green histerids *Saprinus* spp. and the red-headed staphylinid *Creophilus erythrocephalus*. Later stages ("butyric fermentation" and "dry decay") tend to be dominated by beetles, first the large silphids *Ptomaphila* spp. (or *Diamesus* sp. in the far north), then *Dermestes* spp., and finally the scarabaeids *Trox* spp. In the arid zone, the advent of the last two groups is hastened and they consequently acquire greater relative importance. The silphids tend to drop out and cosmopolitan species of *Dermestes* become particularly abundant in the arid interior, as are species of *Trox*. The latter are essentially fur feeders and can complete their life cycle on nothing but wool clippings lying on the ground, or even discarded wool

clothing. Some dermestids are also able to digest wool (Waterhouse 1952).

The presence of a dead vertebrate has a severe inhibitory effect on the normal soil fauna and flora directly beneath it, and the soil community, which is scarcely involved in carcass decomposition, will largely avoid such an area for more than 12 months after the carcass has decomposed (Bornemissza 1957).

Dead bodies of invertebrates and very small vertebrates tend to be consumed mostly by ants, but I have seen tenebrionids and even dung beetles feeding on these.

2.4 AUSTRALIAN ARID-ZONE FORMATIONS

Slatyer and Perry (1969) list various arid subformations and the percentages of total land area they occupy. These were grouped within three principal formations — woodlands, shrublands, and grasslands. I will adopt some of these subdivisions in the present discussion and add a few primarily non-vegetational categories which are significant from the entomological point of view, namely gibber plains, sand ridges, creek beds, dry salt lakes, and dry soil. The insect fauna of these associations has not received any detailed study, but some preliminary observations have been made and some information can be gleaned from the literature on specific groups. Only a few of the more conspicuous insect elements can be mentioned here.

Aquatic habitats in the arid zone, such as water holes and salt lakes (when filled) are not included here but are discussed as part of the general subject of inland waters in section 5.1.

2.4.1 MALLEE

Occupying nearly a quarter of the total land area of Australia, and about one third of the arid zone, mallee is the single most extensive vegetational formation on the continent. In spite of this, its insect fauna has not been the subject of any study, probably because mallee provides little grazing land or commercial wood, and few ornamental species. Buprestid beetles are the most conspicuous insects associated with the mallee trees (*Eucalyptus* spp.). Many of these beetles seem to time their emergence as adults with the irregular, sometimes synchronized flowering of the species of mallee in South Western Australia (S. Barker, personal communication). In South Australia, the very large buprestid *Julodimorpha bake-welli*, a mallee root feeder, emerges every year briefly around Christmas time (H. Mincham, personal communication). Eggs of buprestids are laid in different parts of the tree, according to the species, and the larvae are borers in the wood. Adults usually feed on pollen (although some buprestid adults are leaf feeders). They usually but not necessarily feed on the flowers of the same species of tree from which they emerged. If feeding on dried wood, the life span of buprestids may be as long as twelve years (Morgan 1969).

Greenslade and Greenslade (1973) note that the mallee insect fauna is intermediate in its moisture requirements between that of mesic and true arid zones.

2.4.2 MULGA AND OTHER ACACIA SHRUBLANDS

The shrub-grassland association dominated by the tall shrub *Acacia aneura* is the most arid of all the predominantly woody formations. Extensive areas of annual and perennial grasses and low shrubs also occur in mulga.

In a survey of the adaptations of native vertebrates to mulga, Davies (1973) raises some points which are probably applicable to insects also. He notes that the abundant species are generalized ones, not the desert specialists. This is of course a reflection of the hypothesis proposed earlier that r strategists dominate arid formations in terms of biomass per species, but K strategists undoubtedly exceed in numbers of (generally rare) species. Davies notes further that many native mulga species have surprisingly regular breeding seasons, suggesting that if a species' requirements are low enough, mulga can provide reliably recurrent resources. The impor-tance of creeks and hills in increasing the physical homeo-stasis of the community (with regard to water and temperature, respectively) is also stressed by Davies (section 2.4.7).

Practically the only mulga-associated insects which have been studied are the termites discussed by Watson *et al.* (1973), who mention some 20 species associated with this formation near Alice Springs, the most important genus being *Drepanotermes.* Termites are more closely associated with true mulga formations in this area than with other range types.

Tindale (1961) describes the life history of the geometrid *Chlenias inkata* on *Acacia aneura* in the MacDonnell Ranges. This moth is ant-adapted and will be mentioned in connection with ants in section 4.5. It was also mentioned with regard to its long pupal stage in section 2.3.1. Undoubtedly these adaptations reflect two of the dominant selection pressures in mulga: drought and ants. The moth's flightlessness (in the female) and its other specializations indicate it to be one of the *K* strategists in this formation.

Although I have seen no special account of mulga-associated ants, there can be little doubt that these insects dominate mulga formations as predators, seed harvesters, and collectors of honeydew. The honey ants *Melophorus inflatus* and *M. bagoti* are noted by Tindale (1961, 1966) as being especially associated with *Acacia aneura* and its homopterans, particularly on flood plains.

The older literature on economic and taxonomic aspects, mentions numerous insects associated with *Acacia* species without specifying the formations involved. Thus Froggatt (1923) lists 63 species of insects as feeding directly on *Acacia* trees or shrubs; these could of course be only a small fraction of the associated fauna. Duffy (1963) lists about 60 species of Cerambycidae occurring on *Acacia* in Australia. The most conspicuous moths are anthelids and notodontids such as the bag-shelter moth *Ochrogaster contraria.* Butterfly representation is monopolized by the family Lycaenidae, 15 species being listed for *Acacia* by Common and Waterhouse (1972), with additional ones on the toxic epiphytic mistletoes. The latter plants also support species of the pierid genus *Delias.* The gall-forming thrips genus *Kladothrips* is confined to *Acacia* (Reed 1970), as are undoubtedly many other insects.

Some *Acacia,* at least, have cyanogenic glucosides in the leaves (Finnemore and Gledhill 1928) and species feeding on them must presumably have some way of dealing with this chemical defence.

The large ground weevil, *Leptopius duponti,* feeds as a larva on acacia roots, and its calcareous pupal cases are found abundantly in the soil along the arid western coast of South Australia (Lea 1925).

Acacia shrubs (*A. ligulata,* etc.) are frequent along the fringes of the Nullarbor Plain. Their associated cossid moths were described by Tindale (1953). The larvae feed externally on the roots, some species remaining more or less stationary in silken chambers; they consume very little wood, merely gnawing at the root to keep sap flowing. Females of some species are flightless and use pheromones to attract males. Gravid females are among the heaviest insects known (Tindale 1966).

Common (1970) suggests that concealed feeding (feeding within stems and roots, or deep in the soil) by larvae is an important adaptation of the Australian lepidopterous fauna to arid conditions, and could explain the abundant representation of such families as Hepialidae, Cossidae, Castniidae, Oecophoridae, and Xyloryctidae.

External root (ectophytic) feeding by larvae seems to expose them to attack by the spectacular entomophagous fungi, *Cordyceps* spp. Victims of these fungi in Australia are usually hepialid caterpillars of the genera *Trictena* and *Abantiades* (Harris 1946), although other soil-inhabiting insects are also affected (Norris 1970).

2.4.3 SALTBUSH AND OTHER SHRUBS

Formations of saltbush (*Atriplex*) and other chenopodiaceous shrubs can be quite extensive on poor soils, the Nullarbor Plain being the largest single tract of this type of formation. In spite of their well-known palatability to cattle and sheep, superficial observation suggests that these shrubs may not be rich in associated insect life. However, Froggatt (1910), in a summary of the knowledge of saltbush insects up to that time, listed several species that feed on *Atriplex*. He particularly noted considerable defoliation by larvae of the agaristid *Apina callisto* and the noctuid *Agrotis infusa* (the Bogong moth), both of which are general feeders on winter annual forbs. Two weevils of the genera *Elaeagna* (Cryptorhynchinae) and *Belus* (Belidae) appear to be specialist feeders on *Atriplex*.

The lycaenid *Neolucia serpentata* is a specialist feeder on *Atriplex* and *Rhagodia* (McCubbin 1971) and the chenopod *Bassia* is mentioned by Clark (1970) as a food source for the plague locust.

Chenopodiaceous formations provide important habitats for some morabine grasshoppers, although these do not necessarily feed on the shrubs themselves, but on various ephemeral shoots that emerge on the bare ground between them after rains (Blackith and Blackith 1966). Species of the morabine genus *Keyacris* are often associated with saltbush country, as well as some races of the *viatica* "group" (White et al. 1967; Blackith and Blackith 1969). A chromosome race of the same group feeds on *Salicornia* (a salt-tolerant shrub growing around the edge of salt lakes) and is sustained by this plant during drought periods in spite of the high salt content of its sap (Blackith and Blackith 1966).

Among other arid-zone shrubs mentioned in the entomological literature are: (1) the malvaceous *Sida* cited by Key (1959) as an exclusive food of the grasshopper *Ecphantus quadrilobus*; and (2) species of *Psoralea* (Papilionaceae) and *Eremophila* (Myoporaceae), mentioned as providing honeydew (through the medium of homopterans) to the widespread ant, *Iridomyrmex purpureus* (Greenslade 1970). These woody shrubs can evidently serve the same purpose as trees (section 4.5) in supplying ants with much-needed honeydew in arid areas.

Arid Australia, particularly the western part, is blessed with a great variety of flowering bushes of the genera *Hakea, Grevillea, Eremophila, Crotalaria, Nitraria, Cassia,* etc. which attract a wealth of nectar-feeding insects. Since the flowering of these shrubs is timed by non-biotic factors (i.e., the right combination of moisture and temperature) they tend to bloom simultaneously. This characteristic of desert environments has led to the evolution of marked oligolecty among desert pollinators throughout the world (Baker and Hurd 1968; Heinrich and Raven 1972). To compensate for simultaneous blooming, flowers tend to vary in structure, in the amount of the caloric reward, in colour, and in the times of day at which they remain open (as in some *Hibiscus*). It has already been mentioned (section 1.4.3) that some bees fly at night in Australia.

There is evidence, quite incomplete at present, for oligolecty among the Colletidae, the dominant bee group. For instance, the tubular flowers of *Eremophila* (Myoporaceae) are visited by hylaeine and colletine bees (*Hylaeus* spp. and *Leiproctus* spp.) which have independently evolved elongated palpi that penetrate the deep narrow corolla (T. F. Houston, personal communication). The megachilid genus *Lithurge* has coarse hairs on the scopa and appears to specialize on coarse pollen of large-flowered Malvaceae (*Hibiscus, Gossypium*, etc.) (Michener 1965; Houston, personal communication). In general, among Australian bees, the family Myrtaceae provides proportionately the greatest number of food plants and the genus *Acacia* (Mimosaceae) the least.

Ant pollinated plants are to be expected in Australian deserts, although none have yet been found.

2.4.4 SPINIFEX AND OTHER GRASSES

The second-largest vegetational formation in Australia, after mallee, is the hummock grassland formed by species of *Triodia* and *Plectrachne*, occupying about 23 per cent of the continent's land area on sandy soil. The sharp, densely interlaced leaves and stems of the spinifex form an impenetrable barrier to larger animals and a haven for insects and small reptiles. It is likely that a distinct insect fauna is associated with the hummocks, which provide both shelter and a food source. Gross (1952) lists the cockroaches *Zonioploca alutacea, Anamesia punctata,* and *Desmozosteria zebra* as

Triodia insects, probably using the hummocks for shelter, whilst Key (1959) mentions the morabine genus *Warramunga* as restricted to spinifex. Some of the species of this genus feed on *Triodia* whereas others merely use the plant as shelter. Blackith and Blackith (1966) describe how one species that eats *Triodia,* stuffs relatively long needles of the grass into its gut without chewing them. The pieces emerge intact in the faeces but with their cell contents having been digested by the grasshopper.

The ubiquitous northern termite, *Nasutitermes triodiae,* may dominate the landscape with its mounds in spinifex areas and feeds on these grasses, but is not restricted to them. It is probable that this termite forms the staple food of many of the spinifex-inhabiting lizards of the genus *Ctenotus* studied by Pianka (1969) (see section 2.2.1). Several species of these lizards are specialized for existence in spinifex areas, and there can be no doubt that the majority of the insect inhabitants of spinifex are equally specialized. However, no study at all has as yet been carried out on them.

In general, termites and grasshoppers are the principal herbivores in arid grasslands (section 2.2), but many other groups of insects have become adapted to grass feeding, including many Anthelidae, the pyraloid subfamily Crambinae, large ground weevils (*Acantholophus,* etc.), harvester ants feeding on seeds, *Chirothrips* feeding on grass flowers, and many others.

An extensive vegetational and edaphic description of Australia's grasslands is to be found in Moore (1970).

2.4.5 GIBBER PLAINS

This type of formation, also called stony desert and often interspersed with sand ridges, is typical of large expanses of Central Australia. The soil appears impenetrable by large arthropods, and vegetation is very sparse, consisting of lichens and small shrubs of *Sida, Bassia,* etc., located mostly in depressions. This unpromising landscape has nevertheless produced a number of specialized grasshopper genera collectively called "gibber grasshoppers" — *Raniliella, Cratilopus,*

Exarhalltia, Phaneroceros, Buforania, and others (Key 1959). Good examples of desert-adapted *K* strategists, they are usually sluggish, flattened creatures closely resembling the pebbles and lichens on which they occur.

The existence of insectivorous lizard species restricted to gibber plains (T. F. Houston, personal communication) once again points to the presence of a reliable but still unstudied insect fauna in this formation.

2.4.6 SAND RIDGES

The parallel sand ridges which occupy most of the true sandy deserts of Central Australia appear to be extraordinarily rich in insect life, probably because of the suitability of sand for digging shelters and nests, and for the growth of many flowering shrubs and trees, such as *Grevillea* spp. and the desert poplar, *Codonocarpus.* These plants attract a profusion of pollinating insects and ants. The sand appears to be honey-combed with the burrows of crickets, spiders, ants, ant-lions, scorpions, and other animals.

The "piedish" beetles of the genus *Helaeus* (Fig. 9) are the most conspicuous insects on inland sand dunes at night. They forage over the surface and are clearly well protected against predators. Food consists of any dead organic matter and both adults and larvae forage on the surface in the same way. In the daytime the larvae dig down into the sand, but the adults are dependent on vertebrate burrows for shelter.

2.4.7 CREEK BEDS

The importance of the creek system as a water reservoir in arid areas is stressed by Davies (1973). The water table beneath the sand or gravel surface of creeks rises by a much greater amount than one would expect from the actual rainfall gauging. Afterwards it falls slowly. Consequently, the effect of a moderate rainfall can be felt in a creek bed, even at a short distance beneath the sand surface, for several months after a rain. Thus, there is more water available to plants growing along creek beds than elsewhere and the general

Figure 9 A piedish beetle (*Helaeus* sp., Tenebrionidae). The paper-thin lateral flanges are correlated with a maximum degree of predator-foolhardiness, since these beetles wander fully exposed on sand dunes at night. The flanges probably serve two purposes: (1) that of offering inexperienced or non-learning predators some expendable tissue to chew on before the defensive-gland secretions can take effect, and (2) that of imparting a distinctive silhouette against the pale sand background as a warning to experienced predators. [Photo the author]

Figure 10 The cockroach *Euzosteria mitchelli* (Angas) with oothecum. Ground-dwelling, usually wingless cockroaches may achieve a very large size in Australia and are involved in leaf-litter breakdown. Exposure to visual predators has often, as in this case, resulted in the evolution of bold, species-specific signal colours through apostatic selection. [Photo C. Lourandos, courtesy Division of Entomology, CSIRO]

productivity of desert ecosystems is largely dependent on the effectiveness of the creek system.

When large grazing animals are present they tend to spend most of their time around water courses and under the shade of trees, even if they forage widely for food. Most of their defaecation and urination occurs in these shelter areas. The result is that their presence (and perhaps also that of birds nesting in trees) has the effect of concentrating nutrients in the creek area. Consequently, the creek system serves to concentrate not only water, but also nutrients produced throughout the ecosystem.

Animal productivity is, of course, dependent on that of plants and the significance of the creek system to insects may perhaps be exemplified by Tindale's (1938) account of how a member of a group generally adapted to moist conditions can survive in the desert.

The ghost moths (Hepialidae) are inhabitants of high-rainfall regions except for a few species; one of the exceptions is *Trictena argentata* which is associated with river red gums (*Eucalyptus camaldulensis*). Larvae of this moth occur at depths of 1.2 to 1.5 m at the bases of trees, where tests showed soil moisture content to be 11 per cent by weight. To quote Tindale (1938):

> In this relatively high moisture content of the soil of the larval environment, we seem to see the reason why *Trictena* can be an exception to the rule that Hepialidae occur only in regions of relatively constant and reliable high rainfall. As the moth appears on the wing for only a brief, irregularly timed period just after heavy rain when the desert blossoms and the air is temporarily moist, it does not suffer from the effects of drought. The eggs hatch rapidly after falling to the ground, and the young larvae retreat deeply into the moist sandy soil of the river bed, modifying their position so as to remain in a suitable climatic environment, despite the arid conditions reigning above them on the surface of the ground.

These moths fly in large swarms during the night following the first heavy summer rain. Each female scatters up to 50,000 eggs over the ground as she flies (Tindale 1966).

Tindale (1935) noted that the adult of *Trictena argentata*

can maintain its body temperature up to 10° C higher than ambient by flapping its wings. In view of the moth's very brief flight period, and its need to synchronize with rainfall, a relative independence of ambient temperature is an obvious advantage.

2.4.8 DRY SALT LAKES

Undoubtedly the most sterile in appearance of all arid-zone environments are the dry salt lakes. These are located primarily in South Australia and Western Australia. However, as in the case of the gibber plain, appearances are deceptive, and even this seemingly barren habitat has its insect fauna.

The drying salt acts as an effective trap for insects that accidentally come into contact with it. This phenomenon provides food for a number of predators which lurk about the salt crust. Most prominent among these in Lake Eyre are ants of the genus *Melophorus*, which R. W. Taylor (in litt.) believes may also feed on seeds blown onto the salt. They were previously thought to live on algae (Madigan 1930). However, G. F. Gross (personal communication) found neither seeds nor algae in several excavated nests, but only dead insects with a large proportion of Hemiptera, especially Cydnidae. Mitchell (1973) described the entrance mounds of these nests as being regularly spaced (overdispersed) at about 10 m intervals on the salt crust. There are two sets of galleries, one near the surface and one just above the water table 40 to 70 cm down. The ants are able to survive the irregular flooding of the lake by sealing their nests, whilst the entrance mounds (about 20 cm high) protect the nests from minor inundations. Mitchell further remarks that the insects trapped on the wet salt tend to be species which normally don't occur on the adjacent shore vegetation and surrounding sand hills, implying that they are long-distance fliers deceived by the watery appearance of the lake at night or simply lured by the "white sheet effect".

Also among the salt crust predators is a salticid spider (*Habrocestum* sp.) which lives beneath overhanging crusts of salt (G. F. Gross, personal communication).

The ants are preyed upon by a lizard, *Amphibolurus maculosus,* which is restricted to the salt-lake habitat (Mitchell 1973). There is thus an exclusive food chain on the salt lake, whose base consists of the insects trapped by the salt.

Some of the insect inhabitants of flooded salt lakes are mentioned in section 5.1.

2.4.9 DRY SOIL

Arid soils in general have a low nutrient content concentrated near the surface, making them particularly vulnerable to degradation by surface erosion (profile truncation). Australian arid soils, in addition, have an exceptionally low phosphorus content which in turn affects their nitrogen status (Jackson 1957). Nitrogen fixation appears to be at a low level, for reasons which are not entirely clear, in spite of the abundant presence of legumes and even of nitrogen-fixing lichens (Ross 1969).

As previously mentioned (section 2.2), litter decomposition may be rapid in Australian arid communities (as opposed to sclerophyll forests, section 4.4.1), and is believed to be due firstly to termite activity (because of these insects' relative independence of rainfall frequency) and secondly to microorganisms, mites, and collembolans, which become active after light rains that are insufficient to influence plant growth.

The Collembola of arid soils in South Australia have been the subject of some recent investigations by Wood (1970) and Greenslade and Greenslade (1973). Wood found that the density of small anthropods (an average of 4,490 individuals per m² of surface area) was much lower than for any other known type of biome except a Central Asian desert; even the Antarctic soil possesses more than 30,000/m². About half the microarthropod fauna studied by Wood consisted of mites, somewhat less than half were Collembola, and the rest were Crustacea (Copepoda and Cladocera).

According to Wood (1970), most of the Collembola were of a single species of *Folsomides* that he considered to be an indicator of arid soils. However, Greenslade and Greenslade (1973) showed that in fact at least two species of *Folsomides* are involved and that they are not as restricted to arid soils as Wood believed. Several other species of Collembola, all Isotomidae, are associated with dry soils, their principal adaptation to this environment being an ability to pass rapidly from an active to an inactive state, and vice versa, depending on changes in soil moisture caused by rainfall. P. Greenslade (personal communication) kept one species of *Folsomides* inactive in dry soil for as long as five months, after which activity could rapidly be induced by addition of water to the soil. Entomobryid collembolans which occur mostly in wetter soils, but overlap with the arid species in mallee, lack the ability to become dormant and attempt to continue activity during dry periods.

2.5   INSECTS AS FOOD FOR ABORIGINAL MAN

The influence of European man on insects (Chapter 3) takes the form of habitat alteration or destruction. The influence of Aboriginal man, on the other hand, was largely one of predation.

The Australian Aborigines were at the hunting and gathering stage of human cultural evolution when Europeans first arrived and practised no cultivation and very little storage of supplies. Their only major effect on the environment resulted from their frequent use of fire as a hunting aid (Tindale 1959). They could feed all year in natural ecosystems by taking advantage of successive periods of abundance of a great variety of plants and animals (see lists in Lawrence 1969). They lived throughout Australia, even in the most arid parts, but population density was much higher around permanent water sources. The basic economic unit was the family or extended family (Lawrence op. cit.), not the tribe. McKeown (1944) describes many of the hunting and gathering techniques used.

Insects formed an essential part of the human diet, providing animal fat and carbohydrates, as well as some vitamins which would otherwise have been lacking. During periods of temporary insect scarcity, scurvy outbreaks occurred (Tindale 1966). The early European explorers in the Centre, lacking the superior ecological knowledge of the native peoples, suffered agonies and even death from this disease in spite of the fact that the remedy (for instance, honey ants) was often close at hand (honeydew is not just a sugar solution, but a complete food). In caloric content alone, insect biomass is far superior to meat, 100 g of fried termites, for instance, delivers over 500 calories, whilst the equivalent weight of beef contains only 127 calories (Bodenheimer 1951). Some insects or their products are great delicacies and were eagerly sought for their pleasant taste alone. This is particularly true of honey, honeydew, and "manna" (lerps), which were the only sources of concentrated sweetness, equivalent in desirability to sugar and sweets in other cultures.

The insects that were eaten were almost certainly abundant in the ecosystems in which they occurred. In fact, the only two attributes needed for an insect to serve as human food is that it be palatable and that it be temporarily abundant or concentrated enough to reward the effort expended in obtaining it, or its products.

The following Australian insects are recorded as figuring in the human diet. Undoubtedly many others have also served as food from time to time.

(1) Cossid moths. The larvae of these moths are locally abundant as external feeders on roots of *Acacia* and *Eucalyptus* (section 2.4.2). The food plant of *Xyleutes leucomochla,* a species frequently eaten, is the shrub *Acacia ligulata.* In the Arabana language these shrubs are known as witjuti, and from this name originated the well-known term "witjuti grubs" (in various spellings) applied by Europeans to all edible wood-feeding insect larvae in Australia (Tindale 1953).

(2) Hepialid moths. The larvae of these insects are external root feeders, timber borers, or occasionally grass feeders. They are dug out, if external root feeders, or impaled on a hooked stick, if borers, and eaten. Species of the genera *Trictena* and *Abantiades* are most frequently eaten (Tindale

1966). Adults of *Trictena argentata* may also be eaten; they are attracted to fires and conveniently cook themselves in the embers (Tindale 1938).

(3) The Bogong moth (*Agrotis infusa*) (section 5.4.3 and Fig. 12). This species was reported by John Eyre as a favourite food of the Aboriginal tribes of the riverine area of New South Wales. People came from long distances to feast on the adult moths during the latter's regular spring migration. The moths were gathered into baskets, roasted on soil previously heated by a fire, and eaten directly or pounded into cakes with a very high fat content (McKeown 1944). From the accounts of these feasts, it appears that man must have been a significant predator on these moths, together with crows. The engorged crows themselves were eaten by men as they emerged from the hibernation caves.

(4) Other lepidopterans. The literature records several instances of unidentified caterpillars being eaten whenever they became abundant.

(5) Cerambycid beetles. Larvae of these beetles bore in wood and can be picked out with hooked sticks. The species mentioned as food are *Bardistus cibarius* ("bardee"), which feeds on *Xanthorrhoea* spp. (grass tree, yacca, or black boy), *Paroplites australis* in Queensland, *Zeuzera eucalypti* in Tasmania, *Eurynassa australis* (Bodenheimer 1951), and *Agrianome spinicollis* (Duffy 1963). *E. australis* is apparently also eaten as an adult (Linsley 1959). No beetles other than cerambycids are known to be eaten, reports to the contrary being erroneous (see below).

(6) Honey ants. Various species of the genera *Melophorus, Camponotus,* and *Leptomyrmex* store honeydew in individuals which become greatly distended. These repletes are dug out with digging sticks (usually by women) sometimes from a depth of 2 m. Honeydew is obtained by the ants from nectar glands and homopterans on trees and shrubs. Analyses of some insect honeydews have revealed the presence of all essential amino acids, proteins, minerals, and vitamins, as well as sugars (Way 1963).

(7) Other ants. Ants of all sorts were readily eaten by

Aborigines. McKeown (1944) cites an account of ants being scraped off the leg of a person who had placed her foot on a nest, the handfuls thus obtained being passed directly into the mouth. Frequently pupae were dug out and prepared in various ways. There are several accounts of feeding on the green tree ant, *Oecophylla smaragdina,* on Cape York Peninsula and in Arnhem Land, where this ant is extremely abundant. The leaf nests are gathered and the contained larvae formed into balls and eaten directly (McKeown 1944, quoting T. G. Campbell) or the entire nests and their contents of immatures, adults, and inquilines are placed in a mesh basket, crushed, and water passed through. The water is then drunk, producing what observers have described as a "pleasant acid drink" or a drink "like lemonade".

(8) *Trigona* bees. These bees nest in trees and store honey in cerumen pots, not in cells. Although stingless, the bees fiercely defend their nests by biting and depositing a sticky secretion (propolis) on the intruder; this coupled with the height of the nests makes honey gathering no easy matter. Early accounts speak of native bees in southern regions, and it is possible that their present restricted northern distribution may have resulted in part from displacement by the introduced honey bee, *Apis.*

(9) Psyllidae. Many species of psyllids when feeding on leaves produce a protective covering in the larval stage made up of sugar and starch ("lerp-amylose"). These coverings are called lerps (an Aboriginal word originally recorded as "laarp"). Those occurring on red gum and coolibah, in particular, are sought as a source of sugar.

(10) Cicadas. Cicadas of unidentified species are eaten on emergence from the soil in New South Wales and near the Hermannsburg Mission in Central Australia. Cicadas are also said to deposit edible "manna" on white gum (Bodenheimer 1951). This must refer to what Froggatt (1903a) describes as a "fine spray of liquid" discharged from the anus of the "red-eye" (*Psaltoda moerens*), and which falls in a fine shower below heavily infested apple gum (*Angophora lanceolata*).

(11) Termites. Accounts conflict as to the importance of termites in the human diet in Australia. Froggatt (1903b)

describes how termites are "winnowed" from nest debris near Kalgoorlie by using a wooden trough, the immature workers being eventually separated from the rest of the contents. Tindale (1966) and Lawrence (1969) also refer to termites as being of dietary importance in arid areas. However, Bodenheimer (1951) states that termites are almost never eaten in Australia and that this is a matter of taste, as they are of crucial importance in the African diet.

(12) Grasshoppers. In contrast to their great popularity in the Middle East grasshoppers are said not to be eaten in Australia (Froggatt, 1903b; Bodenheimer, 1951). However, Tindale (1966) mentions that the people of Bentinck Island (Gulf of Carpentaria) eat one species of plague grasshopper, and McKeown (1944) quotes an account by Carl Lumholtz of people eating roasted grasshoppers.

(13) Other insects. McKeown (1944) and Bodenheimer (1951) cite butterflies, head lice, and cockroaches as additional insects occasionally eaten. The latter are probably hunted by burning spinifex hummocks (Lawrence 1969) and picked up incidentally with the lizards that are the main quarry.

Some early errors have persisted in the modern literature. Bodenheimer (1951) repeats an early observation attributed to F. W. Hope that the larvae of the rutelid scarab, *Anoplognathus viridiaeneus,* are eaten. However, Froggatt (1903b) points out that Hope believed the adults of all "witchetty grubs" to be this beetle, which is of course erroneous. Lawrence (1969) continues to describe lerp (or laarp) as the "excrement of a green beetle in which the larva is deposited". Froggatt corrected this case of mistaken origin for lerp (see above under Psyllidae).

Insects are also ecologically useful to Aboriginal man in serving as guides to the location of water in arid areas. People in the Flinders Ranges follow a black and orange insect to water (R. Ellis, personal communication). Undoubtedly, this refers to the vespoid wasps *Delta, Pseudepipona,* and *Abispa* spp. which regularly visit small pools in arid areas.

Insects also figure prominently in the art, mythology, and totemic logic of Aboriginal peoples, and have been elaborately classified by them.

CHAPTER 3
The Culture Steppe

3.1 GENERAL CHARACTERISTICS OF THE BIOME

The term culture steppe has been in use for some time in
Continental Europe to denote that area of the landscape
which has been modified by man from the original forested
condition to one of open, usually grassy formations, and
either directly cropped by man or grazed by large domestic
herbivores. The formation thus superficially resembles the
natural steppes of Central Asia. I am using the term here in a
somewhat broader sense to include all parts of the landscape
modified by European man directly (not just through the
introduction of grazing mammals). Crop fields, improved
pastures, settlements, ornamental parks, gardens, and roadsides are included. Arboreal monocultures, such as orchards,
pine plantations, and tropical tree crops must be excluded
from the term so as not to stretch the simile too far, but
occasional reference to them is made in the present discussion.
The more recent literature uses the nearly equivalent, but less
euphonious terms "agroecosystem" or "agrobiocoenosis",
which I will apply only to the agricultural areas themselves.

European man in Australia has profoundly influenced
areas outside the culture steppe itself by introducing sheep,
cattle, buffalo, goats, camels, and rabbits — nearly all the
areas affected (except by buffalo) falling within the arid zone
discussed in Chapter 2. According to the Atlas of Australian
Resources, more than half of Arid Australia is used either for
grazing sheep or beef cattle, whilst feral goats and rabbits
roam widely.

The culture steppe occupies most of the land area outside the arid zone and is therefore Australia's second most
extensive biome type. Although populated by many native
Australian insects it is not a native ecosystem in basic structure
or in many of the components of its biota. It is European
man's own particular environment, which he has established
in temperate climates throughout the world, and into which
he has introduced many of the familiar plants, mammals, and
birds of his homeland and (unwittingly) many of the pests
as well.

3.2 COMMUNITY STRUCTURE AND ENERGETICS OF THE CULTURE STEPPE

The culture steppe differs from all other biome types considered in this book by being an immature system, with very
few of its own K strategists. The principal attribute of an
immature system, as outlined by Odum (1969), is a high
proportion of energy going into production as opposed to
respiration (maintenance), with a resulting rapid accumulation
of biomass. This of course makes the system productive of
the assimilating (green) parts of plants which are harvestable
by man, and man's continuous removal of this production
keeps the system at a youthful level.

Another attribute of immature systems is reduced
species diversity, with the majority of species tending to be r
strategists. Grazing food chains are proportionately more
important than in other systems and litter production is
reduced (except by man himself), whilst excrement production is increased.

One school of current thinking in agricultural ecology
seeks to reintroduce the natural defences of plants, which
have been cultivated out of crops in favour of substituting
man-made defences (usually consisting of chemical pesticide
application). Natural plant defences, as outlined in several
places in this book, consist of escape in both space and time,
as well as the elaboration of toxic compounds. Escape in time
can be simulated by crop rotation and the interposing of
sanitation periods in cultivation practises, while escape in

space can be simulated by growing mixed crops. At the same time, resistant strains of crop plants can be bred so as to re-create the plants' own chemical defences. Among the herbi-vores in the system, pollinators are the only kind encouraged. The second most important general limiting factor on herbi-vore populations, after the plants' defences, is predation, and this too can be encouraged by various means.

In pastoral practise, where it is the herbivore level that is to be supported, man's aims are just the opposite of those just outlined — plants are selected for their edibility and second-order consumers (predators and parasites) are discouraged. To a certain extent, the herbivores' own natural defences can be developed, but in practise this often conflicts with their edibility to man. Therefore, research in pastoral ecology is aimed, on the one hand, at increasing the efficiency of energy flow through the system by such measures as speeding up return of nutrients to plants, increasing the harvestability of plants, and increasing water and nutrient input, and on the other, at adopting various practises to control parasites and competitors.

While all the above measures are alternatives to reliance on pesticides, there is no likelihood that the latter can ever be completely eliminated from any artificial ecosystem, and the aim today is merely to reduce pesticide application to certain critical times in the life history of the target organism, these times to be determined by research on the organisms con-cerned. This combination of biological and chemical mani-pulation is known as "integrated control".

Although insects play a vital part in these policies of manipulation, this aspect will not be treated in detail in this book. Rather the emphasis will be the effect of man on insects. What does man's environment, the culture steppe, offer insects in the way of opportunities? How have they been able to adapt to it?

In spite of the voluminous literature on agricultural entomology, there are few works which look at man's environment from the insects' point of view, as an ecosystem to be exploited.

3.3   GENERAL ADAPTATIONS OF INSECTS TO CULTURE— STEPPE CONDITIONS

Viewed as a whole, the culture steppe consists of a patch-work of different habitats — fields, pastures, gardens, etc. — which are constantly changing as a result of man's activities. The patches themselves are usually much larger than corresponding homogeneous units in a natural environment, and offer large amounts of concentrated food (broad targets). A vagile insect (*r*-strategist) has an obvious advantage in having a high probability of finding a favourable patch early enough for a dense population to be built up before the patch disappears again.

There is, however, another aspect of mobility which does not depend entirely on the insect's own powers of dispersal — the ability to take advantage of man's transport facilities. Some species have become cosmopolitan throughout the temperate zones by being carried with foodstuffs, livestock, and timber. In addition, the former practise of using soil and stones as ballast in ships has resulted in the transportation of some soil-associated species which might not otherwise have been introduced (Roberts 1968). Insects can also be carried simply as stowaways in aircraft, where the journey is brief enough to permit an adult to survive it without food. Hughes *et al.* (1972) report that bushflies reach northern Tasmania nearly every summer, in spite of being unable to overwinter anywhere on the island, and suggest that human transport may be responsible. *Aedes vigilax* appears to have been recently carried by plane to Fiji (Marks 1972).

With regard to mosquitoes, the single most important factor which determines their transportability is their ability to breed in small containers. Such mosquitoes, which breed in ephemeral waters in natural ecosystems, can successfully exploit numerous places aboard ship, such as water casks (in former times), concavities in tarpaulins, lifeboats, fire buckets, and especially motor tyres carried as cargo (Laird 1956). Several species, such as *Culex fatigans, C. molestus, C. annulirostris, Anopheles farauti, A. annulipes,* and *Aedes aegypti,* have been widely dispersed by this means.

Chadwick and Nikitin (1968) made a survey of the beetles intercepted by quarantine in the ports of Sydney and Newcastle in the period up to 1965. Virtually all records are between 1951 and 1965. During this time, 468 beetles were intercepted, belonging to 136 species from 46 countries; 418 of these specimens came by sea, 15 by air, 32 by parcel post, two in passengers' luggage, and 1 by unknown means. To gain some idea of the magnitude of this insect traffic, it should be borne in mind that: (1) this is only one order of insects (albeit the one most likely to be transported); (2) practically only one port is involved, as the Newcastle records are extremely few; (3) these are just the beetles intercepted, not the ones that got through; and (4) these figures cover only a fifteen-year period when quarantine inspections were presumably more stringent than in the past.

One of the most recent introductions of a species that subsequently became a pest is that of the weevil *Sitona humeralis,* first noted near Camden, New South Wales, in 1958. It spread very quickly throughout southern New South Wales and appeared in Victoria in 1964 and in South Australia in 1966. In the settled areas of South Australia it has now become extremely abundant, feeding on annual medic and lucerne (*Medicago* spp.) and clovers (Allen 1971). Its rate of spread in the improved pasture areas of southern Australia is therefore about 150 km per year.

At perhaps the opposite extreme is a very large flightless tenebrionid beetle, *Blaps polychresta,* which was brought into Wallaroo, South Australia, some time before 1930, probably in the ballast of a grain ship returning empty from Egypt. Until the mid 1950s this beetle had not progressed more than 50 km from Wallaroo (a rate of about 2 km/yr). Thereafter it began to turn up in a number of ports on Spencer Gulf — Port Augusta, Whyalla, Cowell, and Port Lincoln — and appeared in Adelaide in 1962. It is most probable that the beetle is being transported by grain ships (which call regularly at all these ports) and is not spreading under its own power. The beetle's affinity for buildings, where it sometimes ex-

cavates hollows in mortar or limestone, as well as its dependence on man's transport facilities, makes it a definite
synanthrope in spite of its lack of intrinsic vagility (Matthews
1975).

The increasing similarity, economically speaking, of all
human societies throughout the world, with the production
of much the same crops and other materials, coupled with the
abundant opportunities for transport discussed above, results
in an increasing level of uniformity in the insect fauna of the
culture steppe of all countries. Many of its insect inhabitants
are cosmopolites familiar to entomologists everywhere. This
tendency toward faunal uniformity is further enhanced by
the deliberate policy of many countries, Australia foremost
among them, of introducing insects for the control of weeds
and other insects already present.

For the purposes of the present discussion, I have considered the insects listed in the CSIRO's "Scientific and
Common Names of Insects and Allied Forms Occurring in
Australia" (1966, CSIRO Bulletin No. 285) as the principal
insect inhabitants of Australia's culture steppe, on the
assumption that if an insect receives a vernacular name it is in
some way involved in man's economy (a few, such as butterflies, however, are probably included simply because they are
conspicuous).

Almost 1,000 species are listed. To gain an idea of what
proportion of these is introduced, I have gone through the
first two letters in the alphabetical list of vernacular names,
presumably representing a random sample of 147 species
(arachnids omitted), and determined which of these are
native and which are not. Sixty-eight (46 per cent) of these
species proved to be introduced.

Gross (1954) found that several natural forest formations around Adelaide had no introduced species, whereas
various grasslands in the area had 18 per cent of their insect
fauna represented by introduced species. One formation in
the culture steppe, mostly cryptozoic habitats under rubbish,
had 53 per cent non-native insect species.

Thus, it appears that a maximum of about half of Australia's culture steppe insects are immigrant species. In the

Lepidoptera, Common (1970) notes that most pest species are native, the introduced ones being chiefly pests of stored products, orchards, and vegetable gardens; Wallace (1970) reports that most pasture pests are native species. Some individual taxa prove an exception to this rule, perhaps the most striking one being the Aphidioidea. Of 118 species of aphids known in Australia, only 8 are definitely native, although a proportion of the remainder, whilst foreign in origin, may have arrived by natural means. Fifty are known to have been introduced by European man (Woodward, Evans, and Eastop 1970).

Of course, the broad geographical limits of the culture steppe include many small patches of native or mixed vegetation on steep slopes and other areas which have escaped cultivation or "development", and native insects, including some K strategists, persist in these patches more successfully than do larger animals (see section 3.6). Gross's figures cited above indicate that the closer we get to man himself and his products and wastes, the higher is the percentage of immigrant species. The extreme case is man's own dwellings, with their complement of household pests and parasites which are virtually all cosmopolitan species.

It is possible that the trend toward cosmopolitanism is not so strong in tropical areas. In an analysis of the zoogeography of economic entomology in New Guinea, Szent-Ivany (1961) found that of the 34 major pests of food crops there, only one was an immigrant species. Of the 1,400 recorded pests of cacao in the world, the vast majority are autochthonous species originating locally from secondary rain forest (Entwistle 1972). Tropical crops are largely arboreal (coconut, cacao, coffee, banana, rubber, etc.) or native foods such as sweet potato, taro, yam, etc. Neither of these categories would be expected to attract insects of the culture steppe. Furthermore, trade to and from tropical countries tends to be with temperate areas rather than with each other, and thus there is limited opportunity for transporting insects from one tropical area to another. We can expect that with time such transport will increase, and that eventually there will be a pan-tropical fauna of mobile insects associated with man and his crops, but one that is largely different from that of the temperate culture steppe.

With regard to household pests and parasites, on the other hand, a more truly cosmopolitan fauna is to be expected, as many of these were originally tropical.

I have not been able to make a general survey of the other aspects of *r* strategy, such as high intrinsic rate of population increase and broad limits in food spectra. However, most economic entomologists would probably agree that the majority of pest species display these attributes to a high degree.

3.4 AUSTRALIAN CULTURE-STEPPE FORMATIONS

Few culture-steppe formations have been studied as ecosystems. I will therefore confine myself to two systems which together embody most of the basic principles involved in man-insect associations.

3.4.1 THE ANTHROPOBIOCOENOSIS

This rather cumbersome term has been used in the European literature in reference to the environment of man's settlement areas — his dwellings and those of his domestic animals (which at one time were the same), his storage sites, manufactured and processed products, and rubbish dumps. In the terminology used by Povolny (1971), this is not part of the culture steppe proper, which is called the "agrobiocoenosis". The anthropobiocoenosis is populated by man, his domestic animals, and synanthropes, the latter being defined as spontaneous inhabitants with man against his wish ("homophiles" is another term sometimes used).

The principal opportunities offered by the anthropobiocoenosis derive from man's storage of food, wood, and fibre, and from waste. The latter takes the form of garbage and faeces, plus material not always considered in this connection, namely durable rubbish. The latter offers shelter for numerous arthropods and there can be no doubt that quantities of wood and metal lying about greatly increase the population levels of arthropods and molluscs relying on cryptozoic habitats for shelter (Gross 1954). Water-holding containers favour synanthropic mosquitoes. Man himself, and his domestic animals, offer an energy source for parasites.

Some synanthropic flies are believed to have evolved in tropical areas from symbovines (breeders in cattle dung) and, as a result of the original intimate association between man and his cattle, transferred to man, eventually becoming independent of cattle (Povolny 1971). Flies such as *Musca domestica*, *Phoenicia sericata*, and *Fannia canicularis* are dependent on man's housing outside tropical areas and could not survive there without it. Among the mosquitoes, *Aedes aegypti* seems to have evolved in a similar way. *Musca domestica* and *Fannia canicularis* now have morphologically distinct races, one truly synanthropic, the other one not (Povolny op. cit.), showing that evolutionary changes have already taken place among synanthropes.

Flies initiating myiasis in cattle, sheep, and man are basically pioneering members of the cadaver microsere. It is a small step from a fresh cadaver to a wounded or diseased part of a living animal where mild necrosis is occurring or (in sheep) where there is merely a soiling of the wool. After the primary flies have initiated myiasis, secondary and even tertiary forms corresponding to the later stages of cadaver succession may come in while the mammal is still living. Norris (1959) cites eight species of calliphorid flies causing primary myiasis or "strike" in sheep in Australia. Six species (three calliphorids and three sarcophagids) cause secondary myiasis, and five (all muscids) cause tertiary myiasis. However, 80 per cent of the primary myiases are caused by the world-wide *Lucilia cuprina*, introduced into Australia since the turn of the century.

It may come as a surprise to learn that the bushfly, *Musca vetustissima*, the most thorough nuisance to man of any fly in Australia, is not really a synanthrope (see sections 2.3.2, 2.3.6). Although there is no doubt that the presence of cattle dung in arid areas has favoured the bushfly, accounts by early explorers such as William Dampier indicate that the fly was abundant even before cattle were introduced; marsupial dung may be a preferred food (Norris 1966). In fact, Gross (1954) notes that around human habitations, even primitive encampments, *M. vetustissima* tends to be displaced by *M. domestica.*

There are other evolutionary avenues to synanthropy beside the intimate man-cattle relationship. Some parasites must have had a long history of coevolution with man. Such must be the case with the taxonomically isolated genera *Pulex, Pediculus,* and *Phthirus.* On the other hand, the bed bug (*Cimex lectularius*) has close relatives among parasites of swallows, swifts, pigeons, and bats (Patton and Cragg 1913; Riley and Johannsen 1938) and probably transferred to man as a result of his previous sharing of cave dwellings with most of these animals. Parasites of domestic animals are *ipso facto* synanthropes even if not directly dependent on man as host.

Other synanthropic insects are somewhat less intimately related to man and their association results from man's long-standing habit of storing food and fibre under shelter (stored products pests). Many are participants in the cadaver micro-sere during its last stages when little but skin, fur, and bones are left (all dermestids, some tineid moths and ptinid beetles). Others have become associated with man by way of birds' nests (other tineids, especially *Tinea pellionella,* and ptinids) (Woodroffe and Southgate 1951) and, of course, many came by way of dead wood and fibre (sometimes as fungus feeders) when man started to use these materials to construct dwellings, furniture, and clothing (lyctid, anobiid, and bostrychid beetles, psocids, and termites). The destructive domestic drywood termite, *Cryptotermes brevis* has recently found its way into tropical Australia (Heather 1970). Finally, general scavengers and omnivores often feed on stored foods, spillage, and glue (cockroaches, ants, silverfish, crickets).

Except for spiders and centipedes, there are relatively few exclusive predators among synanthropes (ants in this role being generally omnivorous). The window fly, *Scenopinus fenestralis*, is the only domestic insect predator that comes to mind.

3.4.2 THE PASTURE ECOSYSTEM

Pastures are essentially of two types in Australia: (1) the improved pasture, established mostly with introduced herbage in areas that would normally support mesic forest (or in irrigated areas); and (2) the unimproved, occupying natural arid lands (discussed in Chapter 2). Unimproved pasture retains most of the basic structure of the native formations, but with a profound alteration of native plant species composition as a result of selective grazing. It is interesting to note that the practice of "agistment" in Australian arid pastoral areas artificially provides the mobility which is one of the essential adaptations maintaining a large biomass in arid biomes.

It will be recalled that large ungulates are efficient ingestors and digestors of primary production and that their introduction into areas which did not previously support them results in a rapid transfer of energy from producer to first-order consumer level and a decline in producer biomass. The important side-effect of this transfer is a greatly increased excrement production. This occurs in large deposits with which most native coprophages are not adapted to deal.

Another consequence of cattle and sheep introduction is the creation of patches of bare ground favouring locusts (section 2.3.1). The first locust plague recorded in Australia was in 1844, in Adelaide. The first in Victoria (in the far west of the State) was in 1848; the first in New South Wales (the Hay district), occurred in 1883; the first in Queensland (Toowoomba), in 1886, and the first in Western Australia in 1917 (Key 1938). The most logical explanation for this sequence is that the colonies or states experienced locust plagues as soon as their pastoral areas began to encroach extensively on arid lands.

The improved pasture is a typical immature system. At the producer level, most available energy goes into production and very little into storage or maintenance. Much of this production (but probably less than half) passes rapidly into the herbivore trophic level, but about one third of this in turn passes out again as faeces. When this proportion is added to that which was not ingested, it can be seen that even in this youthful ecosystem more energy passes through detritus channels than through grazing channels.

It is only recently that investigators have begun to pay close attention to the problem arising in pastures from the accumulation of faecal deposits. To maintain the productivity of the system, the mineral content of these faeces must be recycled through the producer level; this cannot be done efficiently by bacteria alone because of the tendency of faeces to dry out on the surface. Even when conditions do permit decay to occur on the surface, 80 per cent of the contained nitrogen is lost through volatilization of ammonia resulting from bacterial breakdown of undigested protein (Gillard 1967). On the other hand, if this decay occurs in the soil, the ammonia is adsorbed onto soil colloids. Another detrimental consequence of faeces remaining on the surface is the amount of ground area which is covered by dung and hence unavailable for sward growth (Bornemissza 1960).

Whereas flies and termites can convert the matter and energy of faeces lying on the surface into their own biomass (section 2.3.6), they are often not very efficient in doing this and the surface-covering effect persists. At the same time incorporation of minerals into the soil is delayed. Only dung beetles (Scarabaeidae) can dispose of vertebrate faeces in a way which is maximally beneficial to the ecosystem. The surface is cleared and unconsumed material is rapidly decomposed in the soil. Bornemissza and Williams (1970) experimentally demonstrated a beneficial effect of dung beetle activity on plant yield.

In Australia, dung beetles are minimally effective in pasture ecosystems for two reasons. In the low-density unimproved pastures of much of the interior, conditions are too dry for them to be able to survive (section 2.3.6), and it is unlikely that this situation can be changed except through irrigation. In wetter areas, the native dung beetles are ill-adapted for dealing with cattle dung, presumably because they have evolved behaviour appropriate to deal with small faecal pellets that require entirely different handling procedures.

Numerous other insects breed in cattle dung, either feeding directly on dung or as predators on coprophages. Flies, which are the principal coprophages occurring as larvae in surface dung, may be very sensitive to the composition (especially nitrogen content) of their food (Greenham 1972) and often require an additional source of protein for egg maturation to occur. This may be obtained from vertebrate blood or exudations (*Haematobia exigua, Musca vetustissima*) or perhaps from honeydew and pollen.

Finally, insects also feed on the pasture plants themselves. The family to which dung beetles belong, Scarabaeidae, also includes pasture root or herbage feeders. One of these is *Aphodius tasmaniae,* which belongs to a subfamily and genus otherwise entirely coprophagous or detritivorous. In *Aphodius tasmaniae* we see an aphodiine which is coprophagous in the adult stage and detritivorous or coprophagous in the first and part of the second larval stages, but which then becomes an active feeder on live pasture plants (Carne 1956; Maelzer 1962). The older larvae tear off parts of the plants, mostly clover and annual grasses, and take them into burrows where they are eaten. *A. tasmaniae* has greatly benefited from pasture improvement practices primarily because of the increase firstly in the quantity of dung and litter available to adults and young larvae, and secondly in the proportion of leguminous herbage which the older larvae prefer (Carne 1956). The beetle is never found in the dung of indigenous vertebrates, according to Maelzer (1962) and there is a possibility that it is able to survive entirely without excrement since the adult, although exclusively coprophagous, does not need to feed to lay its first batch of eggs. Sufficient protein for egg maturation can apparently be obtained from the plants eaten by the larvae; this unusual adaptation among Aphodiinae may be a response to an original scarcity of dung.

An introduced beetle that has also benefited from improved pasture conditions is the weevil *Sitona humeralis* (section 3.3). It feeds on leguminous herbage in both the adult and larval stages. The latter destroy the root nodules and thereby affect the nitrogen fixation and consequent fertility of the soil. Larval density of this beetle can be as high as 200 per square foot $(0.3m^2)$ (Allen 1971).

The effects on pastures of other groups of scarabaeid larvae were studied by Davidson and Roberts (1968) in the Northern Tablelands of New South Wales, where at least twelve scarab species are commonly encountered, often in mixed aggregates in the field, but with only two to four species abundant at any one time in a given place (Wallace 1970). It was shown experimentally that damage to live plants was considerably reduced when manure was added to the soil, but it is not clear whether this was due to preferential feeding on manure by the larvae or to more vigorous compensatory growth by the plants in the presence of manure. Experiments on one species (Wenzler 1970) indicate that the presence of live plant roots has a much greater influence on larval distribution and aggregation behaviour in the soil than does manure. All evidence so far suggests that most of these scarabs are preferential live-root feeders in the larval state.

The interesting question of whether specific differences in behaviour or food preference permit several root-scarab species to coexist has only begun to be investigated. One can imagine that differences in the depth of feeding in the soil, in preferred moisture content, soil type, preferred proportion of litter vs. live plant roots, preferred plant species, etc., might exist. The last has been demonstrated to occur to some extent (Davidson and Roberts 1968); there are generalized feeders, which consume dead organic matter as well as roots (*Anoplognathus, Rhopaea*) and more specialized live root feeders (*Sericesthis*) (Wallace 1970a). One introduced species, *Plectris aliena,* is strictly limited to light sandy soils (Roberts 1968).

With the exceptions of the introduced black lawn beetle (*Heteronychus arator*), which is a grass feeder in all its stages, those that feed on pollen (*Diphucephala*), and those that do not feed at all as adults (such as the introduced *Plectris aliena*), the adults of scarabs that feed on herb roots or organic matter in the soil as larvae are tree-leaf chafers (for instance, the "Christmas beetles" *Anoplognathus* spp.). These species therefore require a combination of meadowlands and trees in their habitats — a combination which in higher rainfall areas previously occurred under natural conditions only in small subclimax patches. The coming of the culture steppe has vastly increased the extent of this formation and therefore greatly benefited defoliating scarabs.

The non-feeding adults of melolonthine and ruteline scarabs tend to have very short adult flight periods, generally two to four days, a characteristic that minimizes exposure to predators and reduces the latter's opportunities to form concentrations. For this strategy to be maximally effective, all the scarab species in a given area should undergo their flights at the same time. However, it is not known if this is in fact the case. Some *Cerceris* wasps are specialist predators on swarming *Liparetrus* scarabs (Evans and Matthews 1970).

The combination of trees and pastures is also required by the thynnid parasitoids of pasture scarabs. Studies on the biology of these wasps reveal that they are K strategists capable of maintaining only a precarious foothold in the culture steppe. In the Thynninae (family Tiphiidae), the males are winged and the females wingless and usually smaller. In most species, the males feed on honeydew secreted by leaf hoppers and on the nectar from flowering trees, usually *Eucalyptus*. They then feed the females by regurgitation during copulation (Ridsdill-Smith 1970b). The sexes attract each other, evidently by means of pheromones, and copulation is usually accompanied by a mating flight, with the smaller female attached to the male by the end of the abdomen. At the termination of the mating flight the male deposits the female very near the spot where he picked her up; consequently this flight usually does not provide opportunity for dispersal. The females wander about the ground surface searching for scarab larvae. About three days after copulation in *Hemithynnus hyalinatus*, the best-studied species, the female finds a scarab larva by burrowing, paralyses it, and eventually oviposits on it in a prepared chamber as deep as 30 cm in the soil.

The distance between the male feeding area, where the trees are, and the breeding area, where the pasture scarabs are, cannot be more than 800 m in *H. hyalinatus,* and is usually much less.

Only mature scarab larvae or pupae which have accumulated sufficient food reserves to feed the wasp larva are parasitized. There is no evidence of any species-specificity in host selection (Ridsdill-Smith 1970b). One species of the subfamily, the well-known "blue ant" (*Diamma bicolor*), is believed to feed on mole crickets (Rayment 1954).

From the ecological point of view, *H. hyalinatus* and related species are interesting as examples of predators which are remarkably restricted in their ability to take advantage of any increase in the numbers of their prey. There is only one generation per year. The fecundity of the female is very low, i.e., up to nine eggs, with a theoretical maximum of twelve (Ridsdill-Smith 1970a). Even this production is dependent on repeated weekly matings, which in turn depend on the male finding sufficient food for himself and the female. The nectar supply is independent of, or inversely proportional to, the scarab host population level. Add to these factors the restraints on dispersal inherent in the behaviour of the male — the limited distance he will go from a tree, and the deposition of the female in the general area where she was picked up — and the picture emerges of an insect showing characteristics opposite of those believed to be necessary for success in the culture steppe. Whereas mobility is required, it is sedentary. It has complicated its life cycle by tying itself to two independent food sources, and is thus unable to respond to an abundance in just one of them. The conclusion of Ridsdill-Smith (1971) that "there is no evidence of a significant controlling influence of the wasps on the population of these pasture pests" is therefore not surprising.

In some insect species the female is exceptionally sedentary, and the male "compensates" by being highly mobile or migratory (e.g. thynnid wasps observed by I. F. B. Common, cited in Williams 1971). Evidently, the male provides the interdeme genetic exchange necessary even in the most *K*-adapted species (section 1.6).

3.5   IMMIGRATION OF NATIVE SPECIES INTO THE CULTURE STEPPE

It is evident from the foregoing that when natural vegetation is displaced to create culture-steppe formations, the new fauna contains a proportion of species native to the biome which occupied the area previously. The native insects that survive in the culture steppe are either: (1) the usually poly-phagous *r* strategists of the original ecosystem (adapted to temporary habitats such as young successional stages); or (2) more specialized species that happen to find in the new environment food or other requirements which they can exploit after relatively minor genetic changes. There are as yet very few culture-steppe specialist species among insects, perhaps only some *Blaps, Tribolium* flour beetles, one or two museum beetles, some cockroaches, silverfish, human parasites, and a few others. However, domestic or agricultural races of various dipterous species are known to have evolved (Povolny 1971; Bush 1974), and must occur in many other insects as well.

Examples of probable *r* strategists which have success-fully immigrated into the culture steppe are the species of the *Hednota* complex (Crambinae) in Western Australia. These normally occur in grass tussocks scattered among the native woodland formations and are not naturally abundant (Wallace 1970a). When forests are cleared and pastures established in these areas, *Hednota* spp. become major pests. In forest areas of Queensland and New South Wales, the native *Amnemus* weevil and funnel ants (*Aphaenogaster*) are rare in the natural forest formation but become very abundant after clearing to establish clover pastures.

In arid areas, the establishment of irrigated culture-steppe formations can produce disastrous insect "plagues". This is most likely because of the relatively large number of *r* strategists naturally occurring in arid environments especially in the warm areas of the world. Species adapted to take rapid advantage of periods of productivity following rains will not fail to increase to high levels under the *r*-selection conditions of irrigation, which remove the last remaining constraint on their build-up (drought). Wherever irrigated crops have been established in the world, the attendant insect pest problems have been severe (Rivnay 1964).

The Ord River Irrigation Area in the north of Western Australia represents an ambitious project started in the 1940s to grow tropical crops year-round in an arid zone. After an overland trip to the Ord River in the dry season, Jenkins (1945) reported that many potential pest species were already present in the area before commercial crops were planted. Local residents were unable to grow vegetables because of insect pests, primarily the grasshoppers *Gastrimargus musicus, Austacris guttulosa,* and *Locusta migratoria,* and various coleopterous and lepidopterous species.

Cotton growers in the area today have twenty pest species with which to contend (Richards 1964). Different species play dominant roles in different years (Wilson, Basinski, and Thompson 1972). From 1963 to 1968 the cosmopolitan noctuid *Spodoptera litura* was the dominant pest. After this period, a "sanitation" interval (with no cotton planting) was introduced in the dry October to December period, and *Spodoptera* could not sustain its continuous population growth. For one year the noctuid *Heliothis punctigera* became dominant, then in 1970 *Heliothis armigera* took over. The latter also feeds on maize and sorghum, which had been planted during the sanitation period. Thus it appears that measures used to control *S. litura* favoured *H. armigera.* All of these species are polyphagous and have native herbs as alternate hosts, and thus there is no likelihood of any crop rotation scheme succeeding in controlling all of them at once. During the insecticide application period, not more than five days can elapse between successive aerial sprayings. Although such spraying is effective, it is expensive (accounting for about 40 per cent of the cost of cotton) and leads to the development of resistance among the insects. Wilson, Basinski, and Thompson (op. cit.) conclude that biological control "merits serious consideration" as an alternative to routine spraying.

The worst cotton pests in the Ord River area appear to

be introduced species (although originally from arid zones elsewhere). However, several native pest species occur as well, and would undoubtedly rise to the fore should the present dominants be controlled biologically. Effective control by predation or disease is a complex and difficult matter in this type of environment.

Perhaps the worst insect-associated problem man faces in irrigated arid areas is the increase in abundance of mosquitoes and the consequent risk of establishing mosquito-borne arbovirus epidemics (yellow fever, dengue, various encephalitides), some of which are endemic in water fowl. A survey of Australian arbovirus vectors is provided by Doherty (1972).

A somewhat similar pest problem to that in irrigated areas arises when the opposite practice is adopted, i.e., when swamp lands are reclaimed by drainage (Rivnay 1964). The hepialid *Oncopera fasciculata,* in particular, flourishes under these conditions in Australia (Madge 1958) and ceratopogonid midges may greatly increase following filling of mangrove areas. Reasons for the worldwide problem in reclaiming swamplands are not clear, but it may be another example of man's interference favouring certain normally-rare species.

Establishment of a cultivated system on a new soil may greatly favour a native species tied to that soil type. An example is the cricket, *Teleogryllus commodus,* in the southeast of South Australia. This cricket occurs abundantly only on heavy black clay. This soil type was subjected to cultivation of harvested crops before about 1930 but not to pasture. Subsequent introduction of a new, sown pasture clover enabled areas to be converted to pastures. Ploughing which previously destroyed the cricket egg masses, ceased and the cricket then became a serious pest of pastures (Browning 1954).

When an arboreal crop is established in an area formerly occupied by native forest, or adjacent to it, problems are somewhat different. Fugitive open-land species (those adapted to early successional stages) will not be favoured since succession usually goes back only one step — from a multispecific arboreal assemblage to a monospecific stand. This situation greatly favours certain forest insect species that are sufficiently generalized in their food habits to be able to adapt to the introduced plantations.

In Australia, fleshy fruits were relatively rare in native formations being largely limited to tropical forest. Of 54 known species of fruit flies of the subfamily Dacinae (Tephritidae) all but about 12 appear to be specialist feeders, laying their eggs only in one or a few native fruits. Of the remainder, 5 are sufficiently generalized to have been able regularly to include cultivated fruits in their diet (Birch 1965). Of these, the 2 most generalized feeders (*Dacus tryoni* and *D. neohumeralis*), which fed on 66 and 21 native host species respectively, have become the most serious cultivated fruit pests, respectively adding 51 and 25 cultivated species to their diets.

So far we have been considering polyphagous native species that dominate the pest fauna of human cultivations. Occasionally, however, there are specialists which find in the culture steppe a crop or ornamental which is very similar to their native food plant and to which they can transfer with a minimum of adjustment. One Australian example is the fruit fly *Dacus musae,* which was known only from one native banana species, but which moved to cultivated bananas when these were planted (Birch 1965). Some races of the very oligophagous bird-wing butterfly *Ornithoptera priamus* have been able to adapt to a South American species of *Aristolochia* (J. J. H. Szent-Ivany, personal communication).

Movement from taxonomically or chemically related host plants to a cultivated crop also occurs in some feeders on native Rutaceae (such as the pentatomid *Biprorulus bibax* and the butterflies *Papilio anactus* and *P. aegeus*) that are able to feed on introduced *Citrus* (Stride and Straatman 1962; Birch 1965). These Rutaceae presumably share similar attractants. Under experimental conditions, one of the above species, *Papilio aegeus,* can also be induced to oviposit on umbellifers such as celery, parsley, and camphor laurel (the latter a common food plant of some other papilionids).

Umbelliferae and Rutaceae apparently share a number of similar essential oil attractants, and these chemicals, rather than taxonomic relationship, are evidently the important factors. Butterflies may thus be "fooled" by introduced plants and oviposit on them because they contain the same attractants as their native host plant, with resulting death of the larvae (Straatman 1962). It is not clear what factors cause the larvae to starve in such cases, as it is not necessarily host toxicity (Common and Waterhouse 1972).

Another example is that of several species of *Chlenias* (Geometridae) that have switched from *Acacia* to cultivated *Pinus* plantations in south eastern Australia (Tindale 1928).

Some transfers to taxonomically unrelated host plants have evidently occurred naturally (i.e., before the establishment of man's crops), as in the case of the switch from the presumably ancestral rutaceous host to the native legume *Psoralea* (emu foot, etc.) by the widespread inland *Papilio demoleus sthenelus*. Occasionally in New South Wales this subspecies reverts to *Citrus* (Hely 1958; Straatman 1962) on which the Asian subspecies normally feeds (the latter will also occasionally eat *Psoralea* in India – J. J. H. Szent-Ivany, personal communication). Perhaps when the attractants of *Psoralea* are investigated, they will be found to be similar to those of Rutaceae.

It should now be clear that the challenges and opportunities offered by man's environment have been met by certain insects. Even the "insecticidal environment" can be adapted to by way of genetically controlled resistance. The large proportion of native insects in the culture steppe shows that every natural ecosystem probably contains species preadapted to succeed in man-made habitats after genetic adjustment.

But what about the remaining species, the K-strategists intimately tied to ecological formations usurped by the culture steppe?

3.6   EXTINCTION OF NATIVE SPECIES IN THE CULTURE STEPPE

An insect or any other species is in danger of extinction if, firstly, it occupies habitats which have been replaced by culture steppe and secondly, it is unable to survive in the culture steppe because of overspecialization in resource requirements. It is in particular danger if its habitat is of the sort not valued by man and therefore not preserved in parks and reserves. A restricted range is a frequent consequence of *K* strategy, and hence such species are particularly exposed to the risk of extinction.

The organisms most endangered, therefore, are those specialized for living in limited areas of native grasslands, heaths, and marshes. Many insects come under this category, including some mosquitoes (Marks 1972) but the ones best studied in Australia are the morabine grasshoppers. White (1957) describes these insects as being species

> which were certainly associated in an intimate manner with the climax vegetation as it existed before the coming of the white man 100—150 years ago, and which have hence disappeared from all but a minute fraction of their former range as the land was cleared and modified by agriculture.

These insects' reliance on particular plant associations for food and shelter is discussed in section 2.3.3. In some areas, species such as *Keyacris scurra* and *K. marcida* survive only in cemetaries which have been fenced off from grazing mammals and which contain the only remnants of the native *Themeda* grassland. Colonies of morabines sometimes contain as few as several dozen individuals (White 1957).

Orthopterists and lepidopterists everywhere have long been aware of the value of fenced areas — roadsides, railway embankments, etc. — as the last stand of native forbs and grasses and the insects associated with them.* Such areas of

---

* However, it may be that in Australia the nutrients from rubbish discarded along roadsides are in themselves sufficient to destroy native plants, which are adapted to nutrient-poor soils. *See* p. 4 in Specht *et al.*, 1974, *Aust. J. Bot. Suppl. Ser.* No. 7.

herbaceous vegetation are almost never set aside for their own sake in national parks, but are sometimes preserved unwittingly along lines of communication, in military security zones, and in small patches that happen to be associated with forest preserves. Such herbaceous areas, including marshes, should not be overlooked in establishing reserves; they must be totally protected from non-native mammals and from trampling by man and his vehicles.

CHAPTER 4
Forests

4.1 GENERAL CHARACTERISTICS OF THE BIOME

Forest of one sort or another is the natural biome type over most of the quarter of Australia which is not arid. Even in the arid zone, and especially in the south, there is a general tendency for climax vegetation to be dominated by woody shrubs or trees (mallee and mulga, for instance).

Today, however, the non-arid forests have been extensively replaced by culture steppe and it is difficult to say what proportion of the land area is still forested. Clearing is proceeding at a rapid pace, particularly in South Western Australia. Even rain forest, initially of minimal extent in Australia, is being cleared for agricultural and pastoral uses and for urbanization.

The arboreal flora of Australia is dominated by the endemic genus *Eucalyptus,* with some 500 species (absent from rain forest, however). The world-wide genus *Acacia* has its best representation in Australia, where over half its species occur (about 340). Some of the insects associated with *Acacia* as well as the mallee species of *Eucalyptus,* were mentioned in Chapter 2. The present chapter will deal mostly with the more mesic formations of *Eucalyptus*; *Acacia* will be mentioned again only in connection with the ant-tree association (section 4.5), whilst smaller tree genera will receive only casual mention. Tropical forests will be discussed separately (section 4.6.2), as they are formations in which community structure is largely the result of insect activity.

4.2   COMMUNITY STRUCTURE AND ENERGETICS OF FORESTS

Forests are usually climax or subclimax communities, but a climax community is not always a forest. If nutrients, water, or (at high latitudes and altitudes) usable radiant energy are in short supply, then the climax or mature community may be grass, heath, or shrubland (these are sometimes termed edaphic climaxes). Some forest types are maintained by periodic fires. For example, undisturbed wet *Eucalyptus* forests have few of their own seedlings but many characteristics of rainforest beneath the dominant trees (Florence 1969). If this process continues, wet sclerophyll forest will obviously be replaced by rain forest. The reason this does not usually happen is attributed to the effect of recurrent fires.

Forests are usually stated to be the most productive biomes. Rodin and Basilevich (1966) compared net primary productivity per year, and cited higher figures for forests (except taiga) than for grasslands, although salt marshes and sugar cane fields can be even higher. Tropical forests and grasslands are more productive than temperate ones.

As far as animal consumers are concerned, net productivity is not very meaningful, as it does not distinguish between harvestable and non-harvestable production. Of more significance is the fact that less than 10 per cent of the net production of mature forest is grazed (consumed in the living state) (Odum 1969). The rest of forest production eventually ends up in the detritus food chains, which thus tend to be proportionately more important than in grasslands (see Chapter 2).

Therefore, from the grazing consumer's point of view, younger ecosystems may be much more "productive", as the production consists of a larger proportion of harvestable tissue. In mature systems, much energy goes into the production and maintenance of difficult-to-digest woody tissue (Odum 1969) and toxic compounds (Janzen 1974).

Many other consequences of ecosystem maturity are listed by Odum, but the ones that concern us most here are stability and species diversity. Physical stability in forests is primarily a consequence of adequate water intake and the ability of trees to store water and nutrients, and to draw them from deeper in the soil. Shading and the physical barrier to winds provided by trees, dampen temperature and humidity fluctuations. Whereas limiting factors governing the functioning of ecosystems and the storage of water and nutrients tended to be physical in the environments treated in Chapter 2, and controlled by man in those discussed in Chapter 3, in forests they tend to be biotic. The trend toward increasing biotic control in ecosystems reaches its culmination in the tropical rain forest.

Animal diversity in forests is great because: (1) a tree can be exploited in more different ways, both as food and shelter, than can grass or shrubs; (2) the stratification of forests, with a soil layer, litter, herbs, shrubs, and various tree strata, plus epiphytes, provides greater complexity in the structure of the environment; and (3) in a stable environment, organisms have a tendency to become more specialized (that is, their niches become narrower) because of species-to-species interactions and coevolution, and because of all the factors previously mentioned as operating under K selection (sections 1.2, 1.5). There are, however, some forest types even in the tropics with very low species diversity because of edaphic factors (Janzen 1974).

It will be noted that the primary reason for increased animal diversity in forests is the greater complexity of the vegetation, both in structure and in species composition. In other words, the area of the plant-herbivore interface (section 1.4) is increased, even though the amount of available energy may not be.

Within the detritus food webs, the litter-based chains have more energy available in forests than do those based on excrement. Green feed available to mammals is much less and dung production is consequently reduced. On the other hand, excrement of the small-pellet type is constantly raining down on the forest floor and is more exploitable (because of higher humidity) than in drier biomes. As a reflection of the increased diversity of the forest biota, the number of species of coprophages (as opposed to their biomass) is often very much greater than in grasslands.

4.3   GENERAL ADAPTATIONS OF INSECTS OF FOREST—GRAZING CHAINS

In this section I will confine myself to the tree strata. I believe that the best way to outline the adaptations of insects to this habitat type is to take a hypothetical tree and describe the various ways in which it can be exploited by insects, both as food and as shelter. I will begin with the most coevolved forms of association. Examples from Australian insects will be mentioned here if they do not receive closer attention in sections 4.5 and 4.6, where associations especially well represented in Australia are described.

4.3.1   GALL FORMERS

The familiar, "abnormal" plant growths caused by insects and other organisms can affect any part of a plant, from root to flower. Galls are known to be caused by members of seven orders of insects, by far the most important one of which is Diptera, especially the gall-midge family Cecidomyidae, with some 5,000 species in the world.

The gall is the result of a proliferation of plant cells initiated by "cecidotoxins" produced in the saliva of the original gall former. The exact nature of these substances does not seem to be known, investigations until recently having concentrated on relatively simple compounds such as amino acids and auxin-like substances (Mani 1964). However, the galls formed by insects are often of complicated, species-specific form and it appears likely that complex molecules, capable of structural variation, would be needed to convey enough information to the plant to produce the variety of shapes that are known. What appears to happen is that the insect takes control of a portion of the plant's morphogenetic mechanism. There is, in fact, a strong possibility that nucleic acids are involved in some plant-gall-insect relationships (Went 1970), but the potential in biochemical research which this possibility offers has not yet been realized.

Complicated symbiotic relationships often exist between the principal gall former and a number of secondary gall organisms, which in some cases could number over 20 (Mani 1964). The secondary organisms are not necessarily insects. Certain coccid galls on *Leptospermum* (Myrtaceae) frequently bear a conspicuous black fungus, *Septobasidium* spp. (Heterobasidiae) which evidently has a mutualistic relationship with the insect (Cleland 1934–5, p. 329), and in section 4.6.1 a mutualism between a nematode and a gall-forming fly is described.

In any event, it appears that as a rule plants are not killed as a result of the activities of gall-makers. Only parts of the plant's organs are affected, and some of these (such as leaves) may continue normal function, although the overall fitness of the affected plant may be reduced. There are a few known cases in which a plant derives a benefit from the activities of gall-making or gall-inhabiting insects (see below).

There is a rather high degree of host specificity among gall-forming species, as would be expected in a coevolved association. However, this is difficult to estimate since the complete host range of many species is unknown.

There are two clear instances of plants deriving a benefit from gall-associated insects. One involves the swollen-thorn acacias of the New World, discussed in section 4.5, and the other involves the fig wasps, mentioned below. I believe more instances of this sort of mutualism will come to light as more work is done in the tropics and on gall chemistry.

Figs (except some horticultural varieties) are entirely dependent on agaonid wasps for pollination. The female wasps are shaped in such a way that they can penetrate the entrance to the flower (ostiolum), which is guarded by spines that keep out all other insects. The wasps lay eggs in some of the short-styled female-phase flowers, which then become "gall-flowers". As the wasp larvae develop, the flower enters the male phase and produces anthers and pollen. The emerging female wasps gather this pollen into corbiculae or may simply be dusted with it as they escape to other flowers (still in the female phase) which they pollinate. The biology of these wasps is reviewed by Ramirez (1970), who rectifies some previous misconceptions on gall-flower formation, species specificity, and the role of other wasps. He shows that host specificity is virtually absolute in the agaonid-fig association, and is obligate for both partners. A given fig can produce seed only when its agaonid is present. In Australia there are many fig species, but only a few of their associated wasps have been described. These include *Pleistodontes imperialis* on the Moreton Bay fig (*Ficus macrophylla*), *P. froggatti* on *F. rubiginosa,* and *Kradibiella* sp. on *F. coronata* (Cribb 1969). Torymids and several other wasp groups move in after maturation of the fig flower has been induced by the agaonids and feed on plant tissues. They are not parasites and play no part in pollination (Ramirez 1970).

The Australian gall fauna is briefly discussed in more specific terms in section 4.6.1.

4.3.2 LEAF MINERS

Another form of insect exploitation is leaf mining, in which the insect larva tunnels between the upper and lower epidermal layers of the leaf. The prevalence of monophagy and oligophagy among leaf miners attests to the essentially coevolved nature of the relationship with the host plant (Hering 1951). The leaf-mining habit has been evolved independently in a number of insect groups, always among larvae (except perhaps in some Thysanoptera), and the habit is most extensively developed in the Lepidoptera. In some of these, such as the cotton feeder *Bucculatrix gossypii* (Lyonetiidae), and some yponomeutids, oecophorids, etc., the larva is a leaf miner only in the early instars, becoming a skeletonizer after growing to a certain size (Common 1970).

The biology of the jarrah leaf miner, *Perthida glyphopa* (Incurvariidae) was studied by Wallace (1970b). The mature larva cuts an oval-shaped hole in both the upper and the lower epidermis of the leaf and drops to the ground, using the leaf pieces to make a case in which it eventually pupates. Only isolated trees are attacked severely, but even those do not die.

4.3.3 SAP SUCKERS

Members of the order Hemiptera feed by positioning themselves on leaves, stems, or roots, and sucking the sap of the plant. They tend to concentrate on those tissues in which a maximum amount of transfer of nutrients is taking place, particularly new growth but occasionally old leaves from which materials are being withdrawn prior to leaf fall (Way and Cammell 1970). Sucking insects can only ingest materials in solution, such as carbohydrates and amino acids, and this solution occurs mainly during the transport phase of the plant's activities. Aggregations of insects on one part of the plant can draw nutrients from elsewhere. In the case of some aphids, the animals tend to concentrate on one leaf, or part of a leaf, thereby minimizing mechanical damage to the plant. In addition to ingesting normal phloem translocates, some psyllids, particularly *Cardiaspina* spp., appear to be able to induce senescence and consequent conversion of palisade mesophyll to transportable products in the leaves which they are attacking, apparently by secreting a still unidentified substance (Woodburn and Lewis 1973). This process of induced senescence in some cases may be the cause of the severe leaf fall following high-density attacks by the psyllids *Cardiaspina* spp. (Clark 1962), *Spondyliaspis* spp. (McKeown 1945), and *Glycaspis* spp. (Moore 1961).

White (1971 and previous papers) has observed that heavy psyllid infestations coincide with periods of stress in *Eucalyptus* caused by winter waterlogging of roots followed by a dry summer. Under such circumstances there is an unusual amount of nitrogen (as amino acids) being transported in the sap, thereby permitting a build-up of the psyllid populations.

Adult cicadas may occasionally become numerous enough to cause tree mortality (Froggatt 1913), but the reasons for such increases are not known. Nymphal cicadas, which feed on tree roots, can become abundant enough to seriously affect wood production (Edwards, Reichle, and Crossley 1970).

When severe debilitation of a tree occurs as a result of

sucking-insect attack, damage may result as much through water loss because of excess honeydew production, as through direct nutrient loss.

Moore (1961) noted that defoliation of various *Eucalyptus* by *Glycaspis,* tends to be carried out by complexes of closely-related species, each one being rather host specific.

On the whole, it is to be expected that defoliation is counterproductive from the point of view of sucking insects, which are relatively immobile and which depend on leaves for both food and shelter. The lack of vagility of *Cardiaspina albitextura,* for instance, has been described by Clark (1962). Nymphs scarcely disperse from their hatching sites. Adults cannot cross gaps of more than 120 m, and tend to return to the same tree to oviposit. Clark et al. (1967) describe how the adults of this species are unable to find most of the remaining leaves of redgum trees after partial defoliation, and consequently fail to oviposit. Defoliation also takes a heavy toll of nymphs.

Sap sucking insects are important as vectors of plant viruses.

4.3.4 LEAF CHEWERS

The majority of insects attack leaves by chewing them. The readiness with which a plant can be exploited in this way depends on the amount of energy that has been invested in the protection of the leaf tissue. Where there is a general scarcity of nutrients, as in some tropical forests, the destruction of a leaf represents a proportionately greater loss of energy for a plant than it would elsewhere, and leaves will correspondingly be more protected by sclerophyllous tissue and toxic compounds (Janzen 1974). Such protected leaves will stay on a tree for years, in some cases. Forest types that exemplify this strategy are swamp forests (e.g., *Melaleuca* and mangroves), tropical rain forest (section 4.6.2) where each species is subject to attack by specialist herbivores only, and to a certain extent desert trees and coniferous forests. Sclerophyll forest trees (*Eucalyptus,* section 4.6.1) appear to adopt an intermediate defensive strategy, whereby leaves are quite strongly defended by essential oils, tannins, and tough tissue, but are still shed with some frequency (after removal of soluble substances).

Under normal circumstances leaf chewers, like all herbivores, are kept at moderate densities primarily by the plant's defences, but to a certain extent also by intrinsic population density controls (Monro 1967), competition, predation, and weather changes. However, should the plants be subjected to unusual stresses, which are becoming increasingly frequent through man's interference (Carne, Greaves, and McInnes 1974), energy must be diverted from defence against herbivores to other needs. Certain species of insects are adapted to take advantage of this lowering of the plant's defences and are able to multiply to plague proportions. In addition to some of the psyllids already mentioned, examples in *Eucalyptus* forests are stick insects (*Podacanthus wilkinsoni* and *Didymuria violescens*), certain scarabaeid chafers (mostly *Anoplognathus* spp.), and *Perga* sawflies. Certain subclimax rain forest trees are also subject to insect plagues (section 4.6.2), but such outbreaks are rare in more arid forest types and in swamp forests, because such communities are more influenced by physical factors (scarcity of water or nutrients), than by biotic controls.

Species of insects which are adapted to take advantage of the plant's lowered defences are at the same time protected against predation at high densities through selective predator satiation (section 1.3.1), and it is this adaptation which may enable them to best their competitors. The prey population density at which satiation occurs varies inversely with the effectiveness of defence and is lowest in the most strongly defended species such as the *Perga* sawflies (Fig. 2). Such species do not need to have recourse to the defensive strategy of procrypsis at low densities. That is to say, even small aggregations of these larvae are defended by their toxic secretions, the effect of which is enhanced by their habit of clustering on branches in the daytime (Carne 1962, 1969). Identical behaviour is seen in the larvae of some *Paropsis* beetles (Chrysomelidae) (Fig. 4) (Carne 1966a), which discharge a defensive substance containing hydrocyanic acid (Moore 1967). Alternately, some aggregations of defoliators cluster in bags or tents containing a quantity of excrement or stinging hairs, as in the notodontid *Ochrogaster contraria* and the eupterotid *Panacela lewinae*. Silken shelters are also made by some Pyralidae, Oecophoridae, and other lepidopterous families. It has been demonstrated in North America that a secondary function of such shelters is the maintenance of higher-than-ambient temperatures through the greenhouse effect.

If individual defence is minimal, selective predator satiation can occur only at the highest prey densities, probably as a result of the cumulative effect of many small doses of toxins to the predator. Such insects must rely on procrypsis when at densities too low to achieve predator satiation, and must therefore carry out a frequency-dependent "switch" in defence strategy which is accompanied by a corresponding change from procryptic to signal colours when passing from the low- to the high-density kentromorphic phases (Figs. 13 and 14). As explained in section 1.3.2, the signal colours facilitate the formation of avoidance-images in visual predators. In forests, such a strategy is known only in the phasmids mentioned above.

Carne (1966b) proposed that additional advantages result from the gregariousness of certain defoliators through a division of labour, whereby particularly active individuals lead the way in breaking out of egg pods, finding feeding sites, and digging into the soil prior to pupation. Larger aggregates have a greater probability of containing such "leader" individuals and therefore of surviving. However, I do not believe that this division of labour represents one of the advantages of gregariousness, but rather that it is a behavioural device ensuring that aggregations, once formed, function successfully. After all, solitary species are perfectly capable of performing these activities as well. The important point is that in gregarious species the proportion of active (i.e., normal) individuals must be kept down to preserve the

cohesiveness of the group, which depends on passive individuals. Undoubtedly, the proportion of active to passive
individuals`is continuously adjusted by natural selection in
conformance to values maintaining functioning aggregations
of optimum size. Ultimately, the basic *raison d'être* of the
aggregations themselves continues to be, first and foremost,
defence against avian predators.

The loss of primary production caused by defoliators
can be very severe and may greatly exceed the net secondary
production of the animals involved. A single outbreak can
cause timber loss equivalent to five to ten years of growth
(Smith 1972).

4.3.5 NECTAR AND POLLEN FEEDERS

The complex mutual relationships between pollinating insects
and plants are discussed in section 1.4.3, pollination of
Eucalyptus is mentioned in section 4.6.1, and that in tropical
forests in section 4.6.2.

It hardly needs to be said that a great many insects
depend on nectar and pollen in the adult state, even though
they may have such diverse larval habits as wood borers
(Buprestidae), predators (Ichneumonidae), and carrion feeders
(Calliphoridae). Pollen may in some cases provide the protein
necessary for egg maturation.

Bees and some thrips are the only insects depending
entirely on nectar and pollen in both the adult and immature
stages; they are also the most specialized pollen feeders.
Thrips have mouthparts with short, fine, piercing stylets
which are adapted for penetrating small spherical capsules
such as pollen grains and fungus spores.

4.3.6 SEED AND FRUIT EATERS. PLANT TOXINS

Australia seems to contain few specialized seed eaters among
beetles, the family Bruchidae being represented by only fourteen known species. It is probable that some curculionids fill
this niche, and among the cerambycids one genus, at least,
specializes on seeds. This is *Aphanosperma,* which feeds on

the seed capsules of *Hakea* (Britton 1969). The most important seed eaters in Australia are probably lygaeid bugs and harvester ants: in the latter this adaptation appears to be associated with a dry climate (Brian 1965). In *Eucalyptus* forest, insect (mainly ant) attack is believed to account for about 80 per cent of seed mortality (Florence 1969), but the most coevolved seed eaters do not cause extensive destruction. A torymid, *Metastigmus* sp., together with a symbiotic fungus, *Ramularia* sp., infests only one seed per capsule during the flowering period of some *Eucalyptus*; the development of the fruit is not affected (Drake 1974).

Janzen (1971a), in a review of seed "predation" by animals, observed that plants can adopt two types of defence against seed eaters. They can invest energy in building protection for a few seeds in the form of a heavy or sticky coating or toxic substance (sometimes combined), or they can invest energy in producing many small edible seeds and (often) confine flowering and seeding to short, well-spaced intervals, thus exceeding the seed eaters' searching and ingesting capacity during such brief periods. In both cases, seed production must exceed the insects' ingesting capacity. In the former case the seed-eaters able to detoxify the defensive substances are few and hence seed production can be relatively low and be more closely spaced.

Edible fruits are produced by those plants (usually tropical) which rely on vertebrates for seed dispersal. Fruits attractive to birds and primates are colourful and generally succulent (to us), whilst those evolved to attract bats are green and (again to us) distasteful. Fruit flies use the colour of fruit to locate them from a distance. Obviously, such fruits cannot be poisonous; nevertheless, a given fruit-eating insect cannot automatically eat all types of fruit. On the contrary, there is a great deal of specialized monophagy among fruit flies (section 3.5) and other fruit-eating insects. This may be because fruits are not in themselves complete foods (perhaps a selectively advantageous defence by omission of essential nutrients rather than defence by toxins), and insects that depend on them exclusively must be associated with symbiotic bacilli that provide missing nutrients (Bateman 1972). In the case of *Drosophila* spp. that inhabit fallen fruit the association is with complexes of yeast species. Specialization, therefore, may be the result of species-specific symbioses, of insects with bacilli or fungi. Such symbioses in turn depend on the nutrient spectra of different fruit species.

Fruit-piercing adult Lepidoptera, that obtain sugars as a dietary supplement, have been recorded in various parts of the world.

The use of poison by plants as a protection against herbivores is most highly developed in the species-rich tropical forests of the north (Webb 1949, 1952), particularly those growing on poor soils (Janzen 1974), or of ancient plant groups such as mushrooms, cycads (*Macrozamia* and others), conifers (especially *Podocarpus*), and ferns, and would result from long coevolution between herbivores and plants. The last two plant groups named above synthesize substances identical to arthropod moulting hormones (ecdysones) against which insects find it difficult to develop a resistance (Williams 1970). Some Northern Hemisphere conifers are also known to synthesize analogues of juvenile hormone.

When chemical toxins are elaborated by plants, they are effective against generalist herbivores, but there are usually one or two species of insects which have made the biochemical investment necessary to overcome specific toxins. A few examples of insects which have become specialized to feed on toxic plants in Australia, besides those already mentioned in section 1.4.1, are *Galerucella laporteae* (Chrysomelidae), which feeds on the stinging tree *Laportea gigas* (Brereton 1957), and a group of weevils (*Tranes,* Amalyctinae) which specialize mostly on cycads (E. C. Zimmerman, personal communication). Some insects reported by Szent-Ivany, Womersley, and Ardley (1956) to attack *Cycas* in New Guinea are the lycaenid *Luthrodes cleotas,* a pyralid, a chrysomelid, and some unidentified weevils, whilst another lycaenid, *Theclinesthes miskini,* is reported by Common and Waterhouse (1972) to feed on cycads in Queensland. Some lycaenids feed on *Strychnos* spp., the partly cyanogenic *Acacia* spp., and on toxic mistletoes. *Onthophagus dunningi* (Scarabaeidae) feeds on the poisonous mushroom *Amanita verna*, but is not a specialist on this species (Bornemissza 1971a).

Trees of more arid areas seem to rely more on heavy protective seed pods or capsules, such as those of *Eucalyptus* and *Acacia*. The former genus also protects its developing flower with a hard cap. The seed coats themselves are mechanically resistant and are protected from decay by a high concentration of tannins.

The other type of defence, predator satiation by well-spaced flowering periods, is adopted by some Australian trees, although this seems to be in conjunction with heavy seed coats or pods, rather than as an alternative to them. In the southwest of Western Australia, the karri (*Eucalyptus diversicolor*) flowers heavily only once in every four to twelve years (Smith 1969), and irregular flowering is common among the rarer species of mallee (A. C. Kessell, in litt.). In Queensland the Bunya pine (*Araucaria*) sets seed only at long intervals. To be most effective against generalized seed eaters, such a tactic requires synchronized flowering and seed set of all species in an area. It is not known whether *Eucalyptus* spp. synchronize their flowering periods in Western Australia, but some *Acacia* are known to synchronize with mallee (Kessell, in litt.).

The fact that irregular flowering coincides with years of unusual rainfall does not mean that it is an adaptation to weather conditions. The weather merely provides a triggering cue which can be used by the trees to time their flowering, much as unusual droughts are used by some tropical forest trees in spacing their reproduction as a defence against seed eaters (section 4.6.2).

4.3.7 WOOD BORERS

Although wood is more difficult to digest than the cell contents of green tissue, it can still be a source of insect food in all its states from perfect health to crumbling semi-humus. Termites are the principal wood feeders in Australia, but in other orders numerous families have also become adapted for boring in intact wood in the larval state, among them the Cerambycidae, Buprestidae, Scolytidae, Platypodidae, some Curculionidae, Lyctidae, Anobiidae, and a few others among the Coleoptera, and the Cossidae, Hepialidae, some Xyloryctidae and others in the Lepidoptera, and the Siricidae in the Hymenoptera.

A few wood boring groups secrete cellulase and thus are able to directly digest wood (Cerambycidae, some Anobiidae). However, the great majority either feed only on cell contents or rely on symbiotic micro-organisms to digest cellulose (and possibly lignin) and supply additional nutrients. Many, such as most Buprestidae and Scolytidae, position themselves in the phloem and feed on transported nutrients.

In addition to the primary wood borers, there are numerous predators and parasites associated with them, as well as detritus and fungus feeders inside their galleries. These associated insects are frequently found under loose bark, which may also serve as shelter for foliage feeders and their predators (section 4.6.1).

An example of a wood-insect association was placed on display at the XIV International Congress of Entomology in Canberra. Over a period of a fortnight a collection of 273 individual insects of 23 species was bred out from 700 cc of wood obtained from the top 1.5 m of an *Acacia mearnsii* in a Canberra garden. The families represented were the following (with their probable food habits in parentheses): Cleridae (predators on wood borers) — 1; Bostrychidae (wood borers) — 1; Corylophidae (fungus feeders) — 1; Chrysomelidae (stem borers) — 2; Cerambycidae (wood borers) — 4; Curculionidae (wood or stem borers) — 1; Scolytidae (bark borers) — 1; Belidae (wood or bark borers) — 2; Megalyridae, Aulacidae, and Braconidae (all hymenopterous parasites) — 1, 2, and 6 respectively; Tachinidae (a dipteran parasite) — 1.

There is usually a definite succession of insect attacks following upon an initial debilitation of a tree by a foliage feeder. Thus Moore (1959) reports that *Eucalyptus saligna* debilitated by a psyllid, *Spondyliaspis* sp., may then be attacked by the scolytid *Xyleborus truncatus,* which brings in a brown stain fungus which in turn eventually kills the tree. The *Xyleborus* attack is followed by a succession of late-stage borers of the families Anobiidae, Bostrychidae, Brenthidae, and Scolytidae. Empty galleries of some of these borers are then used for nesting by a hylaeine bee, *Hylaeus aralis.*

Sometimes, fire damage or other injury provides the initial entry into a previously healthy tree, as in the case of the buprestids *Diadoxus erythrurus* and *D. scalaris* which attack fire-damaged *Callitris* (Hadlington and Gardner 1959). Some buprestids are known to possess infrared sense organs which are used to enable the insect to locate fire-damaged trees while they are still smouldering (Evans 1966). The common Australian arid-zone buprestid, *Merimna atrata,* comes regularly to fires and could well possess such heat sensors.

The attacks of wood borers favour the entry of fungi into the wood, and in some cases the insects then feed on these fungi (Francke-Grosman 1963). The ultimate development in this association is reached when the fungus is inoculated into the tree by the insect, females of which possess special organs used to house and transport fungal spores. Some fungi have come to rely on this method of dispersal, and the insects in turn rely on the fungus for food. A true mutualism with a high degree of specificity is thus evolved.

This type of mutualism was first described for "ambrosia beetles" (some Scolytidae) that carry the spores in ectodermal mycangia independently evolved in various species on the thorax, elytra, or buccal region of the female. The association has since been found in numerous other families of beetles — Sphindidae, Cucujidae, Boganiidae, Anobiidae, Bostrychidae, Platypodidae, Brenthidae, Curculionidae, and Lymexylidae (Crowson and Sen Gupta 1966; Britton 1970) — and in other orders (Graham 1967).

In the hymenopteran *Sirex noctilio,* introduced into Australia, the larvae are entirely dependent on the fungus *Amylostereum chailletii* for food. Female larvae repeatedly collect the fungus in abdominal hypopleural organs after each ecdysis. The adult female collects the fungus from the last larval exuvium, and stores it in wax platelets in a sac at the base of the ovipositor. The fungus is then cultivated in the sac, with the help of a nutrient, and eventually produces spores which are inoculated into trees together with the wasp's eggs (Morgan 1968).

Wood-feeding termites are at least partly dependent on fungi for food (Lee and Wood 1971). Living trees are sometimes attacked, but perhaps only if previously damaged. *Coptotermes acinaciformis* and *C. brunneus* were observed to attack damaged trees and eventually kill them, leaving only a nest mound in their place (Greaves 1962). *Coptotermes* spp. may be responsible for up to 92 per cent of total timber loss in some mature *Eucalyptus* forests (Lee and Wood 1971, quoting T. Greaves and other authors). In Northern Australia, *Mastotermes darwiniensis,* well known as the world's most primitive termite, attacks many introduced trees. Digestion of wood in termites is entirely mediated by symbiotic microorganisms. In lower termites, including *Mastotermes,* the symbiotes are flagellates, either alone or together with bacteria. In higher termites they are bacteria alone (Lee and Wood 1971).

4.3.8 ROOT FEEDERS

Coming to the end of our survey of a hypothetical tree and the ways in which it can be exploited by insects, we arrive at the roots. Most root feeders on trees are in fact wood borers that work their way down from higher parts and some, such as the prionine cerambycids, specialize on the underground parts of the wood. There are also three ways of feeding on roots externally. The external root-feeding cossids and hepialids (Lepidoptera) have been mentioned previously (sections 2.4, 2.5) and they represent the chewing technique of root feeding. The root tissue is not consumed, but only abraded by the insect's mandibles and the flowing sap imbibed. The second technique is to suck the sap from the roots, a behaviour known in many Homoptera, such as nymphal cicadas, coccoids, aphids, and some fulgoroids. An association between root mealybugs (Pseudococcidae) and a polyporid fungus, in which ants are also involved, has been described in New Guinea by Szent-Ivany and Stevens (1966). The third way is simply to chew the roots, but this occurs mostly in soil-dwelling larvae feeding on herbaceous plants.

4.3.9 PREDATORS AND PARASITOIDS

At the next trophic level in forest grazing chains are the various predators. There can be little doubt that birds are the principal carnivores in forest biomes, many of which have become specialized for feeding on forest insects. The large passerine group is primarily adapted for foliage gleaning. Hymenopterous parasitoids, ants, carabid, cantharid, and coccinellid beetles, dolichopodid flies, mantids, mantispids, reduviid bugs, spiders, centipedes, and lizards are other groups that come to mind.

Feeding on wood-boring larvae requires specialized hunting behaviour and is not open to most of the generalized (or otherwise specialized) predators mentioned above. The feeding specializations required have led to the evolution of several higher groups of insects. Among the beetles the Trogositidae, Cleridae, Cucujidae, Passandridae, Rhizophagidae, and Colydiidae are families wholly or largely specialized for feeding on wood-boring insects, especially other beetles.

The most interesting predators (actually parasitoids) on wood-boring larvae are those ichneumonid and braconid wasps, and Megalyridae (Rodd 1951), which possess very long ovipositors, which they use to penetrate wood and oviposit in a larva or pupa. These wasps are able to "drill" through sound wood in a perfectly straight line to the total length of the ovipositor, which may reach 10 cm in large species. An alternate movement of the apposed valves which make up the ovipositor shaft produces a sawing action causing penetration of the wood. Full penetration may take an hour or more.

Observers have been struck by the accuracy of ovipositing wasps. The egg is nearly always inserted in a larva even if the latter is several centimetres beneath sound wood. For the North American *Megarhyssa* sp., Heatwole, Davis, and Wenner (1964) report that the wasp can locate the exact direction of the host's position through up to 86 mm of wood, and that even the depth of the host (a siricid larva or pupa) is gauged in some way before the drilling operation begins, since wasps do not attempt to oviposit in hosts located at a greater depth than the length of the ovipositor. Heatwole and his co-workers were able to eliminate sonic, visual, and tactile stimuli as possible factors used by the wasp in locating hosts, and olfaction was considered very unlikely in view of the accuracy involved. This left only ultrasound (also very unlikely) or "some unknown sensory mechanism".

In fact olfaction does play a part in host location by ichneumon wasps, as shown by recent experiments in Tasmania on *Rhyssa* sp. by J. L. Madden, L. L. Taylor, and co-workers (CSIRO Annual Reports and wall display in Canberra). Yeasts growing in a fungal metabolite in the frass produced by boring *Sirex* larvae produce an odour which guides the wasps in directing their ovipositor in approximately the right direction. From the odour the wasps are able to determine the age (hence size) of the larva involved (only mature ones are attacked). This olfaction is undoubtedly important in enabling a wasp to locate an infested tree and the general zone of infestation by mature larvae, but it still cannot explain pin-point accuracy through centimetres of wood.

A clue as to the probable nature of the mechanism used by some species has been recently discovered in a braconid wasp by Richerson and Borden (1972). They showed that the wasp locates its host (a scolytid larva) through the latter's metabolic heat. The bark surface above a larva was 0.5 to $1.0^{\circ}C$ hotter than the surrounding area, and experiments with artificially produced "hot spots" proved that heat is the stimulus involved. The wasp possesses sensilla placodea on the antennae which are suspected of being highly sensitive infrared detectors; "plate organs" were noted on the antennae of *Megarhyssa* by Heatwole and co-workers.

In the case of the braconid, the host larva is at a relatively shallow depth beneath bark only. At the much greater depth of siricid larvae it is difficult to conceive that heat conduction through wood could be concentrated enough to produce the "hot spot" effect needed for the accuracy observed; nevertheless this may be the explanation, as observations seem to have eliminated all other possibilities. Given the size of the larva (gauged from the frass odour), its location and depth might then be estimated by the intensity of the hot spot. Obviously, the ovipositor has to be inserted exactly at a right angle to the wood surface, in the middle of the hot spot.

Some wasp parasitoids of wood-boring larvae adopt an entirely different tactic and penetrate the galleries themselves. A certain "habitus" is associated with this behaviour; it involves a porrect head, elongated and depressed body, and short legs (Krombein 1968). Most bethylids, *Cerceris,* and some tiphiids have this body form. A similar build is displayed by the Australian spider wasps of the genus *Epipompilus,* which crawl under bark and parasitize spiders in the latter's own nests (Evans 1972).

The loose bark of some *Eucalyptus* provides an important microhabitat for arboreal predators. These are discussed in section 4.6.1.

4.4   GENERAL ADAPTATIONS OF INSECTS OF FOREST DE-COMPOSER CHAINS

The forest decomposer food chains channel much more energy than do the grazing ones. However, micro-organisms, rather than insects or other large decomposers predominate and make up about 90 per cent of the decomposer biomass (MacFadyen 1964). The role of fungi is crucial — they account for most of the litter breakdown, and equally important, they are responsible for the rapid return of minerals to higher plants by way of mycorrhiza (Went 1970).

In spite of their small contribution to forest-floor metabolism and biomass, the large decomposers handle vast quantities of material. The effect of this handling is proportionately much greater than their own metabolic activity (Phillipson 1966), as the comminution and mixing of the material greatly facilitate the action of micro-organisms. Whilst more energy is channelled through decomposer food webs than others, fewer species are involved (see sections 1.5, 4.2). In addition, the energy sources of decomposer food chains, and the ways they can be exploited, are less varied than they are in grazing food webs. We can recognize four basic categories of energy sources: (1) litter; (2) dead wood; (3) excrement and carrion; and (4) nutrients in plant-held waters.

4.4.1 LITTER

The processes involved in the breakdown of forest litter are partly inorganic (fire and leaching); these may be important under certain conditions — fire in seasonally dry forests and leaching in rain forests. Even the biotic breakdown processes lead to a great deal of volatilization of organic material. More than three quarters of the organic material in leaf litter is thus volatilized as CO_2, H_2O, and NH_3, and less than one quarter ends up as humus (Edwards, Reichle, and Crossley 1970). Humus consists of complex polymers of phenolic materials resulting from lignin breakdown, mostly by fungi, and it can still be a rich source of energy for those organisms adapted to feed on it, such as earthworms and geotrupine beetles. Humus-feeding termites are unknown in Australia (Lee and Wood 1971).

The importance of insect and other large decomposer populations varies considerably in different forest types, and may be least (relatively speaking) in tropical forests, where leaching and microbial activity may be exceptionally intense because of the constantly high humidity (K. E. Lee, personal communication). Among medium and large decomposers in tropical forests, mites and Collembola (and perhaps nematodes) may be proportionately more important in litter breakdown than the larger animals (Madge 1965). In jarrah forests mites and Collembola make up 82 to 86 per cent of the individuals in the humus fauna (McNamara 1955).

However, in any forest type these small metazoans, in spite of their large numbers, are insignificant in terms of metabolism and biomass, as well as in terms of the role they play in food webs (Hall 1967). It is generally recognized, however, that they perform a key role in the mixing and dispersion of bacterial and fungal spores, and therefore in the production of humus.

Food webs in litter are made up of the first-order consumers of plant matter, including fungi, and second-order consumers (predators and coprophages). According to Edwards, Reichle, and Crossley (1970), the herbivores and decomposers make up 81 to 98 per cent of metazoan biomass, and the predators 2 to 19 per cent. The first group is represented by micro-organisms, nematodes, oligochaetes, diplopods, isopods, some Acari, pulmonates, Collembola, Isoptera, Thysanoptera, Aradidae, and larvae of Tipulidae, Mycetophilidae, Bibionidae, Elateridae, Geotrupinae, and (in Australia particularly) several lepidopterous families, especially Tortricidae. The second group is represented by Hirudinea, spiders, phalangids, palpigrades, geophilomorphs, Acari, larvae of Therevidae, Formicidae, Carabidae, Staphylinidae, Cantharidae, and Histeridae (as general predators), Scydmaenidae and Pselaphidae (as predators on mites), Drilidae, Lampyridae, and some Syrphidae (as predators on pulmonates), and finally Scarabaeidae and various flies as coprophages. Of the above groups, only Drilidae are absent from Australia, although Lampyridae are poorly represented.

It appears that elsewhere Carabidae and Geophilomorpha (Raw 1967) or spiders (Moulder and Reichle 1972) are the most important forest litter predators. Observations suggest that ants may be more important in this role in Australia, particularly in dry sclerophyll forests (Wood 1971; Greenslade 1973).

The geotrupine scarabs are very well represented in Australia but tend to be limited to sandy soils and relatively open forests. Contrary to what is sometimes stated in the literature, they are not coprophagous but are litter and humus feeders; some species also feed on underground fungi (Hymenogastraceae). Humus in geotrupine nests has a high nutritive value (H. F. Howden, personal communication).

Special features of *Eucalyptus* forest and tropical forest litter production and turnover are discussed in sections 4.6.1 and 4.6.2.

4.4.2 DEAD WOOD

There is a continuous faunal succession in a dying tree, with a predictable replacement of wood-inhabiting species as death and decay proceed. In the Cerambycidae (Linsley 1959) and probably other groups, there is a progressive reduction in the degree of host specificity among the successor species, to the point where species coming in when the wood is thoroughly dead are relatively indifferent to the taxon of the tree involved, unless the wood contains antibiotic substances.

Dry, dead wood is attacked mostly by termites, anobiids, bostrychids, and lyctids, with some participation by terminal successor species of Cerambycidae and Curculionidae, whilst in moist wood, which is thoroughly pervaded by fungi, we find mostly larvae of various lamellicorn groups (all harbouring intestinal symbionts that digest cellulose) and spore-feeding thrips. Among the former are members of the Passalidae, Lucanidae, Acanthoceridae, Scarabaeidae-Dynastinae, and Cetoniinae.

The effect of termites on dead wood in a dry sclerophyll forest in South Australia was measured by Lee and Wood (1971). Three species of termites consumed about 5 per cent of the litter and ten species consumed about 17 per cent of the dead wood (sticks and logs). *Nasutitermes exitiosus* was responsible for most of the consumption of dead wood.

As in the case of litter, the principal effect of large decomposers in dead wood is to break up the material and make it more accessible to fungi and bacteria, with the result that it is eventually incorporated into the soil and recycled. A secondary effect is the formation of spaces inside fallen logs used as shelter by largely predacious cryptozoan organisms such as ants, spiders, beetles, centipedes, and small reptiles, plus some large decomposers such as diplopods, isopods, and pulmonates.

Some trees, particularly conifers, secrete allelochemic substances into heartwood, thus rendering the wood highly resistant to decay and insect attack, even after the tree dies. The Huon pine (*Dacrydium franklinii*) of Tasmania is one Australian example.

4.4.3 EXCREMENT, CARRION, AND BIRDS' NESTS

Mammals in forest biomes are smaller and undoubtedly incarnate much less biomass per unit area than in grasslands. Nevertheless, they, and other vertebrates, are numerous enough to support a high density of litter-inhabiting copronecrophages, particularly in tropical forests. These scavengers are largely scarabaeine dung beetles, small sepsid and calyptrate flies, and pulmonate molluscs. That mammal faeces are not proportionately as significant as a food source as in grasslands is shown by the fact that even on islands where native mammals (except for bats) are absent (New Zealand, Mauritius), coprophagous beetles are still abundant and diverse in forest litter. Under such circumstances, they must feed on the droppings of birds, reptiles, and large snails, as well as on carrion.

It is also in forests, probably because of the relative scarcity of mammal excrement, that we find most of the significant departures from coprophagy among dung beetles. In tropical American forests a high proportion of them are specialist necrophages, whilst in Australia there is a tendency toward eating decaying mushrooms and litter (section 4.6.1), and occasionally fallen fruit.

Birds' nests in trees provide both food and shelter for numerous species of beetles, flies, thrips, gryllacridids, and some tineoid and gelechioid moths, as well as parasitic groups. Some species are specialized for this habitat. Energy is provided by the excrement, feathers, living and dead nestlings, and scraps of uneaten food dropped by the birds. E. B. Britton (personal communication) identified numerous beetles collected from birds' nests in New South Wales by W. J. M. Vestjens, with *Platydema* spp. (Tenebrionidae) being the most common in both the adult and larval categories

(Fig. 8). Other beetles present as larvae were *Cavognatha* (see below), dermestids, anthicids, and clerids, whilst adults of several other families were represented. Thrips were also abundant in these nests, particularly the two species *Limothrips cerealium* and *Nesothrips propinquus*.

The general subject of the symbiotic association between birds and insects in Australia is reviewed by Chisholm (1952). *Platydema* is mentioned by him as a scavenger, often abundant in nests of finches. The muscid genus *Passeromyia* is a specialized bird's-nest group which includes three species in Australia: *P. steini* which is a scavenger, *P. indecora* which is a subcutaneous parasite on nestlings, and *P. longicornis* of unknown biology (Pont 1974). A remarkably specialized bird's-nest inquiline is the oecophorid moth *Neossiosynoeca scatophaga,* a scavenger and coprophage in the nests of parrots of the genus *Psephotus.* These birds nest only in hollows in termite mounds and are thus closely associated with insects in two different ways (not counting parasites).

Chisholm (1952) refers to a beetle of the South American genus *Taphroiestes* as being found abundantly in weebill and thornbill nests in Victoria. This genus has recently been placed in the family Cavognathidae (Crowson 1973), which also includes *Cavognatha pullivora,* abundantly represented in Britton's material (see above) especially from nests of the Australian magpie (*Gymnorhina tibicen*). It is probable that the "*Taphroiestes*" cited by Chisholm are in fact *Cavognatha.* The family Cavognathidae is restricted to Australia, New Zealand, and Chile, and probably restricted to birds' nests. If so, it is the highest taxonomic category of insects so restricted and must represent a very old association (Crowson suggests that it may have begun in the Mesozoic).

The larvae of Cavognathidae are apparently ectoparasites or ectocommensals on nestlings, and not scavengers. This is to be expected, as the coevolution implied by the long association is not likely to be based on a detritus trophic relationship.

As well as insects that seek birds' nests for food and shelter, there are birds that seek the company of social insects, apparently for protection. Aside from the parrots mentioned above as nesting in termitaria, there are warblers (*Gerygone* spp.) that regularly nest near wasps' nests (probably *Polistes* spp.) in the north of Australia, and one (*G. olivacea*) which nests in heavily ant-infested trees (Chisholm 1952). "Anting" represents a one-sided association between some birds and social insects which is still not well understood.

4.4.4 PLANT-HELD FLUIDS

I am including plant-held waters in decomposer systems because the basic energy source, dissolved or suspended nutrients and micro-organisms, results largely from the decay of plant and animal tissues. Plant-held waters are largely a phenomenon of rain forests or monsoon forests, although pitcher plants will replenish their reservoirs with soil water. The latter, like many insectivorous plants, occur in strongly acidic, boggy soils deficient in nitrogen. Two independently-evolved genera are found in Australia, one on Cape York Peninsula (*Nepenthes,* an Asian genus) and the other in South Western Australia (the endemic *Cephalotus*). The water in pitcher plants acts as a trap for insects lured by nectar and perhaps colour, and as a medium for their digestion or decay. Nevertheless, certain insects, belonging to the dipterous families Ceratopogonidae, Culicidae (*Tripteroides* spp.; Marks 1972), an unnamed calyptrate group (G. B. Monteith, personal communication), and, in Western Australia, Tabanidae (Hamilton 1904), specialize in breeding in pitcher-plant waters. It is said that the plants produce digestive enzymes, but if so these evidently act more to hasten decay already occurring, as they do not affect the live larvae just mentioned.

Many parts of the north and east of Australia, as well as the South West, contain sundews (*Drosera*) and sundew-like *Byblis* — not water-holding, but logically included with pitcher plants — as they trap insects with sticky secretions. Again, specialized insects have taken advantage of the plants' insectivorous habits, in this case predacious mirid bugs of the

Figure 11   The insectivorous pitcher plant *Cephalotus follicularis* Labillardière, endemic to south-western Australia. It has evolved quite independently of the eastern, widespread genus of pitcher plants (*Nepenthes*). Some insects have evolved the ability to feed on the prey trapped in the fluid of pitcher plants. [Photo Division of Entomology, CSIRO]

Figure 12   Aestivating bogong moths (*Agrotis infusa* Boisduval) on the wall of a granite cave near Mt. Gingera summit at 1860 m, Australian Capital Territory. In the season when food plants are unavailable, cool temperatures of montane caves lower metabolic rate, while the reduced number of predators in mountains permits absolute predator satiation to be practised through aggregation. [Photo R. Carrick, courtesy Division of Entomology, CSIRO]

genera *Cyrtopeltis* and *Setocoris* (China and Carvalho 1951; China 1953). I have seen at least one species of these bugs on *Drosera* in Arnhem Land. G. B. Monteith (personal communication) observed that the bugs feed on both the plant itself and the trapped prey.

Among other plants with special structures or enlarged leaf axils for holding water are *Pandanus,* many Araceae, Cannaceae, and ferns (often epiphytic), plus bamboo in which water is held by the hollow stems. In these cases the water does not trap insects, but is presumably used for the plant's metabolic needs. Numerous insects will breed in these waters, including some Culicidae, Heleidae, Chironomidae, Psychodidae, Tipulidae, Syrphidae and Helodidae (Laird 1956), plus some odonatan nymphs (Corbet 1962). Laird states that the adaptations among mosquito larvae needed for existence in leaf-axil waters are an ability to crawl over dry surfaces (to move from drying axils), a prolonged developmental period with much inactivity, cannibalism, a covering of dense hairs, and very long anal papillae. *Aedes kochi* is cited by Marks (1969) as a regular breeder in *Pandanus.*

Pandanus, widespread in northern Australia, provides an important habitat for a fauna of specialized insects that has not yet been investigated. During the dry season in Arnhem Land some *Pandanus* axils yielded numerous individuals of an undescribed species of *Oncocoris* (Pentatomidae), plus a colourful species of earwig; orthopteroid insects known to be associated with *Pandanus* include *Daperria accola* and *Bermiodes nigrobivittatus* (Acrididae), several Tettigoniidae, Gryllacrididae, Gryllidae, and one phasmid (K. H. L. Key, personal communication).

Some species of *Forcipomyia* (Ceratopogonidae) breed in "exudates" of cacao and are important pollinators of these plants (Lee 1963).

Tree holes are breeding places for certain mosquitoes, several species (particularly in the genus *Tripteroides*) being specialized to live in such habitats (Dobrotworsky 1965; Marks 1972). Also occurring in tree holes are stratiomyiid, tabanid, and syrphid larvae (Williams 1968), plus Ceratopogonidae (Lee 1963). Kitching (1971), in a review of the subject, distinguished between hollows formed by the natural growth of the tree and lined by bark (pans), and those that result from injury and thus expose the wood to water (rot holes). The fauna of these two types may be quite different.

One final category of plant waters should be mentioned. The water contained in fallen and broken coconuts, gourds, pods, large leaves, and bark pieces provide temporary habitats for fugitive species. It is probable that mosquitoes now breeding in discarded containers about human habitations, like *Aedes aegypti* and *Culex fatigans,* originally occupied this type of habitat. Breeders in water tanks about houses, like *Aedes notoscriptus,* were probably tree-hole species originally.

4.5   TREES, ANTS, AND ASSOCIATED INSECTS

The majority of ants are dependent for at least part of their food on honeydew produced by homopterans such as psyllids, jassids, and eurymelids; hence these ants tend to remain in the vicinity of woody plants, even if they nest in the ground. Also, many predatory ants depend on tree-inhabiting insects for food.

The predatory ants of the genus *Myrmecia,* in particular, are heavily dependent on trees. Some species of this genus were observed by Douglas and McKenna (1970) and Gray (1971a, b). *M. dispar* is closely associated with *Eucalyptus largiflorens* in New South Wales and Queensland, preying mostly on other ants on the trees. Altogether, Gray found up to ten species of *Myrmecia* sharing the same general area and not showing nest overdispersion (territoriality, see section 2.3.4), and therefore probably not competing with one another. The species differ from each other in prey selection and in their principal foraging seasons. For instance, *M. desertorum* feeds mostly in winter, whereas *M. dispar* feeds in summer. *M. varians* feeds on lerp psyllids and on smaller insects than does *M. desertorum,* whilst *M. dispar* feeds mostly on other ants.

Greenslade (1973), in a study of the ants of Oraparinna National Park (Flinders Ranges), found *Myrmecia* to be almost restricted to the most densely wooded habitats (creek beds and mallee); these formations contained the largest numbers of ants in general. *Iridomyrmex purpureus,* a species heavily dependent on the availability of trees, was found to forage on red gums as far as 200 m away from the nests.

In various parts of the world some *Acacia* species have evolved special structures for housing and protecting ants, the best known being those of the Americas (Janzen 1966) and Africa (Hocking 1970). These structures are swollen thorns. Unlike galls, they are not produced as a result of insect activity, but occur spontaneously. Their evolutionary origin is not known, but it has been mentioned previously that ants, usually *Crematogaster* in the Old World, are frequent "successori" in true galls (section 4.3.1), and it is probable that as the plant derived increasing benefit from the presence of ants, selection favoured the formation of galls without any external stimulus (Hocking 1970). At any rate, Janzen showed that the *Acacia*-ant association can be obligatory for both partners, the ant obtaining food and shelter and the plant deriving protection from phytophagous insects, competitors, vines, and perhaps fire (since the ants clear the surrounding undergrowth). Some of the American acacias have "Beltian bodies" (nutritive pinnule tips) and nectaries supplying the ants with honeydew, thus by-passing the homopteran intermediaries with consequent benefit to the plant by reducing energy loss.

Structures described as nectaries occur also in some Australian acacias. Bagnall (1929) discussed these glands only in connection with minute thrips (*Rhopalothripoides, Froggattothrips*) which live inside them, and does not believe they are really nectaries. In the light of recent knowledge of extra-Australian acacias, and direct observations (e.g., Cleland 1965), we now know that they are in fact nectaries and serve the function of attracting ants, the thrips probably being incidental beneficiaries, as far as the plant is concerned.

As for the supposed absence of ant-favouring structures

in Australian acacias, Brown (1960) proposed that the absence of native large herbivorous mammals obviated the need for the protection which ants give to the plant elsewhere in the world. This idea is supported by Hocking (1970), but in view of Janzen's (1966) observation that it is against invertebrates and epiphytes that the ants are most protective, and the fact that nectaries are present in some Australian acacias, Brown's hypothesis is no longer tenable.

There are also true "ant plants" (myrmecophytes) in Australia – the curious epiphytic *Myrmecodia* and *Hydnophytum* (Rubiaceae), whose bulbous stems, honeycombed with galleries (Fig. 28), house the ant *Iridomyrme caudactus* and its associated lycaenids, *Hypochrysops apollo* and *Ogyris aenone* (McCubbin 1971), or sometimes other ants. These plants occur on a variety of trees in Australia and New Guinea, but tend to be concentrated on *Melaleuca* in swampy areas of Queensland and in other situations of very poor soil productivity. Ants inhabiting these epiphytes appear to have a competitive advantage over the green tree ant, *Oecophylla smaragdina,* and prevent it from becoming established in the tree (J. J. H. Szent-Ivany, personal communication). The epiphytes in turn depend on the debris of the ant nests for mineral nutrients, and because of this exceptional method of obtaining food they are able to survive in areas of low productivity which cannot support ordinary epiphytes (Janzen 1974).

As previously mentioned, ants are exceedingly numerous on many trees in Australia, and many foliage-feeding and sap-sucking insects have evolved protection from them. The ways in which this has been accomplished in the Homoptera and Lycaenidae will be discussed later in this section. There are few data on other insects, but Tindale's (1961) observations on *Chlenias inkata* (Geometridae), which feeds on *Acacia aneura,* may serve as an example of a herbivorous insect adopting defensive (as opposed to appeasing) measures against ants. The larvae of this moth drop down on silken threads when disturbed, the pupae have a thick ant-proof skin, and the wingless female has firmly adpressed spine-like hairs. This species has to live in close proximity to foraging *Melophorus bagoti*.

The general principles of the important association between ants and honeydew-producing Homoptera have been reviewed by Way (1963). When feeding on sap, homopterans have to ingest a large excess of water and sugar in order to obtain sufficient amounts of essential proteins and vitamins. The honeydew produced is thus a form of excretion, and one of the benefits homopterans derive from the association with ants is its removal. In some coccids, lycaenids, and *Cyclotorna*, death from fungi ensues if this excess is not removed. However, the honeydew is not simply a solution of sugars, but usually contains amino acids, proteins, minerals, and vitamins. Webber (1958) reports that blowflies can sometimes obtain enough protein for egg maturation from honeydew. It thus appears that the herbivore has to pay a price for the ants' services by supplying more than just excess carbohydrates and water. Other benefits derived by the herbivore from the association are believed to be protection from enemies such as syrphid larvae, coccinellids, and wasps, dispersion to other host plants, transport to and from shelter, and provision of space around roots for root feeders.

The ants in turn derive honeydew — a complete food, and in arid areas also a vital source of water. Nel (1965) observed that *Iridomyrmex detectus* could not survive in areas of 350 to 1,000 mm of annual rainfall without access to honeydew.

The honeydew-producing insects are often not protected against ants, but "appease" ant aggression by taking advantage of the ants' stereotyped behaviour. Ants associated with homopterans and other insects practise trophallaxis within their colonies and the behaviour associated with receiving honeydew from other insects is much the same as that involved in the exchange of food between ant workers. The transportation of aphids, lycaenid larvae, etc., into the ants' nests is carried out in such a way that it appears that the ant "mistakes" the other insect for one of its own larvae (Malicky 1970). Some lepidopterans predatory on ant larvae thus "trick" ants into carrying them down into the brood chamber where the larvae are kept, and it is amusing to read about the contortions which *Cyclotorna* larvae undergo to induce ants to pick them up (see Hinton 1951).

Ants are said to exercise control over homopteran population levels by witholding protection from, or eating, the individuals which are in excess of their needs (Way 1963). Shortage of space precludes further discussion of ant-Homoptera relationships. Many details are to be found in the papers cited, but specific information on Australian species is meagre.

The ant-lycaenid association has been reviewed in a comprehensive paper by Hinton (1951). It appears that all lycaenid butterflies are evolved from myrmecophilous ancestors, whether myrmecophilous now or not (most still are). Their response to ants is a combination of defence, appeasement, and aggression, depending on the species. All lycaenid larvae have a thick protective cuticle. In addition the more primitive members have a dorsal organ (or Newcomer's organ) producing honeydew, and lateral organs that apparently serve to protect the dorsal organ from overly eager ants (Hinton 1951). However, many lycaenid larvae have lost the dorsal organ and rely instead on "perforated cupola" organs producing a pheromone which is "informative" to ants (Malicky 1970), although it is not clear just what information is conveyed. At any rate, the perforated cupola organs are apparently more effective in protecting the larva than the dorsal organ, and are present in nearly all lycaenid larvae.

Whereas larval lycaenids communicate chemically with ants, some of their pupae use sound produced by cuticular rasping surfaces on the mobile abdominal segments. The widespread sound-producing ability of lycaenid pupae is believed to be directed toward ants (Downey 1966), but I believe this is unlikely as sound communication is not employed by ants themselves. I suspect that vertebrate predators are the intended recipients, and that this represents a case of sonic prey-predator communication (section 1.3.2).

In Australia all lycaenids seem to be associated with

ants, although it is not usually clear to what extent this association is species-specific (see Common and Waterhouse 1972). Two species associated with *Myrmecodia* ants have already been noted. Szent-Ivany and Carver (1967) mention another species in New Guinea, *Hypochrysops arronica.* *Hypochrysops ignita* shelters during the day in "byres" built for it by the ant *Iridomyrmex nitidus* on *Acacia.* Also, *Ogyris zosine*, a mistletoe feeder, may be carried by *Camponotus* and *Oecophylla* species to the bases of trees on which it feeds.

In the unusual case of the widespread *Liphyra brassolis major,* what must originally have been an association of the type outlined above has been transformed into a predator-prey relationship, with the butterfly the predator. In spite of the hostility of the ant prey (*Oecophylla smaragdina*) the thick-skinned slug-like caterpillars penetrate their nests, eat the brood, and subsequently pupate. On emergence, the butterfly is covered with deciduous scales which foul the ants' mandibles.

The moth *Cyclotorna monocentra* (Cyclotornidae) is a more subtle predator which in the first larval instar attaches itself to the abdomen of cicadellid nymphs. In the second instar it becomes transformed into a curious stage with two caudal processes, and proceeds to attract ants, apparently by a pheromone. When an ant (*Iridomyrmex purpureus*) arrives, the caterpillar offers it an anal secretion and begins a lengthy "courtship" eventually culminating in the ant carrying it into the nest, where it feeds for a long time on the ant brood (Hinton 1951, quoting F. P. Dodd in a 1911 paper).

No other Lepidoptera are definitely known to be ant predators in Australia, but Hinton (1951) suggests that the pyralid *Stenachroia myrmecophila* might be a predator in *Crematogaster* nests in trees, and Common and Waterhouse (1972) believe that the lycaenid *Pseudodipsas myrmecophila* may feed on the larvae of *Iridomyrmex nitidus*. In New Guinea, *Liphyra castnia* was found in the nest of *Oecophylla smaragdina* (Szent-Ivany and Carver 1967).

4.6   AUSTRALIAN FOREST FORMATIONS

Ecologists have recognized a large number of forest types in
Australia (see Leeper 1970), but as the insect fauna of these
has not been individually investigated, I will arbitrarily divide
the discussion into *Eucalyptus* ("sclerophyll") forest and
tropical closed forests. I am not able to add anything about
other forest formations to that already mentioned in connection with some arid woodland or shrub types in Chapter 2,
and with swamp forests in section 4.3.4.

It would be of special interest to study the insects
associated with the *Nothofagus* and other southern fern-tree
rainforests, in view of these formations' antiquity and consequent biogeographic importance. Although this subject has
received little attention, a start has been made with an
analysis of the taxonomy and distribution of certain aphids
associated exclusively with *Nothofagus* in Australia and
South America (Schlinger 1974). The Peloridiidae (Homoptera) tend to live in mosses occurring in *Nothofagus* and
similar southern montane associations and are of biogeographic interest (Evans 1959), as are certain curious wingless
aradid bugs with similar distributions (Gressitt 1961).

4.6.1   EUCALYPTUS FORESTS

The wood and foliage feeders on *Eucalyptus* are too
numerous to discuss in their entirety. Some have been mentioned previously in other connections. Suffice it to say that
mesic *Eucalyptus* species have a very extensive specialized
insect fauna. Some of the tree species produce a vigorous
crown growth with continuous replacement of leaves through
epicormic buds, which is believed by some foresters to compensate for damage by insects or fire, actual or potential. If
relieved of their insect pests (as in overseas groves), these
trees overcompensate and produce luxuriant growth which is
too heavy for the structure of the root system. The known
heavy litter production of *Eucalyptus* (see below) may be a
reflection of this vigorous growth. The characteristically
copious production of gum in woody tissue and oil in the
leaves is also a defence against insects.

There are several higher taxa of insects which are almost entirely specialized for feeding on *Eucalyptus* and other Myrtaceae, showing that coevolution between Australian insects and these trees has gone on for a very long time. Among such insect groups are Euryglossinae (Colletidae), Pergidae, Paropsinae (Chrysomelidae), Brachyscelinae (Eriococcidae), Spondyliaspinae (Psyllidae), Eurymelidae, and numerous genera from other families; probably some of the bark-inhabiting groups mentioned below should also be included.

I will confine the presentation here to only four aspects of the insect-*Eucalyptus* relationship: the bark fauna, galls, pollination, and the litter fauna.

(1) The Bark Fauna. There are genera of Carabidae which appear to be largely restricted to the loose bark of some *Eucalyptus,* for example the flattened *Philophloeus* and *Agonochila* (Lebiinae) and various Helluoninae and Pseudomorphinae (the latter myrmecophiles). Darlington (1943) reports that fully one quarter of the Australian Carabidae are arboreal, and that "most of the arboreal species are confined to a peculiar local habitat: the shaggy trunks of *Eucalyptus* and other Australian trees".

Many species of other groups are found under *Eucalyptus* bark, the river red gum (*E. camaldulensis*) having a particularly rich subcortical fauna. Although no quantitative study has been made, the impression gained by the collector is that there is a prevalence of predatory forms, including the carabids mentioned above, reduviids, ants, numerous spiders (some flattened) and their mantispid predators (McKeown and Mincham 1948), and lizards. It is evident that most of the herbivores that sustain this fauna do not feed under bark; it follows that most of the predators must emerge at night onto the foliage to feed. Some undoubtedly also feed on herbivores (weevils prominent among them) which move under the bark for shelter, transit, or pupation, and on emerging wood borers. I know of no explanation for the curious habit of many eucalypts, paperbarks (*Melaleuca*), and some other Australian trees of continuously producing exfoliating bark strips; it is tempting to speculate that this is an adaptation of the trees which provides shelter for the predators of their herbivores.

(2) Galls. The Australian gall-insect fauna, largely based on *Eucalyptus,* differs markedly from that of the rest of the world in taxonomic composition. Gall-making aphids are virtually absent, and Cynipinae are very poorly represented (hardly surprising in view of the absence of native *Quercus*). Most of our hymenopterous gall formers are chalcidoids. "Honeydew galls", which are a common feature of American trees and the principal source of honeydew for many ants and bees there, are rare in Australia and are replaced in this function by psyllids, jassids, and nectaries. Eriococcid gall formers are very highly developed and produce some spectacular gall shapes (Froggatt 1921). Species of the weevil genus *Apion* can produce galls of curious shape on *Callitris* (Moore 1972). Australia has some of the very few buprestid gall formers (Froggatt 1892), and gall-forming thrips are practically restricted to Australia and Indonesia (Reed 1970).

The galls of *Apiomorpha* and other Eriococcidae are of different forms in different species; the two sexes of the same species usually produce separate types of galls, the male ones being smaller and often bell- or trumpet-shaped. This genus provides a particularly good example of species-specific gall shapes, requiring a sophisticated chemical communication system between insect and plant, and probably involving nucleic acids (see section 4.3.1). It would be interesting to investigate the explanations, both in terms of chemistry and of natural selection, for the variety of shapes. Why for instance do some species, like *Apiomorpha hilli,* form galls "wonderfully like the seed capsules or fruits of [*Eucalyptus miniata*]" on which it feeds? (Froggatt 1921). Has the insect taken over a part of the tree's normal morphogenetic mechanism as an expedient? Could this be some kind of mimicry or crypsis?

Currie (1937) described the extraordinary symbiosis between agromyzid flies of the genus *Fergusonina* and nematodes (*Anguillulina*). The nematodes are transported inside the body of female flies and deposited with the fly's eggs in flower buds in *Eucalyptus* spp.; the nematodes cause the formation of a gall on which the fly larvae feed. The association between fly and nematode is an obligate mutualism. The life cycle of one of these flies has been illustrated by Norris (1970, p. 117).

Moore (1961) has described the association between members of the psyllid genus *Glycaspis* and *Eucalyptus* spp. and traced an evolutionary sequence in the psyllids which corresponds to one of the proposed classifications of the host groups of *Eucalyptus*. The most primitive *Glycaspis* are foliage gall formers, whilst later ones evolve through various shapes of "lerps" (tests).

(3) Pollination. The close relationship between *Eucalyptus* or other Myrtaceae and euryglossine colletid bees in Australia has been pointed out by Michener (1965). The colletids have radiated more extensively in Australia than anywhere else in the world, and most of them are oligolectic pollinators on Myrtaceae. These plants usually have open, cup-shaped flowers which can be fed upon by insects with short mouthparts (e.g., colletids and buprestid beetles). This oligolecty does not extend to the species of trees (except as a reflection of temporary apostasy). Other cases of known oligolecty on Australian plant families or genera are mentioned by Michener (op. cit.) (see also section 1.4.3). In *Eucalyptus*, pollination by vertebrates (lorikeets, honeyeaters, bats, pygmy possums, gliders, and perhaps *Tarsipes*) may be more important than pollination by insects and it is possible that flower structure and colours, as well as the tendency of blossoms to be concentrated at the top of the foliage crown, may be adaptations to bird and mammal pollination to which some insects have also adjusted (Carlquist, 1974).

(4) The Litter Fauna. *Eucalyptus* litter production is high relative to other forest types (Florence 1969). For a given amount of bole growth, these trees produce much more (particularly woody) litter than do other types of trees. This is partly a consequence of vigorous crown growth, and partly one of production of exfoliating bark strips. I have suggested

above that both of these activities of *Eucalyptus* are responses to insects.

A second important characteristic is the slow decomposition of *Eucalyptus* leaf litter (Wood 1971). The reasons for this are not clear, but can probably be traced to an exceptionally high C/N ratio in the litter, and to a low phosphorus content (as little as 1/10th that of other temperate forests) (Florence 1969). Polyphenols in the leaves, as well as other toxic substances such as tannins, are another factor affecting their initial edibility. Finally, the absence of suitable native earthworms, isopods (McNamara 1955), millipedes, or other macrofauna may be a factor in reducing turnover rates in some cases (Wood 1971).

The possibility of vacant large-decomposer niches in Australian forest litter is suggested by the plague numbers achieved by a recently introduced Mediterranean millipede (*Ommatoiulus moreleti*) at Bridgewater, S.A. and by the fact that at least three groups of insects which are not normally leaf-litter feeders have adopted this habit in Australia (not always in *Eucalyptus* forests). In Southern Queensland a dung beetle genus (*Cephalodesmius*) provisions its nest with fallen *Eucalyptus* leaves and flowers (G. B. Monteith and R. I. Storey, personal communication). This type of saprophagy is unknown in other members of the subfamily Scarabaeinae and probably permits the beetles to achieve higher population densities than would be possible when feeding on excrement alone (compare the case of *Aphodius tasmaniae,* section 3.4.2).

Secondly, in inland parts of Queensland and New South Wales cockroaches of the genera *Macropanesthia* and *Geoscapheus* may be significant agents of litter breakdown in *Callitris* and *Casuarina* woodlands (G. B. Monteith, personal communication). Adult insects occur in large numbers in some areas and dig spiral burrows into which they drag dry leaves and litter for their own feeding and for that of young nymphs. After rains these large cockroaches may undergo spectacular migrations over the ground surface.

Thirdly, the proportion of lepidopterous (mostly tortricid, pyralid, and oecophorid) species which feed on leaf litter as larvae is higher in Australia than elsewhere. This is probably because these normally live-tissue feeders are adapted to deal with the toxic substances in the *Eucalyptus* leaves.

Other groups abundant in leaf litter in Australia and other tropical or south-temperate areas, are aradid bugs and thrips. The highly specialized aradids possess extremely long stylets (normally held coiled in the head) which are used to penetrate lengthwise along fungal hyphae. Thrips, on the other hand, have short stylets adapted to penetrating fungal spores (see section 4.3.5). The frequent occurrence of the latter in the upper layers of *Eucalyptus* leaf litter is emphasized by Mound (1974).

Decomposition of *Eucalyptus* litter was investigated in two forest sites on Mt. Kosciusko by Wood (1971), one a dry *E. pauciflora* — *E. dalrympleana* association and the other a wet *E. delegatensis* association. By using bags of different size mesh he was able to show that exclusion of meso- and macrofauna retards decomposition, but leaching and micro-biota together (these effects not being separable) account for at least 70 per cent of litter weight loss, most of which occurs in the first three months. In dry sclerophyll forest medium and large decomposers were relatively few and had very little effect in the first nine months, but in wet forest these organisms attacked *E. delegatensis* leaves after three months. Primarily responsible for this were earthworms, which broke leaves into pieces, and larvae of Tortricidae (Lepidoptera) and various Diptera, which skeletonized the leaves. Other large-decomposer/herbivore groups present were Scarabaeidae, cicada nymphs, Diplopoda, and Isopoda. *E. delegatensis* leaves were significantly more palatable to large decomposers than were those of *E. pauciflora* in identical situations, showing that leaf species is an important factor even in dead litter decomposition.

The most numerous large predators in both forest types were ants, although in biomass these were outweighed in wet forest by Chilopoda and Japygidae. Whilst the role of ants in forest floors is mostly that of predation, in some sclerophyll forests they are partly responsible for a high level of seed harvesting as well (Florence 1969).

Termites are not important in the sites investigated by Wood (1971), but in drier sclerophyll forests in South Australia, where the litter has a high wood content, termites were found to consume approximately 5 per cent of the leaf content and 17–40 per cent of the wood (Lee and Wood 1971 and K. E. Lee, personal communication).

4.6.2 TROPICAL CLOSED FORESTS

Generally speaking, there are three major types of tropical closed forests in Australia: (1) those of very low species diversity growing in stagnant or saline waters (*Melaleuca* and mangrove forests), or on nutrient-poor soils; (2) the seasonal or monsoon forests growing in areas with a well-defined dry season; and (3) the rain forests. The first group grow under unusual or severe edaphic conditions, whilst in the second group moisture is a limiting factor during part of the year. In the third group there are no obvious physical limiting factors except space.

These forest types have not received any study as complete communities and it will be necessary to summarize here what has been learned regarding similar forest types overseas, particularly from the works of Janzen (1970, 1971a, 1973, 1974).

Tropical forest plants growing under conditions which permit survival of only a few specialized species are invariably strongly defended by toxic secondary compounds such as latex, essential oils, resins, tannins, and many other chemicals. The fruits are either highly poisonous, or edible but produced at very long intervals. Examples are mangroves, strongly protected by tannins, *Melaleuca*, with medicinal substances in the leaves (Janzen 1974), and various gymnosperms of the Podocarpaceae growing on white-sand soils in New Guinea and probably some areas of Australia. The conditions under which the above plants grow select for strong defences. Because of the general shortage of nutrients the destruction of a leaf is a proportionately greater loss to the plant than it would be under more favourable conditions; at the same time the reduced animal diversity makes this defensive tactic more effective. However, insects specialized to feed on plants like mangroves and conifers do exist, and the question arises as to what prevents such insects from decimating the largely monospecific stands of their food trees. Undoubtedly, it is the high cost of breaching the plants' defences, perhaps combined with intrinsic population density controls and predation.

Characteristics to be noted in connection with these forest types are: (1) that their regeneration after destruction is extremely slow; (2) the life span of an individual leaf is longest under the poorest soil conditions; and (3) communities are very stable, in spite of greatly reduced species diversity.

Monsoon forests are particularly evident in Northern Australia and one of their dominant characteristics is the deciduousness of many (but not all) of their trees. Leaf drop at the beginning of the dry season is believed to prevent transpiratory loss at times of water scarcity, but it could also be a defence against insect attack. Many insects cannot go into dormancy or diapause during the dry season. Temperatures are too high and the consequent continued high metabolic rate requires a continuing energy input. Another reason is the difficulty of choosing a site that will guarantee a moist environment over the whole of the dry season. An active adult shifts from place to place as moisture conditions change, and spends time hunting for food and scattered hosts on which to lay eggs. It also takes advantage of new leaf growth in the deciduous trees, which occurs before the wet season actually begins. The normal condition in which an insect passes the tropical dry season, therefore, is as a moderately active adult in reproductive diapause (Janzen 1973). The progressive die-out of adult insects as the dry season advances (characteristic of the Arnhem Land grasshopper fauna, for instance; K. H. L. Key, personal communication), attests to the high attrition rate that these insects suffer. Such mortality is not critical as long as an adequate proportion of the population survives to the next wet season.

Deciduousness in the trees, therefore, would seem to be a defence against the increased voracity of insects which are seeking moisture and food during the dry season; moreover it requires them to locate their food trees anew each wet season. It is also a way of "turning off" insects reproductively during that season, thus reducing their numbers.

The third type of forest considered here, the tropical rain forest, is similar in general structure throughout the world and is characterized by high species diversity. It is now believed that the community structure of tropical rain forests is determined entirely by the reactions of plants to the pressure of herbivory. In particular, the great distance between conspecific tree individuals, which is a defence against specialized herbivores, permits many trees of different species to grow in the intervening spaces (Janzen 1970).

Analysis of tree species composition in rain forests reveals that the smaller size-classes contain trees that tend to be grouped in monospecific clumps. In progressively larger size-classes species tend to become more and more solitary, with maximum distances occurring between the largest individuals of the same species. In other words, small trees tend to have their own species as nearest neighbour, whilst large trees tend to have any species but their own as nearest neighbour. Evidently, many trees are seeded in clumps, but some process occurs during development that eliminates these clumps through selection against individuals situated too close to conspecifics.

In some cases, this thinning out process may result from suppression of their own seedlings by some trees, such as *Grevillea robusta*, which produce a diffusable toxin in the soil (Webb 1968). This auto-allelopathy is seen in some infra-climax species and perhaps increases the fitness of survivors during the intense competition occurring in light breaks. As a general rule, however, overdispersion of conspecific trees in climax rain forest is because of attack by host-specific herbivores; these have a greater chance of finding a new food plant, particularly a seed or seedling, if it is located close to a previous food plant (Janzen 1970).

It would appear that tropical rain forest trees escape herbivore pressure through their spacing, as well as through the other defensive tactics previously mentioned (tissue toxicity and lengthy intervals between fruiting).

Toxicity is not as high as in forests suffering a shortage of nutrients, because the loss of a leaf is not proportionately as serious. However, shrubs adapted to grow in the understorey of tropical rain forests are strongly toxic. This is probably because resource scarcity (light in this case) and reduced animal diversity in this layer (Elton 1973) make this tactic worthwhile for the reasons mentioned above.

A lengthy periodicity between fruiting times is brought about by herbivore pressure on those tree species producing edible seeds and which therefore rely on herbivore satiation as a defence. The genotypes that fruit out of phase are selected against by having their seed crops destroyed. However, the trees need some infrequently-occurring environmental cue to synchronize their fruiting; this can be provided by occasional severe droughts. When such cues are not available, the mast-fruiting strategy cannot evolve (Janzen 1974).

Therefore, the major attributes of tropical rain forests — their pattern diversity, profusion of secondary plant substances, and infrequent flowering and fruiting — are all defensive tactics brought about by pressure from herbivores, mostly insects.

The insects' counteractions involve primarily the ability to detoxify or otherwise resist the secondary compounds, and the biochemical investment necessary to do this requires that each herbivore be a specialist on one or a few host plants.

Populations of herbivores are believed to be kept down by the plants' active defence, by the escape of the latter in space and time, and by intrinsic population density control (Elton 1973). The virtual restriction of insect activity to the night time is believed to be a result of selection by visual predators (Elton 1973).

There are occasions when the controls operating on herbivorous insect populations are relaxed in rain forest, and outbreaks occur (Brereton 1957; Gray 1972; Janzen 1974), but it will be noted that in nearly all cases it is subclimax tree species that are involved — those that grow in disturbed areas (Elton 1973).

The different sorts of tropical forest types just discussed will support different types of pollinators. If the trees do not escape herbivores through either time or space, but rely only on toxicity, flowering times can be rather continuous (as in some mangroves) and because dense stands are usually involved, there is no selection for oligolecty. Flowers are therefore available at most times to generalized pollinators.

If escape from seed eaters is through time (that is, by infrequent flowering and fruiting, so that between fruiting periods the seed eaters have little food, and at fruiting time they have more than they can ingest) oligolecty is also disadvantageous. Any specialized pollinator would suffer the same fate as the seed eater against which the tactic is directed. Such mast-fruiting plants must depend on generalized pollinators and have exceptionally showy flowers, or be wind-pollinated. A general trend toward polylecty in tropical forest pollinators has been noted by Heinrich and Raven (1972).

A device which favours pollinators over seed eaters on the same tree species is dioecism, common in tropical lowland forests (Janzen 1971a). Some individual trees will flower but not set fruit; they are essentially acting like males. If we suppose that the ratio of male to female trees is 1:1, then such a species will be twice as common for its pollinators as for its seed eaters.

Only overdispersed plants that do not rely on mast-fruiting will need to select for specialized pollinators to ensure outcrossing over the long distances involved. Such plants will have frequently-blooming, highly specialized flowers that are inconspicuous and offer only enough caloric reward to take care of their few specialized pollinators. The latter will fly very long distances and will learn the location of each suitable flower, so that no subsequent searching behaviour need occur. Each flower is revisited at about the same time each day. This behaviour, including flights of at least 23 km from the nest, was noted in euglossine bees in the Neotropics by Janzen (1971b).

Because of the highly coevolved nature of the relationships between the species inhabiting tropical forests, brought about by genetic feedback over a very long period of time, these forests are integrated units which can occur as biotic islands in much larger areas of identical climate (which may not be strictly tropical), occupied in Australia by wet *Eucalyptus* forest. Once destroyed, these biotic islands cannot be recreated piece-meal (unless there is a feeder community close by) and are lost forever.

The only other aspect of tropical forest ecology that will be discussed here is the decomposition of leaf litter. Limited studies made on soil and litter biota in tropical forests indicate that litter decomposition is generally much faster than in forests of cooler regions (K. E. Lee, personal communication). Figures published by Kira and Shidei (1967) indicate that rainforest litter in Thailand is decomposed about 90 times more quickly than in spruce forests of northern Japan. If the much greater amount of litter produced in the rain forest is taken into account, tropical litter decomposition accounts for about 425 times more volume of material in a given time than does that of temperate forest.

Soil animal populations in tropical forests appear to be much lower than in temperate forests, perhaps in part because the upper soil layer tends to be permanently saturated and practically anaerobic in the former (K. E. Lee, personal communication). Therefore, an unusually large proportion of the observed decomposition is due to leaching and perhaps microbial activity. Nevertheless, soil animals, whilst not actually consuming much litter, still play their usual significant role in physically disintegrating the particles to expose a greater relative surface area to physical and microbial action.

The rapid decomposition of organic matter in tropical forests, and the rapid return of nutrients and minerals to trees with the help of mycorrhiza, mean that at any given moment a relatively small proportion of nutrients and ex-

changeable cations is held ·in the soil, and a greater proportion is present in living tissues, than is true of other ecosystems.* Cutting down the forest therefore results in the
loss of most of these nutrients, those remaining in the soil
being insufficient to support sustained growth of new
vegetation.

We see in the tropical rain forest a type of community
in which nearly all the selective pressures are biotic in origin
— the opposite of the desert communities with which we
began Chapter 2 and which tend to favour r strategists. In
tropical forests the culmination of long-term coevolutionary
processes has produced a maximum number of K strategists.
In the next and concluding chapter we will consider environments which are largely beyond-K.

* The scarcity of labile minerals renders these, when present in
mammal dung and urine, and in mineral springs, exceptionally attractive
to butterflies, bees, and wasps, which will congregate about such unlikely sources in enormous numbers.

CHAPTER 5
Other Environments

Within, or adjacent to, the broad biome categories covered in Chapters 2 to 4 are some habitat types, or biocoenoses, that differ significantly from the general environment prevalent in the biome, and which are large or important enough to be included in a general survey. I am referring to inland waters, marine waters and shore habitats, caves, and high mountains.

Most of the environments treated in this chapter are beyond-K (section 1.2), that is, dominated by one or a combination of extreme physical factors that, although severe, are constant and predictable in their effects, and are continuous over long periods of time. Such environments tend to be inhabited by small numbers of highly-adapted K strategists, often quite sedentary, sometimes blind, and showing life-history characteristics often involving a reduction or deletion of the dispersal phase or other non-adapted phases of the life cycle (P. J. M. Greenslade 1972, and personal communication). The principal energy source in these environments is often detritus rather than primary production, and as such it is subject to fluctuations that place a premium on energy conservation. There may thus be an active selection against energy wasting structures and life-history stages normally involved in dispersal or other irrelevant activities. However, the principal reason for the reduction of vagility in the first place is probably preservation of locally-adapted genotypes favoured by K selection in general (section 1.6).

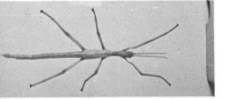

Fig. 13

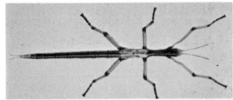

Fig. 14

Fig. 15

Figures 13—15 Defence-strategy switches in orthopteroids. (13) Low-density kentromorphic phase of the stick insect *Podacanthus wilkinsoni* Macleay, showing procryptic coloration. *Australian Journal of Zoology.* [Photo Division of Entomology, CSIRO] (14) High-density phase of *Podacanthus wilkinsoni* displaying signal colours which facilitate avoidance-image formation in visual predators. This colour-pattern switch indicates that the insect's normal defences, inadequate to induce predator satiation at low densities (when procrypsis is relied upon), succeed in doing so when multiplied by the greatly increased numbers of the high-density phase. *Australian Journal of Zoology.* [Photo Division of Entomology, CSIRO] (15) Female *Acripeza reticulata* Guerin in display attitude, unveiling normally-masked signal colours. The male also displays in the same way. As in the stick insect in figure 14, the normal procrypsis is abandoned in favour of a display of signal colours, in this case as a temporary stratagem following the insect's awareness of having been perceived by a predator. The function of the signal depends on the predator's experience and on the grass-hopper's population density (see text and figure 1). [Photo Densey Clyne]

Fig. 16   Fig. 17

Fig. 18   Fig. 19

Figures 16–19   The use of eyespot patterns in adult Lepidoptera. (16–17) A sudden unmasking of large eyespots in the emperor gum moth, *Antheraea eucalypti* Scott, may startle or frighten a visual predator, an effect which has been demonstrated experimentally in other moths. [Photo R. V. Southcott] (18) The two eyespots and the false antennae on the hind wings of these *Lampides boeticus* (Linnaeus), here shown *in copula*, will not startle a predator but will confuse it as to which is the front end of the insect. The "tails" here are realistic false antennae, small enough not to interfere with the procryptic pattern of the wings. In some other butterflies where procrypsis is not so important, tails may become enlarged into supernormal antennae with enhanced confusing effect. [Photo R. V. Southcott] (19) Peripheral small eyespots on the wings of *Hypocysta metirius* Butler. Such eyespots are very often associated with a procryptic pattern in butterfly wings. They are small enough not to interfere with procrypsis and do not have either a startle or deceptive function, but probably serve to divert beak thrusts to non-vulnerable parts of the insect. [Photo Densey Clyne]

Fig. 20

Fig. 21

Fig. 22

Fig. 23

Fig. 24

Fig. 25

Figures 20—25 Defensive adaptations of lepidopterous larvae. (20—21) The larva of *Uraba lugens* Walker stacks the head-capsule exuvia of previous instars on its prothorax. This probably serves to impart a distinctive appearance for the benefit of predators having had experience with the insect's stinging hairs, shown enlarged in figure 21. [Photos R. V. Southcott] (22) Larva of a cup moth, *Doratifera* sp., in which batteries of stinging hairs are incorporated in a highly distinctive pattern of shapes and colours. The insect is sluggish and feeds exposed — sure signs of a very effective individual defence. [Photo R. V. South-cott] (23) Mature larvae of *Papilio aegeus* Donovan relying mostly on procrypsis, but also having red spines visible at close range and able to protrude red osmeteria (seen in lower individual) which release acidic defensive substances. Earlier instars of this species go through a different colour pattern which imitates a bird dropping. [Photo C. Lourandos, courtesy Division of Entomology, CSIRO] (24—25) Suddenly revealed eyespots, as a result of muscular contraction, and a false head at the tail end of the larva of *Neola semiaurata* Walker, probably frighten birds. [Photo Densey Clyne]

Figure 26 Overdispersion in mounds of *Amitermes vitiosus* Hill near Cannon Hill, Arnhem Land. The regular spacing of the mounds, brought about by inter-colony antagonism, aids in resource partitioning of two-dimensional habitats under certain conditions. [Photo J. A. L. Watson, courtesy Division of Entomology, CSIRO]

Figure 27 "Watchtower" mound of an undescribed *Nasutitermes* allied to the spinifex termite, near Cannon Hill, Arnhem Land. [Photo the author]

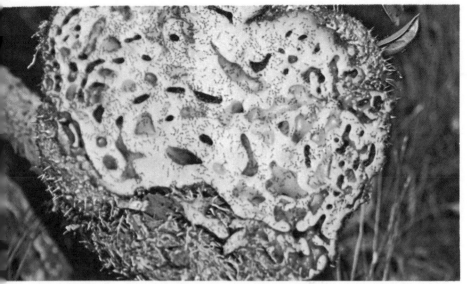

Figure 28 The epiphytic myrmecophyte *Myrmecodia* sp. cut open to reveal labyrinthine passages housing a symbiotic ant colony. Since the ants bring nutrients to these epiphytes in the course of their normal activities, the plants are able to grow in formations of very low productivity not able to support ordinary epiphytes, such as *Melaleuca* swamp forests. The shelter provided by the plant enables the ant to best its competitors on the tree. The relationship is thus mutualistic. [Photo Densey Clyne]

Figure 29 The green tree ant, *Oecophylla smaragdina* (Fabricius), a dominant ant in trees and in some places on the ground throughout northern Australia (where it is somewhat greener in colour than in this picture, which was taken in New Guinea). Visible are the silken threads obtained from the larvae and used to tie leaves together to form the nest. [Photo R. V. Southcott]

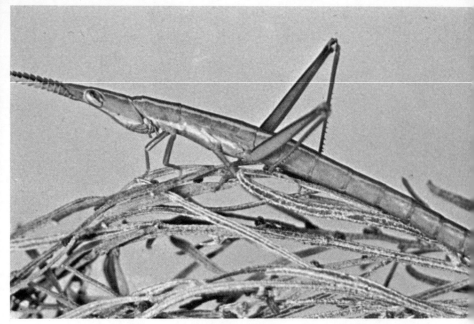

Figure 30 The morabine grasshopper *Moraba virgo* Key. This is the only short-horned grasshopper known to display thelytoky (obligate parthenogenesis) and is even more restricted in its food-plant spectrum than other morabines. [Photo Division of Entomology, CSIRO]

Figure 31 Thermoregulatory colour phases of the male of the alpine grasshopper *Kosciuscola tristis* Sjöstedt. The low temperature phase at the left is melanic, as are certain other alpine grasshoppers. This facilitates heat absorption from the sun's rays. Unlike other grasshoppers, however, *K. tristis* will become paler at higher temperatures (right figure) and thus avoids getting too hot. The colour change is brought about automatically at different temperatures as a result of pigment granule migration in epidermal cells. *Australian Journal of Zoology.* [Photo Division of Entomology, CSIRO]

5.1   INLAND WATERS

The taxonomy and natural history of the invertebrates of Australian inland waters have been surveyed in a book by Williams (1968). It is my purpose here to review the general ecological features of inland waters as they affect insect adaptations. Since water is a "foreign" medium to insects considered as a whole, adaptations to aquatic habitats tend to be dominated by the need to meet physical requirements. The dynamic plant-insect interface, which is so important in terrestrial environments, is much reduced or nonexistent as an evolutionary influence, and the principal biotic selection pressures are those that result from predator-prey relationships and competition. These therefore exert most of the coevolutionary forces.

The principal environmental characteristics of inland water bodies that affect insects appear to be the following.

(1) Duration of the Water Body. Whether a body of water is permanent or temporary, and if the latter, how temporary, appears to be the single most important factor determining which insect species will be present. To be able to breed in temporary waters an insect has to adopt one of two general tactics: it must either be able to withstand periods of foul water or drought, or it must breed so fast that it has a high probability of reaching the adult dispersal phase before the water becomes foul or disappears. The first tactic works only in cases of predictable and relatively short seasonal droughts (K selection), whilst the second is necessary for breeding in unpredictable, transient waters — varying periods may ensue between rains, or between the conditions permitting accumulation of rain water (r selection).

Both tactics have been described in Western Australia Odonata by Hodgkin and Watson (1958) and Watson (1967). The drought-enduring dragonfly nymphs are exemplified by species of the genus *Synthemis,* that inhabit summer-dry bogs and can survive for some months in damp soil. The second tactic (rapid breeding) is shown by at least nine widespread fugitive species of dragonflies, exemplified by *Hemicordulia tau,* which can complete its life cycle in as little as 36 days at high temperatures. They generally cannot tolerate dry conditions in the nymphal instars.

Truly ephemeral waters of less than a month's duration, and frequently also of small volume, are inhabitable by *r*-strategist mosquitoes. The most fugitive of these insects can breed in just a few ml of water and in a period as short as three days (Laird 1956). In some species, the eggs must undergo a period of desiccation and diapause before hatching. Other requirements enabling breeding in ephemeral waters are a tolerance of high temperatures (above 40° C) and wide salinity variations, as well as an ability to feed entirely on bacteria. Bacteria begin multiplying immediately in ephemeral waters and are thus quickly available. Predators and competitors tend to be few in such waters, and transient-water mosquito larvae achieve very high population densities. In Australia, the most fugitive mosquito species appear to be *Culex annulirostris, Anopheles annulipes,* and *A. farauti* (Laird 1956), but synanthropic species such as *Culex fatigans* and *Aedes aegypti* are probably similar.

Temporary waters can also be inhabited by insects that are aquatic in the adult stage and thus able to abandon a pond once it starts to evaporate. Some Notonectidae, Corixidae, Mesoveliidae, and Dytiscidae are examples.

Air-breathing is frequent in temporary waters and bogs, for even if these do not dry out altogether there are periods when the water becomes too foul for aquatic respiration. Air-breathing aquatic insects will either swim to the surface for air, have long breathing tubes, pick up oxygen bubbles from submerged algae, or pierce vascular-plant tissues. This piercing ability is found in six families of Diptera (including the mosquitoes *Mansonia* and *Coquillettidia* spp.) and three of Coleoptera (Chrysomelidae, Curculionidae, and Elmidae) (Hinton 1953). Australian members of the weevil genus *Bagous* have also been mentioned in this connection (Britton 1970). Bog-dwelling odonatan nymphs are able to use aquatic respiratory organs, such as rectal gills, caudal lamellae, and even wing pads for air breathing providing these remain moist (Corbet

1962). Air breathing in poorly-oxygenated water can be dispensed with by chironomid larvae possessing haemoglobin ("blood-worms").

In permanent waters the immature stages of insects may require several years for development. Breathing is usually by gills or plastron or by cutaneous exchange (in running waters). Air breathing is seldom required, but all the breathing organs mentioned can function aerially as well as aquatically. The skin and gills must be kept moist, but the plastron has the advantage of being able to function both in well-oxygenated waters and in dry air, and is frequently seen in terrestrial insect eggs adapted to occasional flooding (Hinton 1961, and section 2.3.5).

Watson (1969), in a survey of the dragonfly fauna of the North West District of Western Australia, pointed out the importance of the duration of water bodies in determining their faunal composition. He categorized waters in the district as: (1) ephemeral and still, with wide fluctuations in temperature and oxygen concentration, (2) permanent and still, and (3) streams (all permanent). The last two categories are relatively constant in temperature and oxygen concentration. Of the 30 species of dragonflies surveyed, ten inhabited all three categories of waters. These are geographically widespread species ranging far from water in the adult state. The remaining 20 species were largely confined to the combined categories (2) and (3), the current of the water not being an important factor; they had a limited adult dispersal range. These species showed restricted and disjunct geographical distributions. Whilst there are no flightless dragonflies, the lack of mobility associated with K strategy is manifested in these insects by a reluctance to fly far from the water in which they developed.

(2) Salinity. Many intermittent inland water bodies have a high salt content and r strategists inhabiting them must be euryhaline. We have already seen that they are also tolerant of wide fluctuations in temperature and oxygen concentration. Among mosquito larvae, high salinity tolerance seems to be correlated with short anal papillae, and euryhaline species

like *Culex annulirostris* have variable papillar lengths according to the ambient salinity (Laird 1956). A certain amount of osmoregulation is possible among some aquatic insects.

The groups tolerant of the highest salinity in Australian inland waters are some Tipulidae, Ceratopogonidae (especially *Culicoides multimaculatus*), Culicidae (especially *Aedes vigilax* and *A. australis*), Chironomidae (especially *Tanytarsus barbitarsus* and *Procladius* spp.), some aquatic Pyralidae, the caddis fly *Symphytoneura wheeleri*, the dytiscid *Necterosoma* sp. (Bayly and Williams 1966; Williams, W. D. 1968; Bayly 1970), and perhaps some Hydraenidae (Britton 1970).

The most salt-tolerant dragonfly in Australia may be the widespread opportunistic species *Ischnura aurora* (Bayly and Williams 1966).

(3) Water Current. The principles of stream-insect biology were reviewed by Hynes (1970). Mountain streams are one of the severe and stable beyond-*K* environments and as such contain some highly specialized faunas of ancient groups ("highly-adapted primitives") which tend to recur throughout the world (e.g., Plecoptera, Coleoptera-Myxophaga, baetid Ephemerida, net-spinning Trichoptera, Simuliidae).

Whilst swiftly-flowing current is the most obvious environmental limiting factor, few insects are actually exposed to it for long; most of them can avoid it by adhering closely to stone surfaces, staying on the downstream side of objects, and especially burrowing into the bottom gravel, which they often do to a considerable depth, thus protecting themselves against both "flushes" and droughts. Insects which do regularly expose themselves to currents have special suckers or a limpet-like shape (larvae of Blepharoceridae, Simuliidae, Psephenidae, and Helodidae) or simply claws coupled with small size (Myxophaga). The high oxygen tensions and low constant temperatures of streams, are reflected in a scarcity of air-breathing groups (such as mosquitoes) in the fauna, in loss of ventilation movements of gills, cutaneous breathing, use of the plastron (Elmidae, some Myxophaga), and in cold stenothermy. Typically, life histories involve extensive dormant periods, long larval life, and ephemeral adult life (except when the adult is also aquatic, as in beetles). Dispersal of adult forms is minimal, even when they are winged.

By far the most important food source in streams is suspended detritus washed down from the terrestrial parts of the watershed, upstream lakes, or snow fields. Only the few forms adapted to clinging to exposed stone surfaces, such as Psephenidae, can feed on the algal film which is the stream's only primary production. Many stream insects have evolved plankton-catching structures in the form of hair fringes on mouthparts and legs, mucus strands, and spun nets. Simuliids may feed entirely on suspended bacteria.

The Australian stream-insect fauna is little different from that of the rest of the world except that it appears to be relatively impoverished. Beetles, however, may perhaps be better represented proportionately than elsewhere, as the Elmidae are particularly numerous and Helodidae, Psephenidae, Hydraenidae, Ptiliidae, Georyssidae, and Sphaeriidae are all represented (Dryopidae may be absent) (Britton, 1966, 1970). In general the Myxophaga do not appear to be as well represented as in South America and Africa (Reichardt 1973).

(4) The Water Surface. Several groups of insects have become adapted as surface skimmers and skaters, feeding on small organisms that accidentally fall into the water. They include a number of Hemiptera (Gerridae, Veliidae, Hydrometridae, Mesoveliidae and Hebridae), Coleoptera (Gyrinidae), and many Collembola. A trigonidiid cricket has evolved this behaviour in Fiji in the absence of torrent-inhabiting veliids (Laird 1956). The underside of the surface film is used by one family of beetles, the Spercheidae (Britton 1970).

(5) Predation by Fish. Fish appear to be extraordinarily efficient as predators on aquatic invertebrates, and there is a marked difference in the biotic composition of water bodies after Gambusia, in particular, have been introduced (Hurlbert, Zedler, and Fairbanks 1972). Phytoplankton increases markedly, producing a pseudo-eutrophic effect which is actually

the result of a drastic reduction in organisms, mostly insects and Crustacea, which feed on phytoplankton. It is probable that this is not a stable situation, and that eventually other herbivore species that can largely avoid fish predation become established. In any case, predation by fish must have a profound effect on the specific composition of aquatic insect faunas, although I am not aware of particular information on Australian bodies of water.

The main significance to insects of aquatic higher plants is that they provide cover from predators. This, together with the source of gaseous oxygen they offer to species with tissue piercing organs, and as bubbles, outweighs any importance that these plants may have as food sources for insects. Unicellular or filamentous organisms — bacteria, algae, protozoa, and yeasts — are more important in this regard. In general, the trophic role of aquatic invertebrates is determined more by the particle size of their food than by its origin.

5.2   MARINE WATERS

Insects have not been very successful in moving into the marine environment. This is not for physiological reasons, as insects can adapt to life in saline waters and to all other physical factors involved. The reason is probably that marine niches available to arthropods are already filled by Crustacea (who have been there a much longer time), and that the great advantage insects normally have over other arthropods — their ability to disperse by air — is not effective in the marine environment. Marine insects have largely had to abandon their aerial heritage and most are flightless.

Therefore, a combination of permanent physical and biotic factors renders the marine environment beyond-K as far as insects are concerned. Some notable relicts are indeed to be found among the beetle inhabitants of the intertidal zone and marine beaches, such as the limnichiid *Hyphalus,* the weevils mentioned below, and the aphodiine scarab genus *Phycochus* (Landin 1960).

On the smallest coral cays, there is no endogenous production of energy on land because of the absence of vascular vegetation; nevertheless communities of terrestrial animals can be supported there by marine energy sources (Heatwole 1971). To a certain extent, plant and animal matter washed up on the beaches provides energy, but the most important resource is that resulting from the activities of "transfer organisms", particularly sea birds contributing guano, carrion, regurgitated food, feathers, and nesting materials. Resident non-parasitic insects on some Coral Sea cays include several Collembola, one earwig (Labiduridae, Carcinophorinae), one sphaerocerid fly, and one abundant dermestid beetle. There is probably a rapid rate of faunal turnover on any given cay.

The larger coral cays support some vascular vegetation and some are inhabited by man. The mosquito fauna of these has been reviewed by Marks (1969).

5.2.1 THE RESIDENT FAUNA

Summaries of information on marine insects are provided by Mackerras (1950) and Usinger (1957). The major habitats are as follows.

(1) Tidal Marshes. The zones vegetated by marine couch grass (*Sporobolus*) and by *Salicornia* are inhabited by salt-marsh mosquitoes, the most important of which in Australia are *Culex sitiens, Aedes vigilax,* and *Anopheles farauti* (Laird 1956). Mackerras (1950) mentions *Aedes alternans, A. longirostris, Culex vishnui,* and *C. fraudatrix*; some *Culicoides* (especially *C. multimaculatus*) and *Leptoconops* (Ceratopogonidae) also occur. Specialized crab-hole mosquitoes are unknown in Australia, but the subgenus *Skusea* of *Aedes* favours this habitat in the Pacific area. Cixiid fulgoroid nymphs (Homoptera) feed on the roots of marsh grasses, and the grass leaves themselves serve as food for numerous non-aquatic insects not considered in this section.

(2) Brackish-Water Pools. These are pools in rocks which fill mostly with rain water, but which receive salt spray from the sea and which are sometimes saltier than the sea because of evaporation. Corixids are the dominant insects in such pools throughout the world, but Mackerras (1950) and Laird (1956) list many other insects as well. Norris (1970) mentions particularly *Aedes australis*.

(3) Sandy Beaches. Ephydrid and tipulid flies (*Limonia*) and other dipterous groups such as Canaceidae and Tethinidae breed in large numbers on interstitial diatoms and dinoflagellates and in stranded seaweed. To facilitate intake of interstitial flora, some ephydrids fluidize the sand by shaking their bodies (Cheng and Lewin 1974). Specialized tenebrionid genera occur under seaweed (Britton 1970), and carabids, weevils, and aphodiine scarabs are also found there sometimes. Mackerras (1950) lists many insect groups associated with seaweed or terrestrial plants growing on beaches, but only a few are groups specialized at the generic or higher level for living in the sandy beach habitat. Among the latter are cossonine weevils of the genera *Notiomimetes, Psaldus,* and *Wollastonicis,* probably root feeders, that occur along the coasts of Australia, New Zealand, and some oceanic islands (Womersley 1937b). Lea (1900) described a new genus of weevils (*Halorhynchus*) known from Fremantle and Geraldton, W.A., that occurs in sandy beaches. The insects burrow about the roots of saltbush and spinifex. Near Hobart, Tas., Lea (1905) found two species of the scarabaeid genus *Phycochus* at the roots of bracken fern on beaches. All of these littoral root feeders are wingless and most are blind.

Kuschel (1972 and previous works) has stressed the association of external root (ectophytic) feeding with polyphagy and endemism in far-southern and subantarctic weevils, many of the insular ones belonging to the taxonomically isolated subfamily Ectemnorrhininae. These weevils are flightless, soft-bodied, and extraordinarily polyphagous.

The Ectemnorrhininae contain the only known fully marine weevil, *Palirhoeus eatoni*; it feeds on intertidal algae in both the adult and larval stages.

The South Australian species of *Pontomyia* (Chironomidae) is a flightless midge living at the extreme edge of the water along sandy beaches (Womersley 1937a), unlike its tropical congener which is fully marine.

(4) The Intertidal Zone. This zone, with a substrate of sand, rocks, or coral and containing crevices and tide pools, has numerous insects adapted to it, some of which were men-

tioned in the previous section. Some of these live under completely marine conditions and are periodically, or permanently, submerged under water; others retreat with the advancing tides. Numerous midges of the subfamily Clunioninae are the most abundant insects in this habitat and the midge *Pontomyia natans* is one of the few marine insects that never emerges from water. It inhabits pools containing the vascular plant *Halophila,* although it feeds on diatoms. The female is larviform and does not leave its larval tube except to copulate, whilst the flightless male uses its legs to swim (according to some accounts) or to skate on the water surface (Mackerras 1950). Other tidal zone insects are saldid bugs, staphylinid, melyrid, carabid, and elmid beetles, one weevil (see previous section), one limnichiid beetle (see below), a trichopteran (*Philanisus plebejus*), collembolans, and others (see Mackerras 1950, Chadwick 1962, and Britton 1971, for lists and discussions of species). Possibly the highest taxonomic category of purely marine insects is the subfamily Hyphalinae (Limnichiidae), recently created for a new genus and a single new species of beetle (*Hyphalus insularis*) from coral rocks on Heron Island (Britton 1971).

(5) The Open Water. Pelagic water striders of the genus *Halobates* are found in the Pacific up to 1,300 km from land (Gressitt, Coatsworth, and Yoshimoto 1962). They lay their eggs in the open sea attached to floating objects (Usinger 1957) and are thus truly pelagic organisms. They are fiercely predatory and presumably feed on flying insects that fall into the sea and on marine chironomids. They cannot be made to submerge under any circumstances and so do not feed on aquatic organisms. There are many species of Gerridae, Hydrometridae, Veliidae, and Mesoveliidae which occur on marine waters, mostly near the shore, all clearly evolved from freshwater relatives, and all showing a reduction in wing development. However, the genus *Halobates* appears to include the only truly pelagic species among them.

The male of *Pontomyia natans* (Chironomidae) may also be found skating some distance from shore (Mackerras 1950). Since the females of this species are sedentary, it is probable that the advantage to be gained by male pelagic behaviour is interdeme genetic exchange.

A water beetle (unidentified, but probably a species of *Rhantus*) was observed swimming in the sea 27 km off the coast of South America by Charles Darwin on the Beagle (Bayly and Williams 1966).

5.2.2 THE TRANSIENT FAUNA AND LONG-DISTANCE MIGRATORS

Aside from the insects that complete their life cycle in marine habitats there are many that are in transit, either as individuals actively flying or blown out to sea, or as plant or detritus inhabitants trapped in flotsam floating out from streams and rivers after storms. An extensive literature on the trapping of airborne insects in the Pacific is to be found in the pages of *Pacific Insects*.

Some of the stronger fliers, such as the dragonflies *Pantala flavescens, Hemianax papuensis,* and *Aeshna brevistyla,* may appear in large numbers on ships hundreds of kilometres from the nearest land (Smithers 1970). Their appearance *en masse* suggests active migration, rather than just the accidental blowing of strays out to sea (passive transport).

If winds and other atmospheric conditions are favourable, large-scale movements of many insect species may simultaneously occur over long stretches of water. Fletcher (1973) described how on one occasion large numbers of insects arrived on Heron Island, apparently over a route carrying them 110 to 130 km over the open sea.

Some sixteen species or more of butterflies have been recorded as actual or suspected migrants in the Australian region (Williams 1971), but some of these, such as *Pieris rapae* and *Bassaris itea,* merely join flights of mass-migratory species as individuals and it is not clear how long they stay with them. Such "mixed flocks" of butterflies, including even other insects, appear to be quite frequent and may represent a tactic whereby lower-density nomadic species can take advantage of the predator-satiating effect produced by the enormous flights of species such as *Anaphaeis java teutonia* and *Precis villida calybe*. Somewhat unusual is the adoption of the regular mass-migratory habit by a skipper, *Badamia exclamationis*, in the Australian region. The distances covered by migrating Lepidoptera, which fly over both land and water, are a matter of some uncertainty. The record for the longest known non-stop flight is probably held by two noctuid moths that flew across the Atlantic for a distance of approximately 3,200 km (Johnson 1969). Since the moths covered the distance in about four days, the rate of travel must have been about 800 km per day, which would require following prevailing winds. Butterflies are known to be able to alight on the ocean surface and thus perhaps extend their endurance, although Johnson (op. cit.) doubts that this behaviour would have any resting effect. It is probably only adopted when the wind shifts to an unfavourable direction. The direction of migratory flights is governed by innate behaviour, not wind (Williams 1971), but there can be little doubt that winds blowing in the right direction must be utilized by long-distance migrators. Nevertheless, there are observations of butterflies flying at an angle to the wind or battling head winds (e.g., K. A. W. Williams 1968).

When insects fly directionally under their own power they are said to be under the "boundary layer", which will be higher for a large insect than for a small one under the same circumstances. Above this layer an insect can no longer maintain flight in any direction other than that of the wind. Butterflies usually migrate within their boundary layer, whilst moths migrate downwind above it (Taylor 1974). This is because at night atmospheric lift is minimal and air currents are generally oriented horizontally, with the result that for any given insect the boundary layer is higher in the day time than at night. Some insects, such as aphids and probably the bush fly, use daytime atmospheric lift to carry them to altitudes where they will be transported passively (using the wings for lift only) downwind.

It is evident that the specific factors bringing about migratory behaviour differ according to the species involved.

This is shown in part by the differences in the direction of flight and the food regime of migratory butterflies. For instance, *Anaphaeis java* and *Precis villida* fly north in August-November (spring) (K. A. W. Williams 1968), whilst *Cynthia kershawi* flies south (Smithers and Peters 1966). The first named species is an oligophagous feeder on Capparidaceae, whereas the latter two are polyphagous on Compositae and other plants. The skipper *Badamia exclamationis* (which flies south from Indonesia in summer and north in the autumn) is oligophagous on *Terminalia* (Combretaceae). The wanderer (*Danaus plexippus*) is oligophagous on *Asclepias*.

Breeding and feeding may occur at both ends of a migratory route, or dormancy may occur at one end of it (Section 5.4.3).

When sufficient data are available to analyse the factors involved, it may be found that migration in a fixed direction is a tactic enabling a species to maintain high population densities by adjusting to predictably varying, average fluctuations in food density over a wide geographical area. We should thus seek reasons in a temporal context, and not merely in the triggering cues provided by immediate circumstances. In Johnson's (1969) words:

> The need for species inhabiting ephemeral breeding places to continually change them may now be considered as the prime ecological function of migration among insects, and the view that in general a species needs to migrate in order to relieve the pressure of population in the habitat must be revised;. . . the food is usually going to disappear during the normal course of the season and migrants often begin to leave a habitat long before this decline becomes apparent; the migratory process is evidently triggered by the token stimuli that have proved their worth as survival mechanisms, and is not merely a current opportunistic behavioural reaction.

Flotsam transport or rafting is a subject that has not received detailed attention in the Australian region. It requires a positive effort to pick up flotsam out at sea and examine it for live animals. This has been done in the Caribbean region by Heatwole and Levins (1972), who point out that such transport can be frequent in marine areas fed by numerous rivers and streams from which flotsam issues after rainstorms.

One of the most important methods of movement of insects by sea is through transport in ocean-going vessels. Transport in modern ships is discussed in section 3.3, but it should be recalled that in the Pacific area this movement antedates the arrival of European man by a long time.

5.3 CAVES

Absence of sunlight, and therefore of producer organisms (other than chemosynthetic bacteria and tree roots), is an obvious characteristic of the dark zone of the cave biocoenosis, and is shared only with the abyssal zone of the sea and profundal zone of deep lakes (light, in the form of bioluminescence, is not necessarily absent, however). Such ecosystems are entirely dependent for their energy source on influx from other systems, and this influx tends to be largely in the form of detritus. The most important ecological consequences of this stem from the fact that such flow from other systems is irregular. In the case of caves, it fluctuates considerably over time, depending on the presence or absence of bats, which are often migratory (Hamilton-Smith 1967, 1968), the extent of runoff bringing in plant litter, the rise and fall of the water table, changes in the abundance of epigean vertebrates (affecting the carcass and dung supply), and long-term climatic changes. Physical parameters inside caves are relatively constant with regard to the diel cycle, but seasonal fluctuations in above-ground humidity are reflected in the cave environment, especially in the tropics (Hamilton-Smith 1971a). In some caves where there are no cues to epigean seasonal cycles, but where a troglobite needs to synchronize its feeding with them, it may evolve a "circannian" rythm (an endogenous annual rythm) (Poulson and White 1969).

The micro-environment which is offered by bat guano deposits is particularly variable. This fact is stressed by Harris (1971), who contrasts the fluctuations in both physical (temperature) and biotic (food energy) factors in guano heaps with the supposed stability of cave environments.

In the dark zone proper, fluctuations in the energy supply are unpredictable to cave residents through the absence of feed-back communication with adjacent ecosystems; under these circumstances it is difficult to evolve stabilizing mechanisms, particularly as population limits are nearly always set by the food supply. The few caves where population size is not food-limited are those where periodic flooding washes out a proportion of the residents; consequently the limiting factor again has a strongly destabilizing effect.

Under such conditions of instability it is surprising that any cavernicolous specialists can evolve at all, or avoid rapid extinction once evolved. In fact, in Australia there are very few troglobites. Only ten species were listed by Hamilton-Smith (1971b), although recent discoveries have perhaps doubled this number. This is far short of the more than 350 species of troglobites in the United States (Barr 1968), which has a comparable area (but many more caves). This difference may reflect an unusual instability of the Australian cave environment that causes rapid extinction of troglobites, but the most logical explanation is one put forward by Poulson and White (1969). They suggest that it is the instability of the epigean environment of North America (and other temperate areas) that traps animals in caves by causing extinction of their surface populations. The instability referred to is glaciation, and it is in glaciated areas that we find most troglobites. By this reasoning, most Australian troglobites should occur in Tasmania and the south-eastern region. At least as far as the Carabidae are concerned, the most strongly modified cavernicolous species do occur in Tasmania, the mainland ones being only recently evolved (Moore 1964).

Evidently, animals do not become adaptively specialized for existence in the dark zone of caves unless they are forced to do so by being no longer able to survive on the surface. Unless this occurs, caves are inhabited only by hygrophilous or aquatic animals generally adapted for a detritivorous or carnivorous existence in the surrounding area (the troglophiles, always well represented in cave faunas), and by those who use the cave only for daytime shelter and forage over the surrounding terrain, or in the air, at night (the trogloxenes). The latter, best represented by bats and raphidophorid crickets, are responsible for the major proportion of energy input into caves (Hamilton-Smith 1971c). In Northern Australia, the adults of a genus of aeshnid dragonflies, *Gynacantha,* have evolved a curious parallelism with bats in that their hawking time is crepuscular and they use the caves for daytime shelter (J. A. L. Watson, personal communication).

It is unlikely that trogloxenes could ever evolve into troglobites, because of their exclusive dependence on epigean food sources, and except for their very important role as energy transfer organisms, they can be discounted in discussions of the evolution of the cave fauna.

In Australia, the usual change in the epigean environment tending to restrict a troglophile to a cave is the onset of aridity. Initially, a species thus restricted is no different in appearance from an epigean species, even though it is not able to survive on the surface except to migrate from cave to cave (such species have been termed "second-level troglophiles" by Hamilton-Smith 1971c), but if they continue to survive in the cave they become subjected to selective forces which bring about highly predictable changes in their appearance and life history. These changes eventually lead to a disappearance of adaptations to light (eyes and pigment) and dispersal (wings). They also lead to rigorous measures conserving energy by lowering respiratory and metabolic rate and to genetic changes permitting survival at very low population densities. In beetles, they frequently lead to a shortening or disappearance of the larval stage (Poulson and White 1969; Britton 1970), but this is because the advantage in having a larva in the first place (the opportunity to adapt to two different environments) no longer exists, and it would be wasteful to adapt both larva and adult for a similar cave life. In any case, the scarcity and unpredictability of food supplies require that the insect be ready at all times to capture food, and in caves the adult is best adapted for this purpose. At the same time, low population densities require that a maximum number of conspecific encounters be potentially fruitful, which they would not be if larvae were involved.

The morphological and physiological changes invariably accompanying adaptation to obligate cavernicoly have usually been ascribed to a relaxation of selection for useless organs and systems, a sort of "degeneration through disuse" (Barr 1968; Poulson and White 1969), but it seems more likely that they are the result of active selection to conserve developmental energy, particularly as there must be times of extreme food scarcity in caves.

Since caves represent well-defined habitats which are different from surrounding areas, the insular analogy can be applied to the dynamics of their faunas (e.g., Culver 1970). The area of a single cave is usually small, but when dealing with a number of interconnected caves it is possible to note a distinct "area effect" — a positive correlation between area and numbers of resident species. Interconnectivity will reduce extinction rates by supporting higher population levels of a given species. Rates of immigration into caves are highest for small organisms able to move through interstitial spaces in the ground, particularly aquatic organisms.

The terrestrial cave biocoenosis derives its energy from three general sources: (1) faeces, carcasses, blood, and food scraps of bats and other trogloxenic animals, together with accidentals, using the cave as shelter; (2) dead vegetation washing in; and (3) tree roots. I don't know to what extent chemosynthetic bacteria are important as a source of energy. In aquatic cave environments, bacterial clays are a vital source of vitamins and antibiotics (Poulson and White 1969). Some cavernicoles feed on fungi growing on some of the sources listed above, but the fungi themselves cannot be considered a source of energy influx to the system. Of the three sources, the first is the most abundant.

To become a troglobite an organism must rely on the most constant type of food supply, not necessarily the most abundant. The first two sources listed above are subject to irregular and long-term fluctuations and therefore unsuitable for specialized feeding by troglobites. Hamilton-Smith (1968) and Barr (1968) agree that it is highly unlikely that guanophiles (coprophiles) could become troglobites because of the irregularity in the supply of faeces. Troglobites are nearly always predacious, reflecting the fact that although there is fluctuation in particular basic energy sources in caves, there is usually *some* source available at any given time and a constant influx of prey in the form of trogloxenes and accidentals. It follows that troglobite predators must be generalists.

Live tree roots may be frequent in shallow caves and are unusual among cave energy sources in that they represent primary production; they are therefore more reliable than detritus-based sources. They should on this account lead to a certain amount of troglobitism, and in fact this appears to have been the case. Some unpigmented Meenoplidae (Homoptera, Fulgoroidea) recently found in caves in South Western Australia (J. Lowry, personal communication) are perhaps the first known example of Australian root-feeding troglobites. Elsewhere cixiid fulgoroids occupy this niche.

Richards (1971), in an ecological study of the caves of the Nullarbor Plain, classified cavernicoles according to their food habits, usual location in the caves, and degree of adaptation to cave life. Only about 6 per cent of the species were troglobites (6 species, including only one insect, the cockroach *Trogloblatella nullarborensis*). All of these appear to be predators (an unusual habit for a cockroach). Altogether, 44 per cent of all species were predators, 49 per cent detritivores, and 7 per cent parasites. The most numerous category, in numbers of individuals, were coprophages and necrophages. About one quarter of the total number of species occurred in guano, but only 11 per cent were actually coprophagous. The rest of the guanophiles fed on fungi or were predatory, (e.g., carabids of the genus *Speotarus*). Fully one-quarter of the Nullarbor cave fauna is accidental, consisting of epigean species entering or falling into the caves. This indicates that there is a continuous flow of potential colonizers, and of prey, into the cave environment.

Hamilton-Smith (1967) makes the point that in an otherwise featureless area like the Nullarbor Plain, caves can exert a significant influence on the total biology of the region by providing shelter, nesting sites, and moist refuges for the epigean biota.

For cave waters to have been colonized, they would have to have been in direct connection with either the sea or with inland water bodies at some time. It is a notable feature of the Nullarbor caves that their waters, which are saline, are entirely devoid of animal life, evidently through absence of such a connection at any time in the past (Richards 1971).* Two of Australia's few troglobites (not insects) are tropical aquatic forms (Hamilton-Smith 1971a).

The presence of bioluminescent chironomids, *Arachnocampa* spp., in Tasmanian and New Zealand caves invites comparison with the marine abyssal zone, where bioluminescence has become general among the nekton. In theory, when one dark-zone dweller becomes luminescent, most of the others must follow or be placed at a disadvantage. The original blind forms should disappear and be replaced with new species possessing highly-developed eyes. That this has not generally occurred in caves indicates that the latter do not offer the necessary conditions of extreme long-term stability reigning in the marine abyssal zone.

Blind dytiscid beetles inhabiting underground waters (not cave waters) have recently been discovered in New Zealand. They are not yet known in Australia, but will undoubtedly be discovered when the technique for collecting them is applied (pumping underground water through a filter).

Some mosquitoes of the genus *Culiseta* breed exclusively in underground waters in the burrows of the land crayfish *Engaeus* spp. (Dobrotworsky 1965).

5.4 HIGH MOUNTAINS

The uplifting of air masses along mountain slopes produces

* Published accounts reporting a species of blind gudgeon in Nullabor caves are unfounded (C. J. M. Glover, personal communication).

adiabatic cooling and precipitation of moisture. Air on mountains in dry climates cools faster when rising than air in moist climates (MacArthur 1972). Mountain ranges, even if low, are always of interest to the biologist as conditions on them are different from those of the surrounding lowlands, producing something of an insular effect for the montane biota. Altitudinal zonation of the flora and fauna is nearly always perceptible. Space limitations preclude discussion of Australia's montane communities with the exception of the most extreme types — the alpine and aeolian zones, which occur above the snow gum (*Eucalyptus niphophila*) line in the Snowy Mountains and Victorian Alps. No other mountains in Australia are high enough to possess an alpine zone, and only two tropical mountains are high enough here to have true cloud forest or mossy forest (Bellenden Ker and Mt. Carbine, North Queensland), both unstudied. Where such forests occur in New Guinea, there is an extraordinary "epizoic symbiosis" involving weevils and many other organisms which live on them (see Gressitt and Sedlacek 1970).

5.4.1 THE ALPINE ENVIRONMENT

The special features of this environment are as follows:

(1) Extreme temperature differences between day and night, and between insolated and shaded surfaces during the day. Key and Day (1954) found that at 1,950 m on Mt Kosciusko the air temperature on a March day ranged from about $-1°$ to $12°$ C, whilst the difference in ground temperature between sunny and shady positions could be as high as $20°$ C, surface temperatures rising to about $33°$ C in the sun. On intermittently cloudy days the temperature in exposed situations rises and falls rapidly.

(2) Prolonged periods of cold — during winter, during the night, and during cloudy spells.

(3) Abundant moisture from atmospheric condensation or melting snow.

(4) A flora largely limited to herbs (*Poa-Celmisia* climax, with numerous brightly-flowering associates) (see Costin 1959) and lichens. As an energy source, this flora is probably

less important than the inflow described in the next paragraph.

(5) A large proportion of the energy entering alpine and especially aeolian communities is in the form of flying insects, pollen, and seeds carried by winds from lower altitudes (Edwards 1973). Mani (1968) described the abundance of this inflow, or "fallout", in the Himalayas, where it sustains the majority of the alpine scavengers and predators. If snowfields are present, the seeds, pollen, and flying insects are trapped in the snow and held in "cold storage" until the thaw. At that time, alpine insects crowd along the snow's edge and consume this detritus as it is released. The snowfields thus act like salt lakes (section 2.4.8), that is to say, as giant traps. Those items not consumed flow into the meltwater streams and return to the lowlands, sustaining stream organisms on the way.

Litter decomposition in an alpine herbfield on Mt Kosciusko at 1,950 m was investigated by Wood (1971). He found that decomposition of *Eucalyptus* leaves brought into the area was rapid, largely because of the activity of earthworms (which are exceptionally abundant at this altitude) and other large decomposers such as scarabs. Small decomposers (particularly Chironomidae) are also abundant but nematodes and predators of all sizes are relatively scarce. Wood believes that most decomposition occurs at the edges of melting snowfields during a short time in the spring, when moisture is abundant and ground-surface and meltwater temperatures rise as high as 18° C above the normal 0.5° C occurring under the snow itself. After the snow disappears, surface temperatures in the daytime settle down to a steady 1 to 2° C below air temperature in the shade. For about half the year, ground temperatures at this altitude lie between 0 and 2° C, and air temperatures are usually below freezing.

5.4.2 INSECT ADAPTATIONS TO ALPINE CONDITIONS

It should be clear from the foregoing statements that the most critical environmental factor in alpine zones is temperature fluctuation during the animals' active periods — not heat or cold in themselves, but the way they vary rapidly from place to place and from time to time. The prolonged cold of winter, and of the night, is much less significant, as it occurs during the animals' inactive periods.

There are three ways of meeting the problem of temperature fluctuations. One, described by Mani (1968) but not yet specifically studied under Australian conditions, is hypolithy (staying under stones). Obviously, the underside of stones and the shaded ground in general undergo less marked temperature fluctuations than the exposed ground. Animals showing this adaptation, which is by far the most important among alpine insects, display a marked cold stenothermy — they have a very narrow range of temperature tolerances with both upper and lower limits of the range occurring at low absolute values, i.e., near the freezing point; they are very sensitive to heat. Collembola, often abundant in alpine environments, are cold-stenothermic in that habitat. At lower altitudes in the subalpine zone where nocturnal insects can be active, they may also show cold stenothermy even when not hypolithic. For instance, the primitive cicada *Tettigarcta crinita,* which occurs at about 1,500 m on *Eucalyptus pauciflora,* is apparently very sensitive to warmth and will avoid it by staying on the shaded side of branches in the daytime (McKeown 1951).

The second way of dealing with alpine temperature fluctuations is by behavioural thermoregulation. Active insects whose food requirements oblige them to move about on exposed surfaces, regulate temperature by moving from sunny to shady positions, and vice versa, according to whether the body is cooler or warmer than the optimum temperature (the standard method of thermoregulation in active ectotherms). Such insects are, of course, always diurnal and often facilitate radiant heat absorption by being strongly melanic. Key and Day (1954) mention several Australian high-altitude grasshoppers which are black or nearly so. In the early morning, grasshoppers climb up on grass clumps or shrubs to catch the first rays of the sun. The normal active body temperature of such insects is of course much higher than in the first group, and there is a pronounced eurythermy. It can readily be seen that during the hottest part of the day melanic insects will be faced with the problem of getting too hot. Their movements at all times will be governed more by their thermoregulatory requirements than by their food requirements. A solution to this problem has been reached by the grasshopper *Kosciuscola tristis*, which is the most conspicuously abundant insect above 1,800 m on Mt. Kosciusko. This grasshopper is nearly black at temperatures below 15° C, above which it begins to turn blue or green (depending on the sex); it is a rather pale colour at temperatures above 25° C. (Fig. 31). This means that *K. tristis* is relatively independent of ambient temperatures and can spend more time orienting its movements to its food requirements. The colour changes in *K. tristis* result from pigment granule migrations in the epidermal cells and are endogenously temperature-controlled (Key and Day 1954). A similar mechanism of thermoregulatory colour change occurs in some non-alpine dragonflies (O'Farrell 1963, 1964).

The third way of dealing with the temperature problem is physiological thermoregulation (endothermy), as in homoiotherms. Bumblebees (*Bombus*) are capable of conserving metabolic heat, and some species can forage in temperatures just above freezing, yet maintain a thoracic body temperature of 32 to 33° C (Heinrich 1972). Bumblebees do not occur in Australia, and I do not know whether any native bees have evolved this adaptation. Partial endothermy is also known in moths (section 2.4.7 and Heinrich op. cit.).

The general question of alpine pollination has received some recent attention. Basically, the problem is that there are few pollinating species, and if alpine plants are to diversify they must share the same pollinators. This can be done by successive flowering of different plant species over a season, producing the continuous succession of blooms so typical of alpine regions. To counter the effect of the dominating flower phenomenon (section 1.4.3), simultaneously-blooming flower species may mimic one another (Macior 1971). The caloric reward must be higher than at lower altitudes to make up for the pollinator's greater energy expenditure at low temperatures (Heinrich and Raven 1972). Pollination is diurnal, and bees (except for *Bombus*, when present) are generally less important than lepidopterous and dipterous pollinators (Mani 1968). In Australia, satyrs (browns) of the genera *Oreixenica* and *Heteronympha* contain typical alpine species which feed on *Poa* grasses as larvae. The polyphagous papilionid *Graphium macleayanum*, although also widespread at lower altitudes, is a conspicuous element of the alpine fauna on Mt. Kosciusko (J. J. H. Szent-Ivany, personal communication). High-altitude orchids in southern Australia comprise the majority of those species which attract male ichneumon wasps (Jones 1972, and section 1.4.3), and one would expect plants to use other unusual insect pollinators at high altitudes.

Some other high-altitude adaptations among insects discussed by Mani (1968) are: (1) increasing monophagy among herbivores at higher elevations (due to ecosystem maturity?); (2) a predominance of predatory species because of the great influx of aerial jetsam (but this was not found in the litter fauna by Wood, see above); (3) fewer species in general, but these in greater abundance; and (4) a predominance of Collembola in early successional communities, but of Acarina in climax ones. I have no evidence as to whether these trends are to be seen in Australian high-altitude communities.

5.4.3 SUMMIT SEEKING IN LOWLAND INSECTS

In many parts of the world it is well known that adults of certain lowland insects migrate in large numbers over long distances in the autumn to high mountains, where they spend the winter in hibernation, with or without diapause. Certain coccinellid beetles are the best known for this behaviour.

In Australia, summit seeking appears to occur in summer, rather than winter, and has been recorded in cantharid beetles (Zeck 1920) — unrelated to coccinellids, but similarly predatory and unpalatable — and in the bogong moth (Fig. 12). These were observed to aggregate in the Blue

Mountains and the Australian Alps, respectively. Whether summit seeking occurs in summer or winter, the principle is the same — the season spent in montane hibernation or aestivation is the one during which the insect's food is scarce. Summit seeking appears to be one tactic for maintaining high adult population densities over unfavourable periods. The high mountains provide cooler temperatures that reduce metabolic activity and therefore energy needs. At the same time, they offer shelter which is unoccupied by resident populations and they possess few resident predators (that is to say, few predators able to concentrate in high numbers). Mobile predators on the other hand, especially birds, pose a constant threat to summit seekers but, apparently, one that does not cancel out the advantage of this behaviour. The concentrations of individuals offered by summit seekers during migration and aestivation provide a possible example of the predator satiation strategy, although the usual predictability of the movements would rob this strategy of much of its effectiveness.

The bogong moth (*Agrotis infusa*) is found along the 460 to 760 mm isohyets on the western slopes of the Great Dividing Range in New South Wales. It feeds on winter annual forbs (Common 1954). During spring, when most of these plants are dying back, the adult moth undergoes an extraordinary southward migration carrying it hundreds of kilometres to the Australian Alps, where it aestivates in very large numbers in granite caves above 1,500 m (Fig. 12). In the late summer and autumn it returns again to its feeding grounds and lays eggs. Two species of mermithid nematode parasites have adjusted to the bogong moth's habit of returning to the same caves every year. The worms emerge from the moths and complete their development in the caves during the insects' absence, reinfesting the latter with larvae when they return in the spring. This adaptation by the nematodes emphasizes the predictability of the moth's movements and shows that the migratory habit has been in existence in its present form for a very long time.

Summit seeking should not be confused with "hill

topping", which is a behavioural device seen in butterflies, similar to the "rendezvous-behaviour" of many other insects and serving to promote reproductive isolation (Zwolfer, 1974). In Northern Australia aggregations of danaine butterflies are common during the winter dry season (G. B. Monteith, personal communication), as in other tropical areas of the world. In this case such aggregations probably serve a defensive purpose.

Notes to Text

Allen, P. G. 1971. *Sitona humeralis* Steph. (Coleoptera, Curculionidae) in South Australia. Dept. Agric., S.A., Agron. Branch Rep. 35:1–13.

Anderson, S. 1974. Patterns of faunal evolution. *Q. Rev. Biol.* 49: 311–32.

Andrewartha, H. G. and Birch, L. C. 1954. *The Distribution and Abundance of Animals.* Chicago: University of Chicago Press.

Ayala, F. J. 1971. Competition between species: frequency dependence. *Science, N.Y.* 171, 820–4.

Ayala, F. J. and Campbell, C. A. 1974. Frequency-dependent selection. *A. Rev. Ecol. Syst.* 5:115–38.

Bagnall, R. S. 1929. On a group of minute Australian Thysanoptera (Tubulifera) and their association with the so-called leaf glands on *Acacia. Trans. R. ent. Soc. Lond.* 77:171–6.

Baker, H. G. and Hurd, P. D. 1968. Intrafloral ecology. *A. Rev. Ent.* 13:385–414.

Barr, T. C. Jr 1968. Cave ecology and the evolution of troglobites. *Evol. Biol.* 2:35--102.

Bateman, M. A. 1972. The ecology of fruit flies. *A. Rev. Ent.* 17: 493–518.

Bayly, I. A. E. 1970. Further studies on some saline lakes of southeastern Australia. *Aust. J. mar. Freshwat. Res.* 21:117–29.

Bayly, I. A. E. and Williams, W. D. 1966. Chemical and biological studies on some saline lakes of south-east Australia. *Aust. J. mar. Freshwat. Res.* 17:177–228.

Beale, I. F. 1973. Tree density effects on yields of herbage and tree components in south west Queensland mulga (*Acacia aneura* F. Muell.) scrub. *Tropical Grasslands* 7:135–42.

Berg, R. Y. 1975. Myrmecochorous plants in Australia and their dispersal by ants. *Aust. J. Bot.* 23:475–508.

Birch, L. C. 1965. Evolutionary opportunity for insects and mammals in Australia. In Baker, H. G. and Stebbins, G. L., eds. *The Genetics of Colonizing Species.* New York and London: Academic Press.

Birch, L. C., Dobzhansky, T., Elliott, P. O., and Lewontin, R. C. 1963.

Relative fitness of geographical races of *Drosophila serrata* (Malloch). *Evolution* 17:72–83.

Blackith, R. E. and Blackith, R. M. 1966. The food of morabine grasshoppers. *Aust. J. Zool.* 14:877–94.

Blackith, R. E. and Blackith, R. M. 1969. Observations on the biology of some morabine grasshoppers. *Aust. J. Zool.* 17:1–12.

Blocker, H. D. 1975. The impact of invertebrates as herbivores on arid and semi-arid rangeland. *J. Range Management* (in press).

Bodenheimer, F. S. 1951. *Insects as Human Food.* The Hague: W. Junk.

Bodenheimer, F. S. 1954. Physiology and ecology of desert animals. In Cloudsley-Thompson, J. L., ed. *Biology of Deserts.* London: Institute of Biology.

Bornemissza, G. F. 1957. An analysis of arthropod succession in carrion and the effect of its decomposition on the soil fauna. *Aust. J. Zool.* 5:1–12.

Bornemissza, G. F. 1960. Could dung-eating insects improve our pastures? *J. Aust. Inst. agric. Sci.* 26:5–6.

Bornemissza, G. F. 1971a. Mycetophagous breeding in the Australian dung beetle, *Onthophagus dunningi. Pedobiologia* 11:133–42.

Bornemissza, G. F. 1971b. A new variant of the paracopric nesting type in the Australian dung beetle, *Onthophagus compositus. Pedobiologia* 11:1–10.

Bornemissza, G. F. and Williams, C. H. 1970. An effect of dung beetle activity on plant yield. *Pedobiologia* 10:1–17.

Bourlière, F. and Hadley, M. 1970. The ecology of tropical savannas. *A. Rev. Syst. Ecol.* 1:125–52.

Brereton, J. LeG. 1957. Defoliation in rain forest. *Aust. J. Sci.* 19: 204–5.

Brereton, J. LeG. 1962. Evolved regulatory mechanisms of population control. In *The Evolution of Living Organisms.* Symposium R. Soc. Victoria, 81–93.

Brereton, J. LeG., Richards, B. N., and Williams, J. B. 1969. Australian ecosystems and their origin. In Webb, L. J., Whitelock, D. and Brereton, J. LeG., eds. *The Last of Lands.* Milton, Qld: Jacaranda Press.

Brian, M. V. 1965. *Social Insect Populations.* London and New York: Academic Press.

Britton, E. B. 1966. On the larva of *Sphaerius* and the systematic position of the Sphaeriidae (Coleoptera). *Aust. J. Zool.* 14: 1193–8.

Britton, E. B. 1969. *Aphanosperma,* a new genus of Cerambycidae (Coleoptera) from woody fruits of *Hakea* spp. in Australia. *J. Aust. ent. Soc.* 8:33–6.

Britton, E. B. 1970. Coleoptera (Beetles). In *The Insects of Australia.* Melbourne: CSIRO and Melbourne University Press.

Britton, E. B. 1971. A new intertidal beetle (Coleoptera: Limnichiidae) from the Great Barrier Reef. *J. Ent.* (B) 40:83–91.

Brown, W. L., Jr 1960. Ants, acacias, and browsing mammals. *Ecology* 41:587–92.

Brown, W. L., Jr. and Taylor, R. W. 1970. Superfamily Formicoidea. In *The Insects of Australia*. Melbourne: CSIRO and Melbourne University Press.

Browning, T. O. 1954. Observations on the ecology of the Australian field cricket, *Gryllulus commodus* Walker, in the field. *Aust. J. Zool.* 2:205–22.

Bush, G. L. 1974. The mechanism of sympatric host race formation in the true fruit flies (Tephritidae). In White, M. J. D., ed. *Genetic Mechanisms of Speciation in Insects*. Sydney: Australia and New Zealand Book Co.

Buxton, P. A. 1924. Heat, moisture, and animal life in deserts. *Proc. R. Soc. Lond.* 1924:123–31.

Calaby, J. H. and Key, K. H. L. 1973. Rediscovery of the spectacular Australian grasshopper *Petasida ephippigera* White (Orthoptera, Pyrgomorphidae). *J. Aust. ent. Soc.* 12:161–4.

Carlquist, S. 1969. Studies in Stylidiaceae: new taxa, field observations, evolutionary tendencies. *Aliso* 7, 13–64.

Carlquist, S. 1974. *Island Biology*. New York and London: Columbia Univ. Press.

Carne, P. B. 1956. An ecological study of the pasture scarab *Aphodius howitti* Hope. *Aust. J. Zool.* 4:259–314.

Carne, P. B. 1962. The characteristics and behaviour of the sawfly *Perga affinis affinis* (Hymenoptera). *Aust. J. Zool.* 10:1–34.

Carne, P. B. 1966a. Ecological characteristics of the eucalypt-defoliating chrysomelid *Paropsis atomaria* Ol. *Aust. J. Zool.* 14:647–72.

Carne, P. B. 1966b. Primitive forms of social behaviour, and their significance in the ecology of gregarious insects. *Proc. ecol. Soc. Aust.* 1:75–8.

Carne, P. B. 1969. On the population dynamics of the eucalypt-defoliating sawfly *Perga affinis affinis* Kirby (Hymenoptera). *Aust. J. Zool.* 17:113–41.

Carne, P. B., Greaves, R. T. G., and McInnes, R. S. 1974. Insect damage to plantation-grown eucalypts in north coastal New South Wales with particular reference to Christmas beetles (Coleoptera: Scarabaeidae). *J. Aust. Ent. Soc.* 13:189–206.

Carroll, C. R. and Janzen, D. H. 1973. Ecology of foraging by ants. *A. Rev. Ecol. Syst.* 4:231–57.

Carson, H. L. 1970. Chromosome tracers of the origin of species. *Science, N.Y.* 168:1414–18.

Casimir, M. 1962. History of outbreaks of the Australian plague locust, *Chortoicetes terminifera* (Walk.), between 1933 and 1959, and analysis of the influence of rainfall on these outbreaks. *Aust. J. agric. Res.* 13:674–700.

Cavill, G. W. K. and Hinterberger, H. 1960. The chemistry of ants, IV. Terpenoid constituents of some *Dolichoderus* and *Iridomyrmex* species. *Aust. J. Chem.* 13:514–19.

Chadwick, C. E. 1962. Some insects and terrestrial arthropods from Heron Island, Queensland. *Proc. Linn. Soc. N.S.W.* 87: 196–9.

Chadwick, C. E. and Nikitin, M. I. 1968. Some insects and other invertebrates intercepted in quarantine in New South Wales, pt 1. Coleoptera. *J. ent. Soc. Aust.* (N.S.W.) 5:35–56.

Chaffer, N. 1930. The Cicada Bird (*Edoliisoma tenuirostre*). *Aust. Zool.* 6:204.

Charley, J. L. and Cowling, S. W. 1968. Changes in soil nutrient status resulting from overgrazing and their consequences in plant communities of semi-arid areas. *Proc. ecol. Soc. Aust.* 3:28–38.

Cheng, L. and Lewin, R. A. 1974. Fluidisation as a feeding mechanism by beach flies. *Nature, Lond.* 250:167–8.

China, W. E. 1953. Two new species of the genus *Cyrtopeltis* (Hemiptera) associated with sundews in Western Australia. *West. Aust. Nat.* 4:1–8.

China, W. E. and Carvalho, J. C. M. 1951. A new ant-like mirid from Western Australia (Hemiptera, Miridae). *Ann. Mag. nat. Hist.* ser. 12, 4:221–5.

Chisholm, A. H. 1952. Bird-insect nesting associations in Australia. *Ibis* 94:395–405.

Clark, D. P. 1970. The plague dynamics of the Australian plague locust, *Chortoicetes terminifera* (Walk.). *Proc. Int. Study. Conf. Current and Fut. Probs. of Acridology*, London, pp. 275–87.

Clark, D. P. and Davies, R. A. H. 1972. Migration and plague dynamics of Australian plague locust. *Rep. Commonw. scient. ind. Res. Org. Aust., Div. Ent.* 1971–2:108–10.

Clark, L. R. 1950. On the abundance of the Australian plague locust *Chortoicetes terminifera* (Walker) in relation to the presence of trees. *Aust. J. agr. Res.* 1:64–75.

Clark, L. R. 1962. The general biology of *Cardiaspina albitextura* (Psyllidae) and its abundance in relation to weather and parasitism. *Aust. J. Zool.* 10:537–81.

Clark, L. R., Geier, P. W., Hughes, R. D. and Morris, R. F. 1967. *The Ecology of Insect Populations in Theory and Practice.* London: Methuen & Co., Ltd.

Clarke, B. 1962. Balanced polymorphism and the diversity of sympatric species. *Syst. Ass. Publ.* 4, *Taxonomy and Geography*, 47–70.

Cleland, J. B. 1934—5. *Toadstools; mushrooms and other larger fungi of South Australia. I, II.* Handbooks of the Flora and Fauna of South Australia. Adelaide: Government Printer.

Cleland, J. B. 1965. The gland on *Acacia* phyllodes and ants. *S. Aust. Nat.* 39:53.

Cloudsley-Thompson, J. L. 1964. Terrestrial animals in dry heat. In Dill, D. B., Adolph, E. F. and Wilber, C. G., eds. *Handbook of Physiology*, sec. 4: Adaptation to the Environment. Washington: Am. Phys. Soc.

Common, I. F. B. 1954. A study of the ecology of the adult bogong moth, *Agrotis infusa* (Boisd.) (Lepidoptera: Noctuidae), with special reference to its behaviour during migration and aestivation. *Aust. J. Zool.* 2:223—63.

Common, I. F. B. 1970. Lepidoptera (Moths and Butterflies). In *The Insects of Australia*. Melbourne: CSIRO and Melbourne University Press.

Common, I. F. B. and Waterhouse, D. F. 1972. *Butterflies of Australia.* Sydney: Angus and Robertson.

Coppinger, R. P. 1970. The effect of experience and novelty on avian feeding behavior with reference to the evolution of warning coloration in butterflies, II. Reaction of naive birds to novel insects. *Am. Nat.* 104:323—35.

Corbet, P. S. 1962. *A Biology of Dragonflies.* London: H. F. and G. Witherby, Ltd.

Costin, A. B. 1959. Vegetation of high mountains in Australia in relation to land use. In Keats, A., Crocker, R. L. and Christian, C. S. eds. *Biogeography and Ecology in Australia.* The Hague: W. Junk.

Craddock, E. M. 1974. Chromosomal evolution and speciation in *Didymuria*. In White, M. J. D. ed. *Genetic Mechanisms of Speciation in Insects.* Brookvale, N.S.W.: Australia and New Zealand Book Co.

Cribb, J. W. 1969. Pollination, with special reference to Queensland plants. *Qd. Nat.* 19:70—5.

Crowson, R. A. 1973. Further observations on Phloeostichidae and Cavognathidae, with definitions of new genera from Australia and New Zealand, *Coleopts. Bull.* 27:54—62.

Crowson, R. A. and Sen Gupta, T. 1966. A new family of cucujoid beetles, based on six Australian and one New Zealand genera. *Ann. Mag. nat. Hist.* ser. 13, 9:61—85.

Culver, D. C. 1970. Analysis of simple cave communities. I. Caves as islands. *Evolution, Lancaster, Pa.* 24:463—74.

Currie, G. A. 1937. Galls on *Eucalyptus* trees. *Proc. Linn. Soc. N.S.W.* 62:147—74.

Darlington, P. J., Jr. 1943. Carabidae of mountains and islands: data on the evolution of isolated faunas, and on the atrophy of wings. *Ecol. Monogr.* 13:37–61.

Davidson, R. L. and Roberts, R. J. 1968. Species differences in scarab-pasture relationships. *Bull. ent. Res.* 58:315–24.

Davies, S. J. J. F. 1973. Environmental variables and the biology of native Australian animals in the mulga lands. *Tropical Grasslands* 7:127–34.

Dethier, V. G. 1970. Chemical interactions between plants and insects. In Sondheimer, E. and Simeone, J. B. eds. *Chemical Ecology.* New York and London: Academic Press.

Dobrotworsky, N. V. 1965. *The Mosquitoes of Victoria.* Melbourne: Melbourne University Press.

Dobzhansky, T. 1966. Are naturalists old-fashioned? *Am. Nat.* 100: 541–50.

Dodson, C. H., Dressler, R. L., Hills, H. G., Adams, R. M. and Williams, N. H. 1969. Biologically active compounds in orchid fragrances. *Science* N.Y. 164:1243–9.

Doherty, R. L. 1972. Arboviruses of Australia. *Aust. vet. J.* 48:172–80.

Douglas, A. M. and McKenna, L. N. 1970. Observations on the bull-dog ant, *Myrmecia vindex. West. Aust. Nat.* 11:125–9.

Downey, J. C. 1966. Sound production in pupae of Lycaenidae. *J. Lepid. Soc.* 20:129–55.

Drake, D. W. 1974. Fungal and insect attack of seeds in unopened *Eucalyptus* capsules. *Search* 5:444.

Duffy, E. A. J. 1963. *A Monograph of the Immature Stages of Austral-asian Timber Beetles (Cerambycidae).* London: British Museum (Nat. His.).

Dunning, D. C. 1967. Warning sounds of moths. *Z. Tierpsychol.* 25: 129–38.

Dunning, D. C. and Roeder, K. D. 1965. Moth sounds and the insect-catching behavior of bats. *Science, N. Y.* 147:173–4.

Edgar, J. A., Culvenor, C. C. J. and Pliske, T. E. 1974. Coevolution of danaid butterflies with their host plants. *Nature, Lond.* 250:646–8.

Edney, E. B. 1974. Desert arthropods. In Brown, G. V., Jr. ed. *Desert Biology,* Vol. II. New York and London: Academic Press.

Edwards, C. A., Reichle, D. E. and Crossley, D. A., Jr. 1970. The role of soil invertebrates in turnover of organic matter and nutrients. In Reichle, D. E., ed. *Analysis of Temperate Forest Ecosystems.* London: Chapman and Hall, Ltd.

Edwards, J. S. 1973. Insect fallout on snow in the Snowy Mountains, New South Wales. *Aust. ent. Mag.* 1:57–9.

Ehrlich, P. R. and Raven, P. H. 1964. Butterflies and plants: a study in coevolution. *Evolution, Lancaster, Pa.* 18:586–608.

Ehrlich, P. R. and Raven, P. H. 1969. Differentiation of populations. *Science, N. Y.* 165:1228–32.

Eickwort, K. R. 1973. Cannibalism and kin selection in *Labidomera clavicollis* (Coleoptera: Chrysomelidae). *Am. Nat.* 107: 452–3.

Eisner, T. 1970. Chemical defense against predation in arthopods. In Sondheimer, E. and Simeone, J. B., eds. *Chemical Ecology.* New York and London: Academic Press.

Eisner, T., Aneshansley, D., Eisner, M., Rutowski, R., Chong, B. and Meinwald, J. 1974. Chemical defense and sound production in Australian tenebrionid beetles *(Adelium* sp.). *Psyche* 81:189–208.

Elton, C. S. 1973. The structure of invertebrate populations inside neotropical rain forest. *J. Anim. Ecol.* 42:55–104.

Engelmann, M. E. 1966. Energetics, terrestrial field studies, and animal productivity. *Adv. ecol. Res.* 3:73–115.

Entwistle, P. F. 1972. *Pests of Cocoa.* London: Longman.

Erickson, R. 1951. *Orchids of the West.* Perth: Paterson Brokensha.

Erickson, R. 1958. *Triggerplants.* Perth: Paterson Brokensha.

Euw, J. v., Fishelson, L., Parsons, J. A., Reichstein, T. and Rothschild, M. 1968. Cardenolides (heart poisons) in a grasshopper feeding on milkweeds. *Nature, Lond.* 214:35–6.

Evans, H. E. 1972. Revision of the Australian and New Guinea species of *Epipompilus* (Hymenoptera, Pompilidae). *Pac. Ins.* 14:101–31.

Evans, H. E. and Matthews, R. W. 1970. Notes on the nests and prey of Australian wasps of the genus *Cerceris* (Hymenoptera: Sphecidae). *J. Aust. ent. Soc.* 9:153–6.

Evans, J. W. 1959. The zoogeography of some Australian insects. In Keast, A., Crocker, R. L. and Christian, C. S., eds. *Biogeography and Ecology in Australia.* The Hague: W. Junk.

Evans, W. G. 1966. Perception of infra-red radiation from forest fires by *Melanophila acuminata* De Geer (Buprestidae, Coleoptera). *Ecology* 47:1061–5.

Ferrar, P. and Watson, J. A. L. 1970. Termites associated with dung in Australia. *J. Aust. ent. Soc.* 9:100–2.

Finnemore, H. and Gledhill, W. C. 1928. Poison plants: the presence of cyanogenic glucosides in certain species of *Acacia. J. Coun. scient. ind. Res. Aust.* 1:254.

Fletcher, B. S. 1973. Observations on a movement of insects at Heron Island, Queensland. *J. Aust. ent. Soc.* 12:157–60.

Florence, R. G. 1969. The application of ecology to forest management with particular reference to eucalypt forests. *Proc. ecol. Soc. Aust.* 4:82–100.

Francke-Grosman, H. 1963. Some new aspects in forest entomology. *A. Rev. Ent.* 8:415–38.

Froggatt, W. W. 1892. Gall-making buprestids. *Proc. Linn. Soc. N.S.W.* 7:323–6.

Froggatt, W. W. 1903a. Cicadas ("locusts") and their habits. *Agric. Gaz. N.S.W. Misc. Publ.* 643:1–15.

Froggatt, W. W. 1903b. Insects used as food by the Australian natives. *Sci. Man* 6:11–3.

Froggatt, W. W. 1910. Insects which damage salt bush. *Agric. Gaz. N.S.W. Misc. Publ.* 1, 331:465–70.

Froggatt, W. W. 1913. Cicadas as pests. *Agric. Gaz. N.S.W., Misc. Publ.* 1625:341–4.

Froggatt, W. W. 1921. A descriptive catalogue of the scale insects ("Coccidae") of Australia, part II. *Sci. Bull. Dept. Agric. N.S.W.* 18:1–159.

Froggatt, W. W. 1923. *Forest Insects of Australia.* Sydney: Forestry Commissioner, N.S.W.

Fuller, M. E. 1934. The insect inhabitants of carrion, a study in animal ecology. *Bull. Commonw. scient. ind. Res.* No. 82.

Ghiradella, H. D., Aneshansley, D., Eisner, T., Silberglied, R. and Hinton, H. E. 1972. Ultraviolet reflection of a male butterfly: interference color caused by thin-layer elaboration of wing scales. *Science, N.Y.* 178:1214–17.

Gibson, D. O. 1974. Batesian mimicry without distastefulness? *Nature, Lond.* 250:77–9.

Gillard, P. 1967. Coprophagous beetles in pasture ecosystems. *J. Aust. Inst. agric. Sci.* 33:30–4.

Graham, K. 1967. Fungal-insect mutualism in trees and timber. *A. Rev. Ent.* 12:105–26.

Gray, B. 1971a. Notes on the biology of the ant species *Myrmecia dispar* (Clark) (Hymenoptera: Formicidae). *Ins. Soc.* 18: 71–80.

Gray, B. 1971b. Notes on the field behaviour of two ant species, *Myrmecia desertorum* Wheeler and *Myrmecia dispar* (Clark) (Hymenoptera: Formicidae). *Ins. Soc.* 18:81–94.

Gray, B. 1972. Economic tropical forest entomology. *A. Rev. Ent.* 17: 313–54.

Greaves, T. 1962. Studies of foraging galleries and the invasion of living trees by *Coptotermes acinaciformis* and *C. brunneus* (Isoptera). *Aust. J. Zool.* 10:630–51.

Greaves, T. and Hughes, R. D. 1974. The population biology of the meat ant. *J. Aust. ent. Soc.* 13:329–51.

Greenham, P. M. 1972. The effects of the variability of cattle dung on the multiplication of the bushfly (*Musca vetustissima* Walker). *J. Anim. Ecol.* 41:153–65.

Greenham, P. M. and Hughes, R. D. 1971. Investigation of a morphometric cline in bushfly populations from north to south in Australia. *J. Aust. ent. Soc.* 10:261–4.

Greenslade, P. J. M. 1964. Pitfall trapping as a method for studying populations of Carabidae (Coleoptera). *J. Anim. Ecol.* 33: 301–10.

Greenslade, P. J. M. 1970. Observations on the inland variety (v. *viridiaeneus* Niehmeyer) of the meat ant *Iridomyrmex purpureus* (Frederick Smith) (Hymenoptera: Formicidae). *J. Aust. ent. Soc.* 9:227–31.

Greenslade, P. J. M. 1972. Evolution in the staphylinid genus *Priochirus* (Coleoptera). *Evolution, Lancaster, Pa.* 26:203–20.

Greenslade, P. J. M. 1973. Ants of Oraparinna National Park. *Nature Conservation Society of South Australia Survey Report*, September 1971, pp. 40–9.

Greenslade, P. J. M. and Greenslade, P. 1973. Epigaeic Collembola and their activity in a semi-arid locality in southern Australia during summer. *Pedobiologia* 13:227–35.

Gressitt, J. L. 1961. Problems in the zoogeography of Pacific and Antarctic insects. *Pac. Ins. Mon.* 2:1–94.

Gressitt, J. L., Coatsworth, J. and Yoshimoto, C. M. 1962. Air-borne insects trapped on "Monsoon Expedition". *Pac. Ins.* 4: 319–23.

Gressitt, J. L. and Sedlacek, J. 1970. Papuan weevil genus *Gymnopholus*. Second supplement with studies on epizoic symbiosis. *Pac. Ins.* 12:753–62.

Gross, G. F. 1952. Desert insects. *S. Aust. Nat.* 27:21–5.

Gross, G. F. 1954. The insect communities of the Brompton Pugholes in relation to those of some nearby climax and disclimax areas. University of Adelaide, unpublished thesis.

Hadley, N. F. 1970. Micrometeorology and energy exchange in two desert arthropods. *Ecology* 51:434–44.

Hadlington, P. and Gardner, M. J. 1959. *Diadoxus erythrurus* (White) (Coleoptera – Buprestidae) attack on fire-damaged *Callitris* spp. *Proc. Linn. Soc. N.S.W.* 84:325–31.

Hale, H. M. 1928. Migrating water beetles. *S. Aust. Nat.* 9:55.

Hall, W. G. 1967. Collembola. In Birges, A. and Raw, F. eds. *Soil Biology.* London and New York: Academic Press.

Hamilton, A. G. 1904. Notes on the West Australian pitcher-plant (*Cephalotus follicularis*, Labill.). *Proc. Linn. Soc. N.S.W.* 39:36–53.

Hamilton-Smith, E. 1967. Fauna of the Nullarbor Caves. In Dunkley, J. R. and Wigley, T. M. L., eds. *Caves of the Nullarbor.* University of Sydney.

Hamilton-Smith, E. 1968. The insect fauna of Mt. Widderin Cave, Chipton, Vic. *Vic. Nat.* 85:194–6.

Hamilton-Smith, E. 1971a. Preliminary notes on the cavernicolous invertebrate fauna of the Mt. Etna Caves area. In *Mt. Etna Caves. Univ. Qd. Spel. Soc:* 65–71.

Hamilton-Smith, E. 1971b. Some aspects of the Australian cavernicolous fauna. *Proc. 8th Natn. Conf. Aust. spel. Fed.* 93–100.

Hamilton-Smith, E. 1971c. The classification of cavernicoles. *Natn. spel. Soc. Bull.* No. 33:63–6.

Harper, J. L. 1969. The role of predation in vegetational diversity. In *Diversity and stability in Ecological Systems.* Brookhaven Symposia in Biology No. 22, Brookhaven National Laboratories.

Harris, J. A. 1971. Simulation of a cave microcosm: a trip in eco-mathematical reality. *Proc. ecol. Soc. Austr.* 6:116–34.

Harris, J. R. 1946. The vegetable caterpillar, *Cordyceps gunnii. S. Aust. Nat.* 23:2–6.

Hassell, M. P. and May, R. 1973. Stability in insect host-parasite models. *J. Anim. Ecol.* 42:693–726.

Heather, H. W. 1970. The exotic drywood termite *Cryptotermes brevis* (Walker) (Isoptera: Kalotermitidae) and endemic Australian drywood termites in Queensland. *J. Aust. ent. Soc.* 10: 134–41.

Heatwole, H. 1971. Marine-dependent terrestrial biotic communities on some cays in the Coral Sea. *Ecology* 52:363–6.

Heatwole, H., Davis, D. M., and Wenner, A. M. 1964. Detection of mates and hosts by parasitic insects of the genus *Megarhyssa* (Hymenoptera: Ichneumonidae). *Am. Midl. Nat.* 71:374–81.

Heatwole, H. and Levins, R. 1972. Biogeography of the Puerto Rican Bank: flotsam transport of terrestrial animals. *Ecology* 53:112–17.

Heinrich, B. 1972. Temperature regulation in the bumblebee *Bombus vagans*: a field study. *Science, N.Y.* 175:185–7.

Heinrich, B. and Raven, P. H. 1972. Energetics and pollination ecology. *Science, N.Y.* 176:597–602.

Hely, P. C. 1958. The food plants of the chequered swallowtail, *Papilio demoleus sthenelus* Macleay, 1826. (Lepidoptera: Papilionidae). *Proc. R. Zool. Soc. N.S.W.* 1956–7, 63.

Hering, E. M. 1951. *Biology of the Leaf Miners.* The Hague: W. Junk.

Hinton, H. E. 1951. Myrmecophilous Lycaenidae and other Lepidoptera – a summary. *Proc. S. Lond. ent. nat. Hist. Soc.* 1949–50:111–75.

Hinton, H. E. 1953. Some adaptations of insects to environments which are alternately dry and flooded, with some notes on the habits of Stratiomyidae. *Trans. Soc. Br. Ent.* 11:209–27.

Hinton, H. E. 1961. How some insects, especially the egg stages, avoid drowning when it rains. *Proc. S. Lond. ent. nat. Hist. Soc.* for 1960:138–54.

Hinton, H. E. 1973. Some recent work on the colours of insects and their likely significance. *Proc. Brit. Ent. Nat. Hist. Soc.* 6:43–54.

Hocking, B. 1970. Insect associations with the swollen thorn acacias. *Trans. R. ent. Soc. Lond.* 122:211–55.

Hodgkin, E. P. and Watson, J. A. L. 1958. Breeding of dragonflies in temporary waters. *Nature, Lond.* 181:1015–16.

Hogan, T. W. 1965. The winter mortality of eggs of *Chortoicetes terminifera* (Walk.) (Orthoptera; Acrididae) during the outbreak of 1955. *Aust. J. Zool.* 13:47–52.

Hook, R. I. van, Jr. 1971. Energy and nutrient dynamics of spider and orthopteran populations in a grassland ecosystem. *Ecol. Monogr.* 41:1–26.

Hotchkiss, A. T. 1958. Pollen and pollination in the Eupomatiaceae. *Proc. Linn. Soc. N.S.W.* 83:86–91.

Hughes, R. D. 1970a. The seasonal distribution of the bushfly (*Musca vetustissima* Walker) in south-east Australia. *J. anim. Ecol.* 39:691–706.

Hughes, R. D. 1970b. The bushfly. *Aust. nat. Hist.* 1970:331–4.

Hughes, R. D., Greenham, P. M., Tyndale-Biscoe, M., and Walker, J. M. 1972. A synopsis of observations on the biology of the Australian bushfly (*Musca vetustissima* Walker). *J. Aust. ent. Soc.* 11:311–31.

Hughes, R. D. and Nicholas, W. L. 1974. The spring migration of the bushfly (*Musca vetustissima* Walk.): evidence of displacement provided by natural population markers including parasitism. *J. Anim. Ecol.* 43:411–28.

Hughes, R. D. and Walker, J. W. 1970. The role of food in the population dynamics of the Australian bushfly. In Watson, A., ed. *Animal Populations in Relation to their Food Resources.* Oxford and Edinburgh: Blackwell Sci. Publs.

Hurlbert, S. H. 1971. The nonconcept of species diversity: a critique and alternative parameters. *Ecology* 52:577–86.

Hurlbert, S. H., Zedler, J. and Fairbanks, D., 1972. Ecosystem alteration by mosquitofish (*Gambusia affinis*) predation. *Science, N.Y.* 175:639–41.

Hutchinson, G. E. 1959. Homage to Santa Rosalia or, Why are there so many kinds of animals? *Am. Nat.* 93:145–59.

Hynes, H. B. N. 1970. The ecology of stream insects. *A. Rev. Ent.* 15:25–42.

Jackson, E. A. 1957. Soil features in arid regions with particular reference to Australia. *J. Aust. Inst. agr. Sci.* 25:196–208.

Janzen, D. H. 1966. Coevolution of mutualism between ants and acacias in Central America. *Evolution, Lancaster, Pa.* 20:249–75.

Janzen, D. H. 1970. Herbivores and the number of tree species in tropical forests. *Am. Nat.* 104:501–28.

Janzen, D. H. 1971a. Seed predation by animals. *A. Rev. Ecol. Syst.* 2:465–92

Janzen, D. H. 1971b. Euglossine bees as long-distance pollinators of tropical plants. *Science, N.Y.* 171:203—5.

Janzen, D. H. 1972. Interfield and interplant spacing in tropical insect control. *Proc. Ann. Tall Timbers Conf. on Ecol. Anim. Control by Habitat Management,* Feb. 24—5, 1972, 1—6.

Janzen, D. H. 1973a. Embryonic field of ecology. *Science, N.Y.* 182: 1125—6.

Janzen, D. H. 1973b. Community structure of secondary compounds in plants. *Pure and Appl. Chem.* 34:529—38.

Janzen, D. H. 1973c. Sweep samples of tropical foliage insects: effects of seasons, vegetation types, elevation, time of day, and insularity. *Ecology* 54:687—708.

Janzen, D. H. 1974. Tropical blackwater rivers, animals, and mast fruiting by the Dipterocarpaceae. *Biotropica* 6:69—103.

Jenkins, C. F. H. 1945. Entomological problems of the Ord River irrigation area. *J. Agric. West. Aust.* ser. 2, 22:131—45.

Johnson, C. G. 1969. *Migration and Dispersal of Insects by Flight.* London: Methuen and Co. Ltd.

Jones, D. L. 1970. The pollination of *Corybas diemenicus* H. M. R. Rupp and W. H. Nicholls ex H. M. R. Rupp. *Vict. Nat.* 87:372—4.

Jones, D. L. 1972. The pollination of *Prasophyllum alpinum* R. Br. *Vic. Nat.* 89:260—3.

Jones, D. A., Parsons, J. and Rothschild, M. 1962. Release of hydrocyanic acid from crushed tissues of all stages in the life cycle of species of the Zygaeninae (Lepidoptera). *Nature, Lond.* 193:52—3.

Kershaw, P. 1973. Quaternary history of rain forest in Australia. *Wildlife in Australia* 10:82—3.

Key, K. H. L. 1938. The regional and seasonal incidence of grasshopper plagues in Australia. *Bull. Commonw. scient. ind. Res. No.* 117:1—87.

Key, K. H. L. 1945. The general ecological characteristics of the outbreak areas and outbreak years of the Australian plague locust *(Chortoicetes terminifera* Walk.). *Bull. Commonw. scient. ind. Res. No.* 186:1—127.

Key, K. H. L. 1957. Kentromorphic phases in three species of Phasmatodea. *Aust. J. Zool.* 5:247—84.

Key, K. H. L. 1959. The ecology and biogeography of Australian grasshoppers and locusts. In Keast, A., Crocker, R. L. and Christian, C. S., eds. *Biogeography and Ecology in Australia.* The Hague: W. Junk.

Key, K. H. L. 1968. The concept of stasipatric speciation. *Syst. Zool.* 17:14—22.

Key, K. H. L. 1974a. Mantodea. In *The Insects of Australia.* Supplement 1974. Melbourne: CSIRO and Melbourne University Press.

Key, K. H. L. 1974b. Speciation in the Australian morabine grass-hoppers — taxonomy and ecology. In White, M. J. D. ed. *Genetic Mechanisms of Speciation in Insects.* Brookvale, N.S.W.: Australia and New Zealand Book Co.

Key, K. H. L. and Balderson, J. 1972. Distributional relations of two species of *Psednura* (Orthoptera: Pyrgomorphidae) in the Evans Head area of New South Wales. *Aust. J. Zool.* 20:411–22.

Key, K. H. L. and Day, M. F. 1954. A temperature-controlled physiological colour response in the grasshopper *Kosciuscola tristis* Sjost (Orthoptera, Acrididae). *Aust. J. Zool.* 2:309–39.

Khare, M. K. 1973. Reassociation of Malpighian tubules in certain beetles. *Entomologist* 106:73–82.

King, C. E. and Anderson, W. W. 1971. Age-specific selection. II. The interaction between *r* and *K* during population growth. *Am. Nat.* 105:137–56.

King, C. E. and Dawson, P. S. 1972. Population biology and the *Tribolium* model. *Evol. Biol.* 5:133–227.

Kira, T. and Shidei, T. 1967. Primary production and turnover of organic matter in different forest ecosystems of the Western Pacific. *Jap. J. Ecol.* 17:70–87.

Kitching, R. L. 1971. An ecological study of water-filled tree holes and their position in the woodland ecosystem. *J. Anim. Ecol.* 40:281–302.

Krombein, K. V. 1968. Studies in the Tiphiidae, X. *Hylomesa*, a new genus of myzinine wasp parasitic on larvae of longicorn beetles (Hymenoptera). *Proc. U.S. natn. Mus.* 124 (3644): 1–22.

Kuris, A. M. 1974. Trophic interactions: Similarity of parasitic castrators to parasitoids. *Q. Rev. Biol.* 49:129–48.

Kuschel, G. 1971. Chapter 27, Curculionidae. In Zinderen Bakker, E. M. van, Winterbottom, J. M. and Dyer, R. A. eds. *Marion and Prince Edward Islands, Report on the South African Biological and Geological Expedition (1965–66).* Cape Town: A. A. Balkema.

Laird, M. 1956. Studies of mosquitoes and freshwater ecology in the South Pacific. *R. Soc. N.Z. Bull.* No. 6:1–213.

Landin, B. O. 1960. The lamellicorn beetles of the Azores (Coleoptera) with some reflexions on the classification of certain Aphodiini. *Bol. Mus. munic. Funchal* No. 13, art. 32, pp. 49–84.

Lane, C. and Rothschild, M. 1965. A case of Müllerian mimicry of sound. *Proc. R. ent. Soc. Lond.* (B) 40: 156–8.

Lawrence, R. 1969. Aboriginal habitat and economy. *Dept. Geogr., Aust. Nat. Univ. Occ. Pap.* No. 6

Lea, A. M. 1900. Descriptions of two new blind weevils from Western Australia and Tasmania. *Proc. Linn. Soc. N.S.W.* 25:391–3.

Lea, A. M. 1905. Blind Coleoptera of Australia and Tasmania. *Trans. ent. Soc. Lond.* 1905:365–8.

Lea, A. M. 1915. An insect-catching grass. *Trans. R. Soc. S. Austr.* 39: 92–93.

Lea, A. M. 1925. Notes on some calcareous insect puparia. *Rec. S. Aust. Mus.* 3:35–6.

Lee, D. J. 1963. The biting midges. *Aust. nat. Hist.* 14:162–3.

Lee, K. E. 1975. Physical effects of herbivores on arid and semi-arid rangelands ecosystems. *J. Range Management* (in press).

Lee, K. E. and Wood, T. G. 1971. *Termites and Soils.* London and New York: Academic Press.

Leeper, G. W. ed. 1970. *The Australian Environment* 4th ed. Melbourne: CSIRO and Melbourne University Press.

Leppik, E. E. 1972. Origin and evolution of bilateral symmetry in flowers. *Evol. Biol.* 5:49–85.

Levin, D. A. and Anderson, W. W. 1970. Competition for pollinators between simultaneously flowering species. *Am. Nat.* 103: 455–67.

Levins, R. and MacArthur, R. 1969. A hypothesis to explain the incidence of monophagy. *Ecology* 50:910–11.

Linsley, E. G. 1959. Ecology of Cerambycidae. *A. Rev. Ent.* 4:99–138.

Lloyd, J. E. 1965. Aggressive mimicry in *Photuris*: firefly femmes fatales. *Science, N.Y.* 149:653–4.

MacArthur, R. H. 1968. The theory of the niche. In Lewontin, R. C. ed., *Population Biology and Evolution.* Syracuse, N.Y.: Syracuse University Press.

MacArthur, R. H. 1972. *Geographic Ecology: Patterns in the Distribution of Species.* New York: Harper and Row.

MacArthur, R. H. and Levins, R. 1964. Competition, habitat selection, and character displacement in a patchy environment. *Proc. Nat. Acad. Sci. U.S.* 51:1207–10.

MacArthur, R. H. and Wilson, E. O. 1967. *The Theory of Island Biogeography.* Princeton, N.J.: Princeton University Press.

McCubbin, C. 1971. *Australian Butterflies.* Melbourne: Thomas Nelson.

McDonald, J. F. and Ayala, F. J. 1974. Genetic response to environmental heterogeneity. *Nature, Lond.* 250:572–4.

MacFadyen, A. 1964. Energy flow in ecosystems. In Crisp, D. J , ed. *Grazing in Terrestrial and Marine Environments.* Oxford and Edinburgh: Blackwell Sci. Publs.

Macior, L. W. 1971. Co-evolution of plants and animals. *Taxon* 20: 17–28.

McKeown, K. C. 1944. *Insect Wonders of Australia.* Australian Pocket Library. Sydney and London: Angus and Robertson.

McKeown, K. C. 1945. *Australian Insects: an Introductory Handbook.* Sydney: R. Zool. Soc. N.S.W.

McKeown, K. C. 1951. Field notes on some insects of the Mount Kosciusko area. *Aust. Nat.* 11:333—7.

McKeown, K. C. 1963. *Australian Spiders.* Sydney: Sirius Books, Angus and Robertson.

McKeown, K. C. and Mincham, H. 1948. The biology of an Australian mantispid (*Mantispa vittata* Guerin). *Aust. Zool.* 11:207—24.

Mackerras, I. M. 1950. Marine insects. *Proc. R. Soc. Qd.* 61:19—29.

McNamara, P. J. 1955. A preliminary investigation of the fauna of humus layer in the jarrah forest of Western Australia. Canberra: Forestry and Timber Bureau Leaflet No. 71.

Madge, D. S. 1965. Leaf fall and litter disappearance in a tropical forest. *Pedobiologia* 5:273—88.

Madge, P. E. 1958. The ecology of *Oncopera fasciculata* (Walker) in South Australia. *Aust. J. Zool.* 6:19—26.

Madigan, C. T. 1930. Lake Eyre, South Australia. *Geogr. J.* 76:215—40.

Maelzer, D. A. 1962. The emergence as a pest of *Aphodius tasmaniae* Hope (Scarabaeidae) in pastures in the lower South-East of South Australia. *Aust. J. Zool.* 10:95—112.

Malicky, H. 1970. New aspects on the association between lycaenid larvae (Lycaenidae) and ants (Formicidae: Hymenoptera). *J. Lepid. Soc.* 24:190—202.

Mani, M. S. 1964. *Ecology of Plant Galls.* The Hague: W. Junk.

Mani, M. S. 1968. *Ecology and Biogeography of High Altitude Insects.* The Hague: W. Junk.

Marks, E. N. 1969. Mosquitoes (Culicidae) on Queensland's coral cays. *Qd. Nat.* 19:94—8.

Marks, E. N. 1972. Mosquitoes (Culicidae) in the changing Australian environment. *Qd. Nat.* 20:101—6.

Matthews, E. G. 1972. A revision of the scarabaeine dung beetles of Australia. I, Tribe Onthophagini. *Aust. J. Zool. Suppl.* 9:1—330.

Matthews, E. G. 1975. The Mediterranean beetle *Blaps polychresta* Forskal in South Australia (Tenebrionidae). *S. Aust. Nat.* 49:35—9.

Matthews, E. G. 1976. Signal-based frequency-dependent defence strategies and the evolution of mimicry. *Am. Nat.* (in press).

Matthews, R. W. and Evans, H. E. 1970. Biological notes on two species of *Sericophorus* from Australia (Hymenoptera: Sphecidae). *Psyche* 77:413—29.

May, R. M. 1972. Limit cycles in predator-prey communities. *Science, N.Y.* 177:900—2.

May, R. M. 1973. Time-delay versus stability in population models with two and three trophic levels. *Ecology* 54:315—25.

Mayr, E. 1965. *Animal Species and Evolution.* Cambridge, Mass.: Belknap Press of Harvard University Press.

Menhinick, E. F. 1967. Structure, stability, and energy flow in plants and arthropods in a *Sericea laspedeza* stand. *Ecol. Monogr.* 37:255–72.

Mertz, D. B. and Robertson, J. R. 1970. Some developmental consequences of handling, egg-eating and population density of flour beetle larvae. *Ecology* 51:989–98.

Michener, C. D. 1965. A classification of the bees of the Australian and South Pacific regions. *Bull. Am. Mus. Nat. His.* 130:1–362.

Mitchell, F. J. 1973. Studies on the ecology of the agamid lizard *Amphibolurus maculosus* (Mitchell). *Trans. R. Soc. S. Aust.* 97:47–76.

Monro, J. 1967. The exploitation and conservation of resources by populations of insects. *J. Anim. Ecol.* 36:531–48.

Moore, B. P. 1964. New cavernicolous Carabidae (Coleoptera) from mainland Australia. *J. ent. Soc. Q'ld.* 3:69–74.

Moore, B. P. 1967. Hydrogen cyanide in the defensive secretions of larval Paropsini (Coleoptera: Chrysomelidae). *J. Aust. ent. Soc.* 6:36–8.

Moore, K. M. 1959. Observations on some Australian forest insects, 4. *Xyleborus truncatus* Er. (Coleoptera: Scolytidae) associated with dying *Eucalyptus saligna* Smith (Sydney blue gum). *Proc. Linn. Soc. N.S.W.* 84:186–93.

Moore, K. M. 1961. Observations on some Australian forest insects, 7. The significance of the *Glycaspis* spp. (Hemiptera: Homoptera: Psyllidae) associations with their *Eucalyptus* spp. hosts. *Proc. Linn. Soc. N.S.W.* 86:128–67.

Moore, K. M. 1972. Observations on some Australian forest insects, 27. Some insects attacking *Callitris hugelii* (White cypress pine). *Aust. Zool.* 17:40–6.

Moore, R. M. 1970. *Australian Grasslands.* Canberra: Australian National University Press.

Morgan, F. D. 1968. Bionomics of Siricidae. *A. Rev. Ent.* 13:239–56.

Morgan, F. D. 1969. Some insects of the Flinders Ranges. In Corbett, D. W. P., ed., *The Natural History of the Flinders Ranges.* Adelaide: Libraries Board of S. A.

Moulder, B. D. and Reichle, D. E. 1972. Significance of spider predation in the energy dynamics of forest-floor arthropod communities. *Ecol. Monogr.* 42:473–98.

Mound, L. A. 1974. Spore-feeding thrips (Phlaeothripidae) from leaf litter and dead wood in Australia. *Aust. J. Zool. Suppl. Ser.* 27:1–106.

Murdoch, W. W. 1969. Switching in general predators: experiments on predator specificity and stability of prey populations. *Ecol. Monogr.* 39:335–54.

Nel, J. J. C. 1965. Influence of temperature and relative humidity on water loss in the workers of the meat ant, *Iridomyrmex detectus* (Smith) (Dolichoderinae: Hymenoptera). *Aust. J. Zool.* 13:301—15.

Nelson, S., Carlson, A. D. and Copeland, J. 1975. Mating-induced behavioural switch in female fireflies. *Nature, Lond.* 255: 628—9.

Norris, K. R. 1959. The ecology of sheep blowflies in Australia. In Keast, A., Crocker, R. L., and Christian, C. S. eds. *Biogeography and Ecology in Australia.* The Hague: W. Junk.

Norris, K. R. 1966. Notes on the ecology of the bushfly, *Musca vetustissima* Walk. (Diptera: Muscidae), in the Canberra district. *Aust. J. Zool.* 14:1139—56.

Norris, K. R. 1970. General biology. In *The Insects of Australia.* Melbourne: CSIRO and Melbourne University Press.

Odum, E. P. 1969. The strategy of ecosystem development. *Science, N.Y.* 164:262—70.

O'Farrell, A. F. 1963. Temperature-controlled physiological colour change in some Australian damsel-flies (Odonata: Zygoptera). *Aust. J. Sci.* 25:437—8.

O'Farrell, A. F. 1964. On physiological colour change in some Australian Odonata. *J. ent. Soc. Aust. (N.S.W.)* 1:1—8.

Otte, D. 1974. Effects and functions in the evolution of signaling systems. *A. Rev. Ecol. Syst.* 5:385—417.

Patton, W. S. and Cragg, F. W. 1913. *A Textbook of Medical Entomology.* London, Madras and Calcutta: Christian Literature Society for India.

Pianka, E. R. 1969. Sympatry of desert lizards *(Ctenotus)* in Western Australia. *Ecology* 50:1012—30.

Pianka, E. R. 1972. *r* and *K* selection or *b* and *d* selection? *Am. Nat.* 106:581—8.

Pimentel, D. 1968. Population regulation and genetic feedback. *Science, N.Y.* 159:1432—7.

Phillipson, J. 1966. *Ecological Energetics.* New York: St. Martin's Press.

Pont, A. C. 1974. A revision of the genus *Passeromyia* Rodhain and Villeneuve (Diptera: Muscidae). *Bull. Br. Mus. nat. Hist. (Ent.)* 30:341—72.

Poulson, T. L. and White, W. 1969. The cave environment. *Science, N.Y.* 165:971—81.

Povolny, D. 1971. Synanthropy. In Greenberg, B. ed. *Flies and Disease.* Vol. I. Princeton, N.J.: Princeton University Press.

Pradhan, S. 1957. The ecology of arid-zone insects. *Arid Zone Res.* 8: 199—240.

Ramirez, B. W. 1970. Host specificity of fig wasps (Agaonidae, Chalcidoidea). *Evolution, Lancaster, Pa.* 24:680—91.

Raw, F. 1967. Arthropoda (except Acari and Collembola). In Birges, A. and Raw, F., eds. *Soil Biology.* London and New York: Academic Press.

Rayment, T. 1954. The prey of the "Blue Ant". *Vict. Nat.*, 71:16.

Readshaw, J. L. 1965. A theory of phasmatid outbreak release. *Aust. J. Zool.* 13:475–90.

Readshaw, J. L. 1973. Numerical response of predators to prey density. *Appl. Ecol.* 10:342–51.

Reed, E. M. 1970. Thysanoptera (thrips). In *The Insects of Australia.* Melbourne: CSIRO and Melbourne University Press.

Rehr, S. S., Janzen, D. H., and Feeny, P. 1973. L-dopa in legume seeds: a chemical barrier to insect attack. *Science, N.Y.* 181:81–2.

Reichardt, H. 1973. A critical study of the suborder Myxophaga, with a taxonomic revision of the Brazilian Torrindicolidae and Hydroscaphidae (Coleoptera). *Arqu. Zool. S. Paulo* 24:73–162.

Reichstein, T., von Euw, J. and Rothschild, M. 1968. Heart poisons in the Monarch butterfly. *Science, N.Y.* 161:861–2.

Richards, A. M. 1971. An ecological study of the cavernicolous fauna of the Nullarbor Plain, Southern Australia. *J. Zool.* 164:1–60.

Richards, K. T. 1964. Insect pests of cotton in the Ord River irrigation area. *Trans. Dept. Agric. West. Aust.* 5:79–86, 120–32.

Richerson, J. V. and Borden, J. H. 1972. Host finding behavior of *Coeloides brunneri* (Hymenoptera: Braconidae). *Can. Ent.* 104:1235–50.

Ridsdill-Smith, T. J. 1970a. The biology of *Hemithynnus hyalinatus* (Hymenoptera: Tiphiidae), a parasite on scarabaeid larvae. *J. Aust. ent. Soc.* 9:183–95.

Ridsdill-Smith, T. J. 1970b. The behaviour of *Hemithynnus hyalinatus* (Hymenoptera: Tiphiidae), with notes on some other Thynninae. *J. Aust. ent. Soc.* 9:196–208.

Ridsdill-Smith, T. J. 1971. Field notes on the occurrence of *Hemithynnus hyalinatus* (Hymenoptera: Tiphiidae) as a parasite of scarabaeids on the New England Tablelands. *J. Aust. ent. Soc.* 10:265–70.

Riley, W. A. and Johannsen, O. A., 1938. *Medical Entomology.* New York and London: McGraw Hill.

Rivnay, E. 1964. The influence of man on insect ecology in arid zones. *A. Rev. Ent.* 9:41–62.

Roberts, R. J. 1968. An introduced pasture beetle, *Plectris aliena* Chapin (Scarabaeidae: Melolonthinae). *J. Aust. ent. Soc.* 7:15–20.

Rodd, N. W. 1951. Some observations on the biology of Stephanidae and Megalyridae (Hymenoptera). *Aust. Zool.* 11:341–6.

Rodin, L. E. and Basilevich, N. I. 1966. The biological productivity of the main vegetation types in the northern hemisphere of the Old World. (Translated from the Russian) *For. Abstr.* 27:369–72.

Roff, D. A. 1973. On the accuracy of some mark-recapture estimators. *Oecologia* 12:15—34.

Roffey, J. 1972. Radar studies of flight activity of locusts and other insects. *Rep. Commonw. scient. ind. Res. Div. Ent.* 1971—2:110—13.

Ross, M. A. 1969. An integrated approach to the ecology of Arid Australia. *Proc. Ecol. Soc. Aust.* 4:67—81.

Ross, M. A. and Lendon, C. 1973. Productivity of *Eragrostis eriopoda* in a mulga community. *Tropical Grasslands* 7:111—16.

Rotherham, E. R. 1968. Pollination of *Spiculea huntiana* (Elbow Orchid). *Vict. Nat.* 85:7—8.

Rothschild, M., von Euw, J. and Reichstein, T. 1973. Cardiac glycosides (heart poisons) in the polka-dot moth *Syntomeida epilais* Walk. (Ctenuchidae, Lep.) with some observations on the toxic qualities of *Amata* (= *Syntomis*) *phegea* (L.). *Proc. R. Soc. Lond.* (B) 183:227—47.

Rothschild, M. 1960. Defensive odours and Müllerian mimicry among insects. *Trans. R. ent. Soc. London* 113:101—21

Schlinger, E. I. 1974. Continental drift, *Nothofagus*, and some ecologically associated insects. *A. Rev. Ent.* 19:323—43.

Scott, J. A. 1973. Survey of ultraviolet reflectance of Nearctic butterflies. *J. Res. Lepid* 12:151—60.

Simberloff, D. S. 1969. Experimental zoogeography of islands. A model for insular colonization. *Ecology* 50:296—314.

Slatyer, R. O. and Perry, R. A. 1969. *Arid Lands of Australia.* Canberra: Australian National University Press.

Slobodkin, L. B. and Rapoport, A. 1974. An optimal strategy of evolution. *Q. Rev. Biol.* 49:181—200.

Smithers, C. N. 1970. Migration records in Australia, 1. Odonata, Homoptera, Coleoptera, Diptera, and Hymenoptera. *Aust. J. Zool.* 15:380—2.

Smithers, C. N. and Peters, J. V. 1966. A migration of *Vanessa kershawi* (McCoy) (Lepidoptera, Nymphalidae) in Australia. *J. ent. Soc. Qd.* 5:67—9.

Smith, F. G. 1969. Honey plants in Western Australia. *Dept. agric. West. Aust. Bull.* No. 3618:1—78.

Smith, P. H. 1972. The energy relations of defoliating insects in a hazel coppice. *J. Anim. Ecol.* 41:567—88.

Straatman, R. 1962. Notes on certain Lepidoptera ovipositing on plants which are toxic to their larvae. *J. Lepid. Soc.* 16:99—103.

Stride, G. O. and Straatman, R. S. 1962. The host plant relationship of an Australian swallowtail, *Papilio aegeus*, and its significance in the evolution of host plant selection. *Proc. Linn. Soc. N.S.W.* 87:69—78.

Szent-Ivany, J. J. H. 1961. The zoogeographical factor in economic entomology in Pacific islands with special reference to New Guinea. *Trans. Papua New Guinea Sci. Soc.* 2:1–11.

Szent-Ivany, J. J. H. and Carver, R. A. 1967. Notes on the biology of some Lepidoptera of the Territory of Papua and New Guinea with the description of the early stages of *Ornithoptera meridionalis* Rothschild. *Trans. Papua New Guinea scient. Soc.* 8:3–35.

Szent-Ivany, J. J. H. and Stevens, R. M. 1966. Insects associated with *Coffea arabica* and some other crops in the Wau-Bulolo area of New Guinea. *Papua New Guinea agric. J.* 18:101–19.

Szent-Ivany, J. J. H., Womersley, J. S. and Ardley, J. H. 1956. Some insects of *Cycas* in New Guinea. *Papua New Guinea agric. J.* 11:1–4.

Taylor, L. R. 1974. Insect migration, flight periodicity, and the boundary layer. *J. Anim. Ecol.* 43:225–38.

Tillyard, R. J. 1926. *The Insects of Australia and New Zealand.* Sydney: Angus and Robertson.

Tinbergen, N., Impekoven, M., and Franck, D. 1967. An experiment in spacing out as a defense against predation. *Behaviour* 28: 307–21.

Tindale, N. B. 1928. Species of *Chlenias* attacking pines (Lepidoptera, family Boarmiidae). *Rec. S. Aust. Mus.* 4:43–8.

Tindale, N. B. 1935. Note on the body temperature of a hepialid moth (*Trictena*). *Rec. S. Aust. Mus.* 5:331–2.

Tindale, N. B. 1938. Ghost moths of the family Hepialidae. *S. Aust. Nat.* 19:1–6.

Tindale, N. B. 1953. On some Australian Cossidae, including the moth of the witjuti (witchety) grub. *Trans. R. Soc. S. Aust.* 76:56–65.

Tindale, N. B. 1959. Ecology of primitive aboriginal man in Australia. In Keast, A., Crocker, R. L. and Christian, C. S., eds. *Biogeography and Ecology in Australia.* The Hague: W. Junk.

Tindale, N. B. 1961. A new species of *Chlenias* (Lepidoptera, Boarmiidae) on *Acacia aneura*, with some Central Australian native beliefs about it. *Rec. S. Aust. Mus.* 14:131–40.

Tindale, N. B. 1966. Insects as food for the Australian aborigines. *Aust. Nat. Hist.* 15:179–82.

Usinger, R. L. 1957. Marine Insects. *Geol. Soc. America Mem.* No. 67, 1:1177–82.

Wallace, M. M. H. 1970a. Insects of grasslands. In Moore, R. M. ed. *Australian Grasslands.* Canberra: Australian National University Press.

Wallace, M. M. H. 1970b. The biology of the jarrah leaf miner, *Perthida glyphopa* Common (Lepidoptera: Incurvariidae), *Aust. J. Zool.* 18:91–104.

Wardhaugh, K. G. 1972. The development of eggs of the Australian plague locust *Chortoicetes terminitera* (Walk.), in relation to temperature and moisture. In: Hemming, C. F., and Taylor, T. H. C. (eds.) *Proc. Int. Study Conf. Current & Fut. Probs. of Acridology:* London. Centre for Overseas Pest Research.

Waterhouse, D. F. 1952. Studies on the digestion of wool by insects. VII. Some features of digestion in three species of dermestid larvae and a comparison with *Tineola* larvae. *Aust. J. scient. Res., Ser. B.* 5:444–59.

Watson, J. A. L. 1967. The larva of *Synthemis leachi* Selys, with a key to the larvae of Western Australian Synthemidae (Odonata). *West. Aust. Nat.* 10:86–91.

Watson, J. A. L. 1969. Taxonomy, ecology, and zoogeography of dragonflies (Odonata) from the North-West of Western Australia. *Aust. J. Zool.* 17:15–112.

Watson, J. A. L. 1972. An old mound of the spinifex termite, *Nasutitermes triodiae* (Froggatt) (Isoptera, Termitidae). *J. Aust. ent. Soc.* 11:79–80.

Watson, J. A. L. and Gay, F. J. 1970. The role of grass-eating termites in the degradation of a mulga ecosystem. *Search* 1:43.

Watson, J. A. L., Lendon, C. and Low, B. S. 1973. Termites in mulga lands. *Tropical Grasslands* 7:121–6.

Way, M. J. 1963. Mutualism between ants and honeydew producing Homoptera. *A. Rev. Ent.* 8:307–44.

Way, M. J. and Cammell, M. 1970. Aggregation behaviour in relation to food utilization by aphids. In Watson, A., ed. *Animal Populations in Relation to their Food Resources.* Oxford and Edinburgh: Blackwell Sci. Publs.

Webb, L. J. 1949. An Australian phytochemical survey, I. Alkaloids and cyanogenetic compounds in Queensland plants. *Commonw. scient. ind. Res. Aust. Bull.* No. 241:1–56.

Webb, L. J. 1952. An Australian phytochemical survey, II. Alkaloids in Queensland flowering plants. *Commonw. scient. ind. Res. Org. Aust. Bull.* No. 268:1–99.

Webb, L. J. 1959. A physiognomic classification of Australian rain forests. *J. Ecol.* 47:557–70.

Webb, L. J. 1968. Biological aspects of forest management. *Proc. ecol. Soc. Aust.* 3:91–5.

Webber, L. G. 1958. Nutrition and reproduction in the Australian sheep blowfly *Lucilia cuprina. Aust. J. Zool.* 6:139–44.

Went, F. W. 1970. Plants and the chemical environment. In Sondheimer, E. and Simeone, J. B., eds. *Chemical Ecology.* New York and London: Academic Press.

Wenzler, R. J. 1970. Locomotor and feeding activity of larvae of the scarabaeid *Sericesthis geminata* (Coleoptera). *Entomologia exp. appl.* 14:270–82.

Wheeler, W. M. 1910. *Ants, Their Structure, Development, and Behavior.* New York: Columbia University Press.

White, M. J. D. 1957. Cytogenetics of the grasshopper *Moraba scurra.* II. Heterotic systems and their interaction. *Aust. J. Zool.* 5:305–37.

White, M. J. D. 1970. Cytogenetics of speciation. *J. Aust. ent. Soc.* 9:1–6.

White, M. J. D. 1974. Cytogenetics. In *The Insects of Australia.* Supplement 1974. Melbourne: CSIRO and Melbourne University Press.

White, M. J. D., Blackith, R. E., Blackith, R. M. and Cheney, J. 1967. Cytogenetics of the *viatica* group of morabine grasshoppers, I. The "coastal" species. *Aust. J. Zool.* 15:263–302.

White, T. C. R. 1970. Airborne arthropods collected in South Australia with a drogue net towed by a light aircraft. *Pac. Ins.* 12:251–9.

White, T. C. R. 1971. Lerp insects (Homoptera, Psyllidae) on red gum (*E. camaldulensis*) in South Australia. *S. Aust. Nat.* 46: 20–3.

Whittaker, R. H. 1970. The biochemical ecology of higher plants. In Sondheimer, E. and Simeone, J. B., eds. *Chemical Ecology.* New York and London: Academic Press.

Williams, C. B. 1970. Hormonal interactions between plants and insects. In Sondheimer, E. and Simeone, J. B., eds. *Chemical Ecology.* New York and London: Academic Press.

Williams, C. B. 1971. *Insect Migration.* London: Collins.

Williams, K. A. W. 1968. Migration of the caper white butterfly in November 1966. *Qd. Nat.* 18:113–15.

Williams, W. D. 1968. *Australian Freshwater Life, The Invertebrates of Australian Inland Waters.* Melbourne: Sun Books.

Wilson, A. G. L., Basinski, J. J., and Thomson, N. J. 1972. Pests, crop damage and control practises with irrigated cotton in a tropical environment. *Cotton Grow. Rev.* 49:308–40.

Wilson, F. 1960. A review of the biological control of insects and weeds in Australia and Australian New Guinea. *Common. Agric. Bureaux. Techn. Communic.* No. 1.

Wilson, F. 1968. Insect abundance — prospect. In Southwood, T. R. E., ed. Insect Abundance, Symposia R. ent. Soc. Lond., 4. Oxford and Edinburgh: Blackwell Sci. Publ.

Womersley, H. 1937a. A new marine chironomid from South Australia. *Trans. R. Soc. S. Aust.* 61:102–3.

Womersley, H. 1937b. On some Australian Coleoptera of the subfamily Cossoninae (Curculionidae). *Trans. R. Soc. S. Aust.* 61: 104–6.

Wood, T. G. 1970. Micro-arthropods from soils in the arid zone in southern Australia. *Search* 2:75–6.

Wood, T. G. 1971. The effects of soil fauna on the decomposition of *Eucalyptus* leaf litter in the Snowy Mountains, Australia. In *Colloquium Pedobiologiae*, 4th Dijon, 1970 (UNRA publ. 71—7), Paris.

Woodburn, T. L. and Lewis, E. E. 1973. A comparative histological study of the effects of feeding by nymphs of four psyllid species on the leaves of eucalypts. *J. Aust. ent. Soc.* 12: 134—8.

Woodroffe, G. E. and Southgate, B. J. 1951. Birds' nests as a source of domestic pests. *Proc. Zool. Soc. Lond.* 121:55—62.

Woodward, T. E., Evans, J. W. and Eastop, V. F. 1970. Hemiptera (Bugs, Leafhoppers, etc.) In *The Insects of Australia.* Melbourne: CSIRO and Melbourne University Press.

Wynne-Edwards, V. C. 1970. Feedback from food resources to population regulation. In Watson, A., ed. *Animal Populations in Relation to their Food Resources.* Oxford and Edinburgh: Blackwell Sci. Publs.

Zeck, E. H. 1920. Swarming of the soldier beetle *Telephorus pulchellus. Aust. Zool.* 1:205—6.

Zwölfer, H. 1974. Das Treffpunkt-Prinzipals Kommunikationsstrategie und Isolationsmechanismus bei Bohrfliegen (Diptera: Trypetidae). *Ent. Germ.* 1, 11—20.

Glossary

Terms used only once in the text, and defined at the time of use, are not included, but terms used repeatedly are included here even if defined at their point of introduction in the text.

Aeolian zone — alpine region dependent on wind-transported food.

Allele — one of a number of alternative expressions of a gene; two occur in each individual.

Allopatry — occupation of geographically separate areas.

Alpine — referring to a montane zone above the timber line.

Ambient — surrounding; encompassing.

Aposematism — use of signals to advertise strong defences.

Apostasy — concentration of attention by a predator (or pollinator) on the most abundant prey (or flower).

Avoidance image — a mental image or conscious memory of the aspect of prey items known to be unrewarding.

Beyond-K selection — set of selective forces operating in physically extreme but highly predictable environments.

Biocoenosis — the smallest natural community unit which it is convenient to recognize, such as a pond or cave.

Biome — the largest natural community unit which it is convenient to recognize, characterised by a uniform structural type (life form) of climax vegetation.

Boundary layer — an air layer above which an animal cannot maintain voluntary directional flight.

Caloric reward — nutrients offered by a flower to a pollinator.

Carrying capacity — maximum population density which can be supported by an environment.

Clone — successive descendants produced parthenogenetically from an original sexually reproducing female.

Coevolution — reciprocal and coordinated evolution of two or more ecologically associated species.

Colony — in social insects, the descendants of a single fertilised female cooperating with her, or another female, to rear more of her offspring.

Competitive displacement — partitioning of environmental resources by two or more species leading to avoidance of competition between them.

Conspecific — of the same species.

Consumer, first-order — a herbivore or plant eater.

Consumer, second-order — a carnivore or predator.

Coprophage — an organism that feeds on excrement.

Crepuscular — active at twilight.

Cryptic species — those difficult or impossible to distinguish morphologically.

Decomposer — an organism feeding on dead organic matter.

Detritivore — a decomposer.

Detritus — dead organic matter.

Diapause — an arrested development governed by environmental events but mediated by hormonal control.

Diel cycle — the 24-hour period of day and night.

Diffraction grating — a file-like arrangement of microscopic ridges spaced so as to reflect only certain wavelengths of parallel light.

Dioecism — having the male and female reproductive organs in different individuals (said of plants).

Disjunct — occurring in widely separated localities.

Diversity — the number (and, in some cases, the relative abundance) of species in an area or in a taxonomic group.

Ecdysis — the shedding of the cuticle from a previous instar.

Echolocation — use of emitted sound to locate objects by means of the sound returning from them.

Ectoparasite — a parasite living on the surface of its host.

Ectophytic — refers to a herbivore feeding on the outer surface of a plant.

Ectothermy — dependence on outside sources of heat.

Endogenous — originating from within a cell or organism.

Endothermy — ability to conserve endogenous heat.

Epigean — above ground.

Epiphyte — a plant with no roots in the soil using another plant for physical support only.

Epizoic — refers to using an animal for physical support without parasitising it.

Euryhaline — able to tolerate a wide range of salt concentrations.

Eurythermy — ability to tolerate a wide range of temperatures.

Eutrophic — in reference to water bodies, with a high concentration of nutrients.

Exuvium (plural: exuvia) — the old cuticle shed at ecdysis.

Fitness — an individual's ability to survive and reproduce in its environment.

Forb — a non-grassy (dicotyledonous) herbaceous plant.

Fugitive species — an r strategist.

Genetic feedback — the mechanism of coevolution.

Genome — the complement of genes possessed by an individual or population.

Grazing — feeding upon, or (in the case of food chains) originating from, live plants.

Homoiothermy — regulation of body temperature by means of physiological mechanisms.

Hygrophilous (also hydrophilic) — seeking moisture.

Inquiline — animal living in the nest of a social animal of another species.

Instar — a growth stage punctuated by the formation of new cuticle.

Ipsisexual — of the same sex.

Isohyet — a line joining areas of equal rainfall.

Isotherm — a line joining areas of equal temperature.

K selection — selection favouring a more efficient utilisation of resources.

K strategist — species able to exploit resources efficiently and interact successfully with coexisting species under stable conditions.

Kentromorphic phase — a morph whose appearance is governed by population density.

Keystone species — a species whose activities are crucial in maintaining the structure and diversity of a community.

Labile — outside organic matter; refers to usable minerals or nutrients.

Locus (plural: loci) — a point on a chromosome occupied by a given gene.

Melanic — with a high concentration of black pigment.

Mesic — refers to conditions or habitats that are moist.

Mimicry — a resemblance between the signals emitted by different individuals or species.

Monophagy — feeding on only one species.

Morph — one of a number of alternative forms in which adult ipsisexual individuals of a population can appear.

Mutualism — a symbiosis of mutual advantage to the participants.

Mycangium — a structure on the body of an insect adapted to house fungi.

Necrophage — an organism that normally feeds on dead animals.

Niche — an organism's role in its community.

Oligolecty — pollination of only one or a few flower species.

Oligophagy — feeding on only a few species.

Parapatry — occupying contiguous geographic regions.

Parasite — an organism living at the expense of only one other organism at a time, but not normally killing the latter.

Parasitoid — an organism living at the expense of only one other organism, eventually killing it.

Parthenogenesis — reproduction by a female without fertilization.

Plastron — a very thin film of gas held against a cuticular surface by closely-spaced hairs, serving for gas exchange between tracheae and an aquatic medium.

Poikilothermy — dependence on behaviour and ambient temperature for regulating body temperature.

Polylecty — pollination of a large number of flower species.

Polyphagy — feeding on many species.

Predation — killing a number of animals for food.

Predator satiation, absolute — a defence depending on being able to exceed a predator's searching or ingesting capacity.

Predator satiation, selective — a defence depending on being able to exceed.a predator's tolerance limits for a particular toxin or frustrating experience.

Procrypsis — the use of colours and shapes to resemble surfaces or objects of no interest to a predator.

Production, primary — the quantity of energy converted by photo- or chemosynthesis into organic substances.

Production, secondary — the quantity of energy assimilated from primary producers by herbivores, minus the latter's respiratory losses.

Productivity — the rate of production.

R selection — selection favouring a high population growth rate because of a temporary abundance of resources.

R strategist — species with high intrinsic population growth rate and mobility, adapted to unstable conditions.

Race — a morphologically or ecologically distinct population of a species occupying its own geographic area or occurring on a distinct host species.

Reproductive isolation — inability of individuals of a population to interbreed successfully with members of other populations even when the opportunity exists to do so.

Saprophage — a decomposer.

Search image — a mental image or conscious memory of the aspect of prey items known to be rewarding.

Semispecies — populations that are reproductively isolated over only a part of their range.

Sibling species — newly-formed species, usually cryptic.

Sign stimulus — a signal eliciting a response in the recipient.

Speciation — as used here, the process of genetic segregation to adapt to environmental heterogeneity, usually but not necessarily culminating in reproductive isolation of the segregates.

Stasipatry — synonymous with parapatry.

Stenothermy — ability to tolerate only a narrow range of temperatures.

Stridulation — production of sound by rubbing two surfaces together.

Subcortical — under bark.

Subspecies — a race that has received a name in formal nomenclature.

Succession — a sequence of natural communities that replace one another in time.

Supernormal (or superoptimal) — refers to the exaggerated mimicry of a sign stimulus which elicits a stronger response in the recipient than the normal stimulus.

Symbiosis — an interaction between organisms of different species which is of advantage to at least one of them.

Sympatry — occurring in the same geographic region.

Synanthrope — a species dependent upon man or his immediate environment, against man's wishes.

Thermoregulation — the control of body temperature.

Troglobite — an animal able to live only in caves and modified for cave life.

Troglophile — an animal able to live all of its life in caves if necessary, but not visibly modified for cave life.

Trogloxene — an animal using caves for shelter, but deriving all or most of its food from epigean sources.

Trophic — refers to nutrition and/or feeding.

Vagility — the ability of a species to disperse, depending on the mobility of at least one of its life stages.

Subject Index

Index of Scientific and Common Names